LOFTY WISEMAN

WHO DARES GRINS

To Dave,
All th very Best -

J Wiseman Lofty

LOFTY WISEMAN

WHO DARES GRINS

BROWN
DOG
BOOKS

Published under licence by Brown Dog Books and
The Self-Publishing Partnership, 7 Green Park Station, Bath BA1 1JB

www.selfpublishingpartnership.co.uk

ISBN printed book: 978-1-78545-120-1

Cover design by Kevin Rylands
Internal design by Andrew Easton

Printed and bound by CPI Group (UK) Ltd, Croydon CR0 4YY

CONTENTS

Here are a few stories that kept me going for 27 years in the SAS. Not everything goes to plan; it's always more exciting when it doesn't. There is too much bad news in the world at present, and I hope this book gives some happiness for a change.

There is humour in every situation; sometime you have to look a little deeper, but it is always there. Maybe it's not immediately apparent, but only humour can offset grief. Like light and dark they complement each other. We must have some bad times so we can recognise the good times. A smile is easier to make than a frown.

Lofty Wiseman

CHAPTER ONE

LEAVING HOME

It all started with the innocent question, "HOW DO YOU JOIN THE ARMY?" Walking home from the local with two mates battling against the elements, alcohol abuse and gravity, this query seemed a good idea at the time, and the answer was to change my life forever. Supporting and picking each other up when required, we staggered homewards. It was a bitter cold night in mid-April 1957. No one with any sense would venture out, and all living things stayed indoors. Although it was freezing I didn't notice the cold. My mind was full of all the stories that my two comrades had told me earlier.

It was Alan's turn to fall over, dragging me and Sydney to the pavement with him, and we decided to stay down and take a break, and lay there reminiscing. It was only a short distance from the pub to our street, normally taking five minutes or less, but this night it took forever.

When the wind dropped so did we. The resistance it offered prevented us pitching forward, it was our crutch.

The evening started quietly enough, with just me and Sydney having a few pints. He was drowning his sorrows after being sacked from a posh hair salon in the West End. Surprisingly, he had lasted three weeks before this incident, which was a record for Sid. He had tried his hand at many things, from chef and plasterer to welder, not finding anything to his liking. He was told to wash a woman's hair and apply a coloured tint. The shampooing was a success but the tinting a disaster. He mixed five parts tint to one of water, instead of the other way around. The woman went hysterical as she saw this orangey-red apparition in the mirror. No amount of washing could remove this vision of Krakatoa erupting. The manager's phoney French accent slipped easily back into his native East Ender's tongue, trying to placate the woman and sacking Sid at the same time. Trying to convince the woman it would grow out in time and telling Sid to get his things took its toll, forcing the manager to slip gracefully to the floor clutching his chest, gagging. Sid, adding insult to injury, said, "Alright, if I wash me hands, and don't forget me 'oliday money."

He left the woman sobbing about the surprise party she was arranging for her husband. Some surprise when she turned up looking like that.

The woman with the dyed scalp was soon forgotten. Sydney's older brother, Alan, joined us. He was a natural storyteller and soon had us mesmerised. Endless stories rolled effortlessly from his silky tongue. I realise now that you should never let the truth spoil a good story, and sat there naïvely absorbing every morsel. Alan had just been demobbed after two years' national service, starting with his basic training in the RASC, to operations against the Chinese Communists in Malaya. He claimed that RASC stood for Royal Army Special Commando, instead of the correct Royal Army Service Corps, which dealt in transport and stores, or was more affectionately known as Run Away, Someone's Coming.

What he did in those two years would put Audie Murphy to shame. No wonder we ruled the world and Great Britain really was GREAT. Sid knew the stories better than his brother, and filled in and elaborated when Alan's memory failed. There I was, a gullible seventeen-year-old, hanging onto the edge of my bar stool and every word said.

I also had many jobs since being expelled from school two years earlier. Me and the headmaster never saw eye-to-eye. I had a problem with being told what to do and hated authority. After many, many jobs, I was still searching for satisfaction, finding nothing to suit so far. Although I didn't know it yet, the seeds were being sown in fertile soil by a master farmer, aided with tons of manure.

There was never a dull moment in our local, with drama and action happening continuously. There were so many distractions that for anyone to hold your attention had to be a maestro. The Downham Tavern was a large pub built to serve the thirst of the Downham Estate in SE London. The public bar, according to the *Guinness Book of Records*, was the largest in Europe. In those days it was unfashionable to be hygienic, and no one seemed to clean the place, they just kept the lights low. The faded curtains, having seen better days, were never drawn in case they fell to pieces, and were used as hand towels and handkerchiefs, or for anything else that needed wiping. The floor was like an ice rink, awash with all the spillages. You could tell the locals from the casual visitors, as they skated between the bar, tables and toilets. The glass collectors were like Torvill and Dean. They had to be nimble because it was life-threatening if they took someone's glass with the tiniest amount of drink remaining. Smoke hung in lumps, forcing everyone to squint, and only dispersed when a door was opened. The people who sat furthest from the doors or in corners looked like Japanese fighter pilots squinting in the haze. No signs were needed to indicate where the toilets were, as you could smell them miles away. No one loitered when using these facilities and they were usually still adjusting their dress as they entered the bar. Anything that wasn't screwed down went missing, so there were never toilet rolls, towels or soap present, and light bulbs were a rarity: that's why the curtains took such a hammering.

Imagine a saloon in a Wild West movie and you have some idea of the atmosphere in the Tavern. The staff were a mixture of peroxide blondes with lipstick on their teeth who called you 'dearie', and blokes with a permanent fag hanging out of the corner of their mouths who called you 'guv'. Some couldn't read or write but could add up the price of three pints, two rums and a gin faster than a modern-day calculator. Although they weren't schooled, it amazed me how they could work out a five-horse accumulator or a Yankee Patent, and take the chalk on the scoreboard when playing darts. They rode all the insults and were never lost for words.

Fights often broke out, usually by the crib table, and the frontier spirit was elaborated by a singer giving it everything they had at the other end of the bar. Not even the fifteen for two, off-key notes or sound of blows distracted me: I was in another world. Even if Lord Lucan came riding in on Shergar, I wouldn't have noticed.

When Alan pulled out photos of dead Malayan terrorists, the crowd swelled and concentration intensified. Not even the event at Hiroshima could distract us.

A lot of ex-boxers used the Tavern, congregating by the piano, reliving past bouts and demonstrating their pugilistic skills, vividly going through past fights, round by round, to anyone who would listen. They never seemed to have lost a fight, so I guess the losers used a different boozer. One fight they did lose was when a stray right hook caught Alan smack in the ear while in mid-sentence. He reacted like a scalded cat, punching everything in range.

They were always ducking and diving and throwing punches at an invisible opponent, and this ex-pugilist overbalanced, catching Alan. Well, all hell broke loose, total pandemonium. I used to love watching the fight scenes in the old black and white westerns, and the next two minutes were equally good. Kicking, biting, gouging and spitting were all part of the scene, and this was just the women. Imagine tables and bodies flying everywhere, and do-gooders holding onto the wrong persons, resulting in the innocents getting punched. As our table went over, Sid grabbed the beer and I the photos. Alan dispatched two intruders besides the one who hit him, and peace was restored in minutes. An old pro was carried out in much the same way as the dead terrorist in one of Alan's photos. Picking up his stool and sitting down again, Alan casually runs a comb through his hair and carries on the story where he had left off. What a man: this is what Army training produces.

When a fight broke out, everyone took sides and avenged their anger on anyone who had upset them. The singer was always a good target, or the barman who didn't top up the glasses. After a scrap everyone seemed friendlier, buying each other drinks, and the entertainment improved. Alan had now reached hero status, spurring him on to greater exploits.

So this was the picture: walking home, full of stories, witness to a hero in action, and thinking up an excuse for my father, who either locked me out or was waiting up for his favourite son. Visions of being pinned down by machine guns, burnt by flame-throwers, and eaten by snakes and mosquitoes, were imprinted in my brain. Even facing my father didn't seem dangerous by comparison. This was a grave mistake and I was soon brought back to earth as I attempted to quietly open the front door. My father must have trained with Alan or gone to the same school. One minute knee-deep in empty cases, the next knee-deep in Michaelmas daisies which grew in the front garden. My father had a quick temper and hands to match. If only I had Alan's training, I could have ducked the blow that dropped me. What really used to wind my father up was Lonnie Donegan who was the star singer at the time. One chorus of "Don't you rock me, Daddy O" would send him ballistic. I knew I should have stopped singing before I reached our house. One thing about good old Lonnie was everyone could sing like him. I was easy pickings for the recruiting sergeant, but I hadn't realised this yet.

Everyone is rebellious in their teens, and the big bone of contention for my age group was national service. All the lads in our street swore that they would never go, and the lengths some of them went to to avoid inscription were incredible. Wearing shoes two sizes smaller than they really needed, encouraged them to walk like geisha girls with hard-boiled eggs stuffed up their arse. Drinking copious amounts of syrup of figs and eating chalk just before their medicals played havoc with their test results. Nervous twitches, memory loss, and poor eyesight were also feigned, but the army doctors had seen it all before. Imagine my surprise when national service was scrubbed and I didn't have to go. The last draft was for men born before September 1940, and my birthday was October, so now I'm asking, "What am I missing?" All the ploys and acting talent were wasted, and I felt unwanted, especially with what was happening at home.

Another influencing factor was my mate Pete May who lived just around the corner. We nicknamed him Daisy. He was army barmy and always intended to enlist in the paras. His brother was a paratrooper in the war, and captured at Arnhem. One night while he was helping me tinker with my motorbike sitting in the kerb, his brother roared past on his. There was only one car in our street and it was parked two doors down. It never moved, as we were always letting the tyres down. He hit this at speed and did a double somersault and went twenty in the air, then rolled for 30 yards before he regained his feet using the forward momentum gained, carrying him straight into the Tavern, and never stopped running till he reached the bar. Peter told me the paras trained you to do this and I was well impressed. I learnt later that he was p…ed. He also said that you got an extra ration of meat to build the shoulders up for parachuting. Army life got more appealing.

Our gang used to meet at the front of the "box office" (funeral parlour), and the usual "they'll never get me in the army" banter was always the main topic. Now we weren't required, we started a "what are we missing?"

12

debate. Charlie always said that he would go to jail rather than the army, his reasoning being they don't cut your hair in the nick. He had strong beliefs on human rights, and forcing him into khaki with a crew cut was one of them. We all had long hair slicked down with grease. If we had money, this was Brylcreem; if skint, any greasy substitute like butter or dripping was used. This was fine when it was cold, but rather pungent when the temperature rose. In summer my head resembled a basted turkey. A Boston DA was the style of the day. This was a straight line shaved across the back of the neck with each side combed back to resemble a duck's arse. Combing the hair was the only exercise some of the lads got, and any energetic movement caused the hair to spring up like sore fingers, so this was avoided at all times. That's why we shuffled when walking and brothel creepers were the footwear of choice. Charlie did finish up in jail because of his beliefs: he believed the nightwatchman was asleep. He was a sad case really: his hair fell out before his twenty-fifth birthday, and when he ran away to join the Foreign Legion, they rejected him. There's no sadder sight than a bald-headed Teddy Boy.

Looking back, there were many factors why I signed up. Alan's stories, Pete's ambition, trouble at home, and my motorbike. This was an old side valve BSA with no silencer, chain guard or brakes. I used to ride it with no helmet, gloves or common sense. I had permanent gravel rash all over my body where I fell off with monotonous frequency. My mother refused to feed me as long as I had it, and I was lucky that the police intervened, banning this death trap from the road, or I might have been a victim of starvation. It was my father who alerted the police, because the neighbours complained that every time I kicked it over, all the tellies in the street suffered interference. He warned me that if I rode it to work in the morning he was going to call the cops. Next morning a policeman leapt out in front of me on the way to work. By the time I stopped and he caught up with me, my road tax had run out.

I thrived on hard work and had a go at anything, from baker to blacksmith, labourer to laundry boy. I always had to have a laugh, often at the expense of the governor. I had thirty-two jobs in two years, so you can't say I didn't give Civvy Street a try. I left home one day unemployed and found work in a flour mill. The dust made me sneeze, so I crossed the road and started in a rum distillery. The smell gave me a headache, so I took off again and found work on a building site. I loved the fresh air, and all was well till I fell foul of the foreman. We were hoisting up a load of bricks and he said, "Don't let go." I only caught the first bit and shouted, "Don't what?" He answered, "Let go." So I did. I was back home by four o'clock, still out of work.

My father was the deciding factor. When he asked me what I was going to do with my life, the only answer that came to mind was, "I'm going to join the army". His reply was, "You'll never get in the army, they won't have you". Now, whether he was cleverer than I give him credit for, but this reverse psychology had the desired effect. I would be itching to get my hair cut, and was about to pay my annual visit to the barber when he would say, "Oi, Shirley bloody Temple, get your hair cut." So I wouldn't: I always did the opposite.

Being an East Ender, his favourite pastime was arguing, and we did this continuously. If I said it was white, he swore it was black. My mother was the pacifist and never raised her voice or had an opinion. She was the peacekeeper and got in between us when things got heated.

My dad worked on the river all his life and his homecoming was a ritual. He would wheel his bike into the passage, propping it against the coal cupboard. You couldn't leave anything outside as it would vanish. I was told that the milkman lost his horse once. My job was to make sure the lights were off, hang his bike clips on the handlebars, and take the paper from his saddlebag and put it on the table. He would hang his cap behind the kitchen door on a three-inch nail, and sit in his special chair at the head of the table. The chair was special as it was the only survivable item from the rent office that was destroyed in the Blitz. It was also the place where I stuck my chewing gum. My mother was always hovering in attendance, making sure that everything was within arm's reach for His Majesty. His dinner, warmed up in two plates over boiling water, was served as soon as he sat down. The pepper and salt were six inches to the left and four inches from the milk bottle. The sugar bowl was on the right exactly four inches in front of the bread. His tea was placed directly in front of him, forming a perfect isosceles triangle between all necessities. Slightly offset were his halibut oil capsules, and the newspaper, front page up, folded by his right elbow. My sister's job was to get his glasses that were kept on the top of the gas meter and place them on the paper. Now I honestly don't know how this happened, but when he reached for his halibut oil capsules, completely absorbed in the sports page with his attention riveted on Millwall's progress in the Cup, he failed to notice the contents of the bottle.

I had been working in the shed on an old pushbike and stripped down the gears. I placed all the ball bearings in an old halibut oil container for safe keeping, and guess what? They turned up on the kitchen table three inches from the paper and nine inches to the right of the salt. My father unscrewed the top, tipped out two spherical ball bearings and with nonchalant ease threw them down his throat. He sounded like a bagatelle machine as they rattled around his false teeth. I missed what happened next as I was out of the door heading for sanctuary. To my surprise, so was my father. He usually chased me to the door before giving up the chase. This time he was hard on my heels and kept on coming. I reached the corner, expecting to be alone but alas, he was still in pursuit: in fact, he was gaining on me. We almost ran around the block before his bearings seized up, but I kept on running straight to the recruiting office. I never did rebuild that bike: I was always two bearings missing. Years later to wind up Pop I used to ask him, "Have you recycled my balls yet?"

I forgot to mention the shed incident a few weeks previous. The shed was constructed from an old Anderson shelter with tar block walls at the ends. These tar blocks were 9x6 pine blocks soaked in tar which used to support the tramlines. When they scrapped the trams, they ripped up the rails and the blocks were free to anyone who wanted to collect them. They made excellent firewood, burning readily, giving off great heat and thick, black smoke. My pappy used them as bricks on his shed. Under the bench were all of the green tomatoes that failed to ripen. They were wrapped in newspapers and stored in wooden crates. I learnt later that, once ignited, they also burnt very well. It was while I was repairing my bike at night that the accident happened. There was no light in the shed so to see what I was doing, I lit the paper that wrapped the tomatoes. When it flared up too high, I put it out and lit another piece. A stubborn nut distracted me and before I knew it the whole store of tomatoes was ablaze. This spread to the tar blocks and I stood no chance. I ran into the kitchen and filled the only available container, a milk bottle, and attempted to fight the fire. The tomatoes weren't the only things with red skins. The fire took over and destroyed everything in the shed. All the tools lost their handles, including the lawnmower and the vice, and a pile of overcooked tomatoes lay on the floor where the bench used to be, resembling a giant pizza. I finished up looking like a cross between a medium rare steak and a kipper. I promised to give up smoking forever.

My father, more concerned for my health than his shed, never said a word. He sifted through the carnage for anything salvageable and must have been devastated by the results. I lay low for days but repercussions never came, but I knew this restraint and calm couldn't last forever. My father was a great man but short of patience, and now he was short of tools also. There was another little incident to help make up my mind for leaving home.

I wanted to make a catapult, so I cut a large branch out of the privets that grew in front of the house. I cut a sturdy prong and replaced the unwanted parts back in the hedge. For the pouch I used the tongue from my father's old working boots as he treated himself to a new pair, and the elastic I bought at two bob a yard from our local hardware shop called Allneeds. It performed a treat but came at a price. My father used to have the occasional pint or two and would stagger home clutching the privets for support. Working in the docks, he had access to port wine and duty-free spirits from the visiting ships. One night he was making steady progress, using the hedge for support, till he came across the large hole I had made and through it he went. In the morning he had little recollection of this escapade and went to the coal hole to get his boots. The coal hole was a cupboard under the stairs where, if we had the money, coal was stored. It was never full, so the space at the front was used for storage of boots and coats. He got his new boots and sat down on the stairs to put them on. He took one off again and started fishing around inside. He pulled the lace out and held the boot upside down, still fishing inside, and finally realised that the tongue was missing. I had targeted the wrong boots. So things were getting tricky. What with the trouble the bike caused with the neighbours, destruction of his shed and boots, and Lonnie Donegan, I was on borrowed time. I needed an escape plan.

Alan was only too pleased to give me directions to the recruiting centre at Blackheath, but I was still unsure, but eventually went with my mate Daisy who was intent on joining the Paras. I was left in the capable hands of the recruiting sergeant while Daisy went through the tests and medical. I had never seen such a magnificent specimen. Six foot three of starch and polish, he gleamed. A clipped moustache underlined a big nose set in a large, round, friendly face, and the epaulettes bearing his rank emphasised the width of his shoulders. You could have sharpened your pencil on the creases in his shirt and trousers. He seemed a very nice man and easy to speak to. He thought it a good idea, while I was waiting, to sit a test. I agreed and was sitting at a desk which had a pencil attached by a length of chain. This must have been a valuable army pencil that wrote in code. The test was very straightforward, consisting of simple problems, fractions and multiplication. I was looking for the hidden twists, wondering if army sums were the same as at school. When the Sgt. marked my paper he seemed very enthusiastic, and said with these results I could join the Guards. I found out in later years that to join the Guards you just needed a pulse. When I told him that, if I was to sign up, it would be the Paras or nothing, his friendly manner changed, and I distinctively felt hostile vibes. I was still non-committed but he fixed me up with a medical appointment and told me to go home and think about it. That night I spoke to Alan asking for his advice, and mentioned the sergeant. I inquired why he had three stripes and Alan none. Alan's explanation was a classic. He claimed that because he took part in secret missions, everything was different. If he was captured the enemy wouldn't torture him so much if they thought he had no rank. Clever stuff, this army rank structure: there's more to this than meets the eye.

I went for a medical a week later still undecided, and can only describe the scene as bedlam. The place was full of recruits and guys in white coats. Most of the recruits were national service guys trying to work their ticket. I was ushered into a room full of naked men with three others and told to strip. The guy behind me said, "What, we've only just met and you haven't taken me out for dinner yet." When you're naked amongst strangers you are very self-conscious and don't know what to do with your hands. You try to keep your eyes up and look each other in the face, and it's fatal to put your hands on hips, especially if they don't belong to you. Some guys are exhibitionists and strut around like the farmyard cockerel, but normal blokes are shy. We milled around, avoiding any bodily contact and waited to be summoned into the next room. While waiting we were given a paper to fill in about our personal details. With nowhere to rest on and with limited pens that were shared, this proved very difficult. Must be part of an initiative test, I thought.

One of the questions was, "Are you homosexual?" Many recruits put: "After today I'm not sure". Many of the contagious diseases listed I had never heard of. Again the conscripts admitted to having them all.

In the next cubicle a urine sample was required. To encourage the reluctant, a tap was left running. Many lads filled their sample bottle from this and added all sorts of dirt, debris or grit they could find. Rust from the radiator was favourite. Paper towels were purposely put in the sink and not the bin provided, causing it to overflow, flooding the floor. The whole floor of the medical centre was tiled and when wet was treacherous. So now all these loonies were slipping and sliding and grabbing onto anyone in a white coat with exaggerated vigour.

We were herded along to the next cubicle where the examination was a classic. A doctor, starting at my head, checked ear, nose and throat, then poked and prodded my ribcage and pelvic area, finishing up with my tackle in his hand, and, adding insult to injury, told me to cough. How could you cough at a time like this? I wanted to punch the pervert. It's a helluva way to clear your throat. To this day I have never discovered what they hoped to find by squeezing your credentials while coughing.

The next cubicle was equally amusing. It was located upstairs on the first floor, and we were encouraged to jog to reach our next humiliation quicker. I didn't know what to hang onto, the banister or my dignity. I was still panting when the bespectacled doctor ordered me to bend over the desk and had a good, hard stare up my Khyber. What was he looking for? I wondered. At least when I adopted this position at school to receive six of the best from the headmaster, I had clothes on.

The ultimate was saved to last: we had to give a stool sample. You had the choice to give one now or come back within the week. There's no time like the present so most chose to deliver there and then. We were each handed a small glass phial and a spatula, but no one explained the technique. The toilet area where this happened looked like a scene from the Willy Wonka Chocolate Factory.

Going home on the bus, I sat reflecting on my recent experiences. One side of me was hysterical, the other most upset. It was so funny but also so sad. If it happened now I would think that I was on *Candid Camera*. How could I take the army seriously?

I was real secretive on my activities, and my mother could sense something was not quite right. She actually fed me and gave me a cake, trying to lower my reserve. She was asking me where had I been, who with, and what had I done. I imagined this as an army exercise and played along with the grilling, practising my resistance to interrogation. When my father came home he joined in, and they doubled up on me. I finally cracked after another cake and a cup of tea, telling them of my medical examination. I don't think my father believed me and all my mother could say was, "I hope you had clean pants on."

I eagerly awaited the postman, looking for the letter confirming my medical results and the date for the next interview. This eventually came and I signed on for six years with the Parachute Regiment. My pay was five pounds and fifteen pence, or £5 1s 6d in old money. I received the Queen's shilling, a week's pay and a rail warrant for Aldershot. No one at home believed I was going, and it took my mate to come and cut my hair down to the wood before they paid attention.

There was one more episode that helped me decide and justify me leaving home.

My father came home one night with a batch of tiles that he half-hitched from the dock. They were rigid tiles made from Sorbo. He also acquired some glue which was made from rendered-down carcasses and smelt like death. They were designed to cover the decks on oil tankers, being impervious to all substances known to man.

My two sisters and I were confined to the front room and told to make ourselves scarce while my father, ably assisted by my mother, laid down the new decking. Hours went by and the three of us were starving. The only thing in the front room that offered any amusement was the stain on the ceiling caused by a burst pipe. It had rusty red streaks running through a greenish yellowy patch. We used to imagine all sorts of shapes and figures, from angels to treasure maps. The smell from the kitchen was atrocious. The glue had to be melted before use and was left boiling merrily away on the stove. Just as I thought we would perish by asphyxiation I was summoned by a roar from the kitchen. My father had laid all the tiles down, and because they were a quarter of an inch thick, couldn't open any of the two doors. I had to go around the back and pass a screwdriver through the window so he could prise up a space around the door, allowing it to open. We sat down at the kitchen table, daring not to breathe, as my father ranted and raged about his handiwork. My mother went about getting the tea ready, and as she walked from the sink to the stove she appeared to be getting taller. I put this down initially to the glue causing hallucinations. But as she returned to the sink she was definitely six inches taller. She had stood on the part by the floor that the tiles had been removed from, covering the soles of her slippers with glue. As she walked she lifted the tiles below, sticking to each other and elevating her like 'Wilt the Stilt'. I had to go: farewell, Downham.

The remnants of the glue were thrown in several bins outside with such venom that it split the sides. It just goes to show:

GLUE TEARS BINS

Later this would change to Who Dares Wins.

CHAPTER TWO

RECRUIT TRAINING

I couldn't imagine what a garrison town would look like, but I was soon to find out. Aldershot railway station was a short walk from the town centre, and the litter and number of broken windows were no different from the ones at home. I got directions from the news-stand and strode out heading for Maida Barracks, the depot of the Parachute Regiment. I was surprised at the number of pubs, some with unusual names like The Rat Pit, and Pegasus. I made a mental note of the tattoo parlour located in the amusement arcade. Once I was a Para I wanted to look like one and fancied a big tattoo.

What was really noticeable from any other town was the number of uniformed personnel mixed with the steady flow of pedestrians who used the shops and filled the pavement. Although most were in khaki and olive drab, the headdress was a variety of all different shapes and colours. Peaked caps, pillboxes, bonnets with feathers, berets with plumes, black berets, beige berets and, best of all, red berets. They mingled unaware of the interest and curiosity that they arose in me.

Maida Barracks, built in 1895, was situated at the top of a steep hill, bounded on one side by a gymnasium with rows of red-brick barrack blocks at right angles to this, framing a huge parade ground. I found myself outside the guardroom, my hair cut down to the bone but still with long sideboards, clutching my worldly possessions in two carrier bags. I casually asked a smart-looking soldier in uniform where to go and he exploded. This was my first mistake: how did I know he was the provost sergeant? Provost sergeants are not picked for their kindness: they are the nastiest animals on earth. If they were dogs they would chase sheep. This one had had an arse transplant and the arse rejected him. His nose was like a blind cobbler's thumb, forcing him to shout in short bursts. He couldn't get any closer and stood with his face inches from mine, bawling and spitting, with the veins in his neck standing out like coiled eels threatening to burst. Alan hadn't warned me of guys like this. His words were almost incoherent and his face changed from purple to red and back again. He was screaming like, "I'll show you where to go, you great big streak of p..s. Get down that road and double, double." I nearly slipped on the wax that had been forced from my ears as I attempted to carry out his commands. Thinking that 'double' meant walking bent over, making a smaller target for the enemy, it was difficult to do in drainpipe trousers carrying two carrier bags. Still, training already and not even in uniform yet. My feeble efforts only antagonised my new friend, causing him to shout even louder. He was calling me every name under the sun; at least at home I was only called a toe-rag. I couldn't get away quick enough but my ticket had been marked. Old Crimpey (because he kept a tight grip) had me listed as a potential troublemaker. He must have been clairvoyant.

So I gave old Crimpy a flash of the ivories and disappeared around the corner with all possible speed. My biggest drawback was that when I was in trouble, I couldn't stop grinning. It was an automatic reaction: I really felt like crying. The more they shouted, the broader the grin. This got me in trouble all through my schooldays and was about to do the same in my new career.

The depot of any regiment is run on strict discipline and bullshit of the highest order, and the Paras, not to be outdone, really excelled at this. They had to be the best at everything, and they certainly achieved this, verging on the sadistic. What they had to achieve in ten weeks was to turn a bunch of kids like me into an elite fighting force: what a challenge!

From the outside, the barrack blocks looked dull and depressing, but what a transformation inside, where everything sparkled, shone or shined. The wooden floor was polished like glass, bordered by beds equally spaced along each wall, displaying blankets folded to perfection. Between each bed was a locker topped with equipment, and on the other side a bedside table with mug, knife, fork and spoon arranged neatly on top. In the middle of the room was a fireplace and coal bunker adorned with brooms, bumpers and mops. Each of the fifty bed spaces was identically laid out with precision and accuracy that a surveyor would be proud of. At the top of the stairs were the ablutions, containing many sinks, toilets and showers, each of which sparkled. Hours of hard work had produced this vision, with daily inspections enforcing it. When we were allocated this top floor it was in some state, having been trashed by the outgoing platoon that had just passed out. It was tradition to leave it as it was found to cause maximum effort to bring it back to standard. It certainly moulded us together. My intake formed 157 Platoon, made up of lads from all over the country, and what I will never forget is all the different accents. Scousers, Jocks, Paddies, Taffies, Yorkies, Geordies and Swedes: all were represented. This was all new to me.

We were shown how to make a bed block, which was a special way of folding the blankets and sheets, forming a layered biscuit. It had to be perfectly square and firm. The top blanket on the bed had to be stretched as taut as a drum skin with the block at the top, with pillow, wrinkle-free, laid on top. All this care with the bedding didn't make you sleep any better, and the first few nights were purgatory. All night long the peace was disturbed by snoring, farting and crying. It was the first time away for the majority of the lads and some found it very difficult. This soon changed when we started training. At the end of the day we were exhausted and could have slept anywhere.

I actually enjoyed the space that I was given: I felt secure being surrounded by new friends. At home my bed was alongside my parents, and every night my mother took off her corset and swung it over my bedstead. The dangling suspenders caught me regularly in the face, and it's a wonder I didn't have eyebrows like Henry Cooper.

We were shown how to bumper the floor and polish it. Blacken the coal bunker and polish it. Clean the locker and polish it. Scrape the broom mop and bumper handles, and polish the buckets, dustpans and any other metal surface located in our new home. Everything gleamed.

There was a place for everything that we got issued with. Initially this was clothing, and we were shown how to fold and store it. After a week we were up to scale with all of our equipment, and this had to be laid out or stored in a certain way. There was so much to learn and not enough hours in the day to take it all in. We were also shown how to clean and polish it, but this would fill another chapter.

Everything issued had to be altered in one way or another. We were issued boots made of pimply leather which had to be made smooth. This entailed hours of work with a hot spoon ironing out the pimples. The soles had to have thirteen studs arranged in sequence. How you could ever sneak up on anyone wearing those was beyond me. They even caused sparks on pavements. Berets had to be shrunk, because a new one would keep your shoulders dry. Brown pumps had to be dyed black, and rough, dull brasses smoothed and polished. Normal working dress was denims, and whoever designed these wanted prosecuting. Whoever modelled for these must have been a freak, because they fitted no one, regardless of what size you tried. All the buttons were issued separately and fixed on by metal rings. It took ages removing these buttons before making up your weekly laundry bundle, and even longer replacing them on the clean set. To get a pair of trousers with my leg length, the waist size was enormous and wrapped around my skinny frame twice. You never had the correct number of buttons, having forgotten to remove them all when making up your laundry bundle. Contradictory to common sense was the way we cleaned our rifles, which were .303 Lee-Enfields. When these were issued we were told that they were your best friend and all that crap, and had to be kept dry at all times. "Cradle them when it rains and hold them up when crossing water" was all instilled in us. Yet the first thing we had to do after shooting on the ranges was to pour boiling water down the barrels. It was a criminal offence if you couldn't remember the serial number of your rifle.

Can you imagine this picture of Britain's finest? Pimply-faced and matching boots, dressed in acres of denim, topped off by a dustbin lid-sized beret. Not very romantic.

Only the tie and gloves fitted: everything else had to be cut, stitched or tailored. Our initial issue was: two pairs of pyjamas, two PT vests (one white, one red), two pairs PT shorts, two towels, two sets of denims (blouse and trousers), four pairs of socks, woollen jersey, three hairy shirts, two ties, pair of woollen gloves, cap comforter, button stick, set of boot brushes, and a house wife. We were all excited when the house wife was mentioned, but disappointed to find it was just a sewing kit. All these items had to be washed, ironed and folded before being displayed in the locker. Everything had to have your number stamped or printed on it. There was a set of dyes with a hammer left in the block for this. Later we were issued webbing, helmet and greatcoat.

When we were issued with battledress we had to parade outside the quartermaster's store wearing PT shorts and carrying our braces. The QM started bawling at me: "Who told you to wear your braces, and why are they dangling?" I was taken aback as I still had them in my hand behind my back. His next line was, "Sorry, they're your legs." What a wit. Alan said it was a laugh. We were issued two sets, one for best, which was brand new, and the other set second-hand, which was our working dress. The new set was actually tailored with pleats and all. The working set fitted where it touched and all slack material was pulled to the rear and gathered in under the belt. You could march two paces before the uniform moved.

From the minute you entered depot, you never stopped running; everything was done at the double. The days were long and intensive, and usually went like this.

Up at first light, wash, shave, and make up bed. Then outside to parade for breakfast. After breakfast, clean billet and the ablutions. We had a duty roster, taking it in turns to do this. Next it was stand by your bed for kit inspection. Your kit layout had to be immaculate: it was scrutinised. Anything that did not come up to scratch was recorded and had to be presented at night, parading behind the guard. Spare bootlaces had to be coiled; everything had to be folded the same width. Packs and pouches squared off, mess tins burnished. Even the contents of the rifle cleaning tin were displayed in a certain manner. Next it was parade outside for inspection. Here, formed up in three ranks, we were inspected from head to toe. Sometimes we were told to remove footwear for foot inspection. Nothing went unnoticed. Only the hair under your beret belonged to you, the rest was claimed by the army. We were marched down to the barber's shop where Paddy the Chop had his wicked way. With clippers that got hotter and hotter, he ran them straight over the top with scant regard for feelings or fashion. We all looked like convicts when he had finished with us. They say you must be ambitious in the army and my ambition was to get in the chair early before his clippers blistered my neck. This was a weekly event that we all looked forward to: at least you got to sit down.

Try as I might, I rarely escaped the extra parades. It was down to the guardroom most nights with whatever bit of kit was deemed substandard. Guess who always took the parade? Correct, my old mate, Crimpy. He was delighted to see me. He always came straight up to me standing nose-to-nose, spitting and salivating, looking for the merest of grins. One night I was so rigid with concentration that I passed wind, causing the parade to erupt. I saw a lot of Crimpy in the following weeks and was really glad when he was admitted to hospital with piles. Rumour had it that when he was born, the midwife threw away the best bit. I hope they don't make the same mistake with his piles.

Hours were spent on the drill square which to me was a constant source of amusement. We were shown a movement then practised it till perfect. As we progressed out came the drum and metronome, which was to ensure correct timing. Marching with a swagger exaggerating the movement, chopping the heels in, were all encouraged. In the beginning it was like a *Carry On* film. When the order was Left Turn, someone always turned right. On the order Halt some kept on going. There were bodies everywhere, it was chaotic. One day I was daydreaming while the instructor showed us a new drill movement. I was watching a man on horseback riding up Queens Avenue when the lad in front of me fell to the ground with a clutter. This surprised me, bringing me instantly back to earth as the instructor came steaming towards the prone figure. I started feeling really sorry for him. You don't collapse without permission. I was even more surprised when the instructor ignored the fallen figure and came straight to me. "What do you think you're looking at?" he spits out, shaking with anger. "That horse," I reply shakily. "That horse has an officer on its back so it's called a charger, what is it called?" "A charger, sergeant," I reply, warming to his little game. The lad on the deck had been forgotten and still lay there clutching his neck. "Get to your feet, you malingering pussy," ordered the instructor and it was then that I noticed the pace stick. Every drill instructor has a pace stick which he uses to measure the length of stride while marching. Our instructor had used his to attract my attention by throwing it at me. Unfortunately for the bloke in front, it caught him right across the neck, dropping him instantly. I always said drill is bad for you. This was proved many years later when a mate of mine attended a course in Brecon. They were parading on the square when a car skidded out of control and ran him down, breaking his leg in many places.

Weapon training took up a lot of the time and it was a pleasure to go on the ranges. We had to qualify on rifle, Bren Gun and Sterling sub-machine gun. A Salvation Army van used to come round selling tea and wads, adding to the enjoyment.

Every day we were in the gym climbing ropes, doing press-ups, crunchies and star jumps. Each session got more and more intense, preparing us for a test that everyone had to pass at the end of training. We spent a lot of time marching over the tank tracks wearing full-scale marching order. Again, these marches got longer each time out and the pace quicker. Road walks and runs were frequent, normally used as a wake-up call before breakfast. These entailed following a physical training instructor over the worst and steepest terrain they could find, which helped condition us, and got us fighting fit. All outdoor exercises were conducted in boots. Assault courses are the most knackering of obstacles. Wearing a tin hat, running, crawling, jumping and swinging used every muscle in the body. After three laps you were wrecked. We were set off at intervals and, encouraged to pass the man in front, we built up to six laps. Unique to the Paras is the trinasium. This is like an aerial assault course. You had to climb scaffolding and crawl across narrow planks high above the ground, to see if you were suitable for parachuting, a confidence test had to be passed. Climbing a tower of scaffolding forty feet high, you had to balance on two poles a metre apart, spanning a gap of twelve feet. With arms held out shoulder high you shuffled across the gap. Halfway across you had to step over a shackle and shout out your number, rank and name. There were no safety nets or harnesses, and it was a long way down.

Fieldcraft, NBC training and education all had to be fitted in: our days were crammed. We even had a visit to the garrison theatre to watch *Theirs Is the Glory*. This was a film about the exploits of the paras in the Second World War. With drill, more drill, and still more drill, the time flew by.

Every evening, regardless of the time, we scrubbed and blancoed belt and gaiters, and polished all brasses. Uniforms were ironed, boots balled, all equipment scrubbed, rifles stripped, cleaned, oiled and assembled, bayonet polished: this was routine. Friday night was bull night, preparing the barrack block for room inspection on Saturday. Very little sleep was had this night.

Working flat out for seven days a week made us really appreciate the first free time given in the fourth week. It was Saturday lunchtime and we were standing down till first parade Monday morning: what a treat!!! The only snag was that just before this momentous occasion we had our final jabs, one of which was a cocktail that left you with a temperature for forty-eight hours. It must have been a cocktail of anthrax or cholera, as the reaction was so severe. When we were injected it was mass production. We were paraded in single file in bare buff, and marched into the med centre where there were two rows of medics eagerly awaiting with syringes at the ready. We were herded down the middle and got jabbed in alternate arms. You never turned around, else you got a double shot. One lad got double-tapped and asked the overkeen medic, "Can I swim after this?" "Of course you can," was the answer. "Magic, that will help me pass the swimming test: I'm a non-swimmer."

From super-fit, rippling athletes we were reduced to quivering wrecks. No one went to the cookhouse, choosing to stay in bed for the whole weekend.

The majority of the senior instructors were ex-wartime veterans, hard but fair men. The corporals were younger and full of enthusiasm, trying to outdo each other and dream up new methods of sadism. One minute we were paraded in PT kit, then told to double away and be back in five minutes in full-scale marching order. If anyone was late it was all back again and parade in best BD.

There were two platoons each of about fifty men who started training together. It was very competitive, with each one trying to be better than the other. There was not a lot to choose between drill or weapon training, but there were four tasks that had outright winners. These were milling, stretcher race, steeplechase, and log race. Each of these was very physical, with points awarded which helped decide which was the best platoon. We would stop at nothing to win. From the onset of training we were trained to win at any cost, always be first, never come second. It's very commendable to come second in a marathon, but despicable to come second in a fight.

The milling gave me great pleasure. It was held in the gymnasium and attracted a large crowd. Two men, matched as close as possible in weight and stature, had to stand toe-to-toe and beat the s..t out of each other for one minute. This doesn't seem long but can feel like an eternity in the ring. No boxing skills were allowed, you just had to get stuck in and throw more punches than your opponent. Boxing experience is a great advantage, however, and a trained man will always beat a novice. I was 6'2", weighing in at 10 stone 6 lbs of romping, stomping, airborne hell. My opponent was a few pounds heavier but inches shorter, and sat opposite me on one of the packed benches that surrounded the ring. So, trying to look tough and confident, we sized each other up. You either rush in and get in the first blows, or hang back slightly and counter when they run out of steam. I noticed my opponent had a pronounced nose, helping me to decide my tactics. You watch the other bouts, screaming out encouragement, and before you know it, it's your turn. The bell sounded and this guy rushed out throwing wild punches, I moved to the right, threw a left, and connected with his proboscis. He never recovered from this, giving me an easy victory. Our platoon won overall, making it a great night.

The steeplechase went the same way. It was a massed start over a three-mile cross-country course. I came in second to my mate Joe from Lisburn. We were to become good friends and did everything together.

Carrying a stretcher loaded with sandbags over the tank tracks is not for the faint-hearted. It takes a lot of teamwork getting the balance right between men carrying and men resting. Everyone is wearing full battle order carrying weapons, and changing over frequently ensures you keep the pace going. You must also change sides to give your arms a rest, and most importantly stay in front of the opposition. It's not long before the physical effort and mud take their toll, causing men to fall behind, and some jacking in. This puts extra strain on those remaining. PTIs are shouting and encouraging all the time, offering words of wisdom like, "Come on, you lazy b'stds, I've seen faster-moving glaciers". We won this event, also earning the praises of our instructors.

So, with three events under the belt, we were fully confident of another victory. The log race is the most demanding of all physical activities in training and was saved to the last. Teams of twelve carried a telegraph pole between them across country for six miles, which terminated up a steep hill to the finish. Everyone was attached to the pole by a toggle rope. This was a ten-foot length of hemp rope about one inch in diameter with a wooden toggle spliced in at one end. Rhythm and coordination are the secret to fast progress, and changing positions on the log frequently is the key to speed. Either end of the log is the hardest, as this is where the weight is felt most. We were down to nine men by halfway, but were still a long way in front. The finishing line couldn't come fast enough and to this day I am still trying to get my breath back.

At the end of 10 weeks' basic training the two platoons were amalgamated to one. Out of seventy-odd starters we were reduced to thirty-four. Our next phase of training was learning to parachute. This was the responsibility of the RAF and we were transported to RAF Abingdon for this pleasure. Things relaxed a lot here and we found ourselves in another world. There were knives and forks laid out in the cookhouse, with butter on the table and sauce in proper containers. There was even a canteen with a jukebox in it. I was beginning to think I should have joined the RAF.

Life here was good. We were split into syndicates and mixed with men from all arms of the services. In my group was a Marine who was just like

Alan. He jumped at Suez, bayoneted a dozen enemy, blew up three bridges, and destroyed two tanks. He was a legend in his own NAAFI break. His name was Harry, a national serviceman.

Compared to depot, the training here was easy, but interesting. Learning parachute rolls, canopy control and aircraft drills filled a busy day. The instruction was brilliant, given with no bullying or shouting by very professional instructors.

We were accommodated a few miles from the airfield at a place called Culham in Nissen huts. These had seen better days and reminded me of home. It was coming up for Christmas and the weather was freezing. When you opened the door the cold would rush out. In the centre of the hut was a pot-bellied stove which we stoked up to the brim and never let it go out. Every Saturday morning we had a room inspection, but this was mild compared to Maida. You couldn't clean the windows too well, as they were loose and in danger of falling out. If the inspection was satisfactory, we could go out over the weekend. This particular Friday night we were all set to bulling up the hut, looking forward to some time off. The stove was smoking badly and Harry, who knew everything, was trying to fix it. He stood on the coal bunker and, leaning over the stove, reached up as high as he could, banging the chimney that went up through the roof, clinging onto it with a gloved hand, using the poker, hoping to clear the blockage. I went outside to see if I could spot any obstruction, leaving a room that sparkled. I climbed on the roof and grasped the chimney stack, giving it a good shake, and was surprised that I could lift it. So, shaking it vigorously while lifting, I give it all I've got. Imagine my surprise when I stopped shaking and let go of the chimney. The whole stack disappeared through the roof. With nothing left to hang onto, I nearly fell, but now I could do para rolls my only concern was "what's happened to the chimney?" When I re-entered the hut I couldn't believe my eyes: this was definitely not the spotless one I had left a few minutes earlier. Through the smoke and soot I could hear hysterical laughter and Harry's cries of woe. Everyone was splitting their sides with laughter but Harry was doing some ritualistic war dance, clutching his midriff which appeared to be smoking, and hollering his head off. Apparently, one minute Harry was balancing precariously over the stove, banging the pipe, when it disappeared. He fell over the stove that was glowing cherry red and branded himself with the manufacturer's name across his belly. Just as he was recovering himself, a large section of falling chimney reappeared, catching him squarely on the head with an eruption of soot, forcing him back on the stove once more. Clearing up the mess took hours, but we never stopped laughing. Harry was the centre of attention and for the duration of the courses was nicknamed Sooty. Being a Scotsman someone said, "Getting ready for Burns Night, Harry?" I was warming to this army lark.

The parachuting was scary, but I was more afraid of refusing in front of my mates than leaping out of the door. The choice between a rifting from the instructors or jumping was an easy one to make: when they said, "Jump", you jumped. We all had one thing in common…fear. The motto of the jump school was "Knowledge Dispels Fear", so I must have been really thick because I was terrified. You never forget your first jump, but it's the second one that's most memorable. The first one alerts you to all the dangers, but you don't believe you are 800 feet in the air dangling below a barrage balloon, and a lot of things go unnoticed. But on the second jump you don't miss anything and are aware of everything that's going on. You also know what to expect. This jump is made through an aperture in the balloon cage from 800 feet. Six more jumps from aircraft completed the course, and after four weeks we received our wings.

Although I didn't know it then, I was to do many more jumps, even taking it up as a hobby and paying for the privilege. I also represented the army.

WORDS OF WISDOM

Fear is the best laxative known to man.

There is nothing as frightening as fear.

INTERPRETER'S NOTE

WIMP Wet unconfident malingering pussy.

NAAFI No Ambition and F... All Interest.

POINTS TO PONDER

I met this girl in the NAAFI; she had a dog with her.

Runny nose, broken teeth, torn ear: the dog was rough as well.

FOOD FOR THOUGHT

Stood to attention resplendent with red beret, I looked like a Swan Vestas match.

It was back to good old Aldershot for continuation training, a place where we could strut in front of the new intake displaying our wings. We were soon brought back to earth with a bump when the training restarted, which was more intense than ever. Now we had to live up to the fearsome reputation of the Parachute Regiment. We had to march further, run faster, and look smarter than any other soldiers on earth. This was enforced by a roly-poly, swaggering dwarf who we dared not look at directly and avoided at all costs. Some said his skeleton was made of titanium and his blood contained kryptonite. I thought he was just a big fat, ignorant ba....d. This was our RSM. His responsibility was to ensure we were up to standard for the passing out parade. Rehearsals for this made Trooping the Colour look like a stroll in the park. Every day we marched with fixed bayonets in quick time, slow time, during daytime and night-time. Occasionally the RSM would swagger onto the square and take over the lesson. He would roar out a word of command and in the same breath scream, "As you were!" He would then inform the sergeant, "Take that man's name." "Got it, sir," the sgt replied. "Not that one, the man behind." "Got him as well, sir," was always the retort. The offenders were marched to jail where they spent a few hours being beasted by the provost staff. This was his way of getting everyone's attention: it never failed.

On a full dress rehearsal the RSM inspected us with microscopic intensity. I was still influenced by the Teddy Boy culture and had my trousers taken in. When issued, the trousers didn't move till I had taken a few paces, then they swished around my legs like spinnakers on a sailing yacht. I think the tailoress cut off a few yards of material, but this failed to impress old grumpy, who was threatening to have a coronary. The veins at his temple stood out like writhing eels on a fishmonger's slab. "Get him out of my sight," he bellowed, and poor Lofty was marched to the slammer. He obviously had no dress sense and there I was back with my old mate Crimpy once again. I think he had mellowed since our last meeting; his piles had taken their toll.

The passing out parade went without a hitch and my parents, who attended, were well impressed. My dad was over the moon and now I was his hero. My mum saw a group of recruits returning from a run covered in mud and this started the tears. She wanted to take them all home and feed them.

I forgot to mention that my mate Daisy, the army barmy one, joined two weeks after me. He only lasted three weeks before they slung him out. He had no coordination and marched with his left arm forward at the same time as his left leg, reminiscent of a scene from a Benny Hill sketch.

Before postings, we were given two weeks' leave, so wearing my best BD with newly sewn-on wings I strode out confidently for Downham. My boots were like mirrors, and it's worth mentioning the amount of time that went into getting them to this standard. At least an hour every day since they were issued was spent bulling them, ironing them flat before applying layers of polish rubbed in with a circular action. We called the polish a tin of little circles. We rubbed it in using the index finger, then with a wet cloth took it off again: this is the original spit and polish. One boot always came up better than the other and, try as you might, they were never the same. With metal tips at heel and toe and thirteen studs each, they weighed in at a few pounds. They were my pride and joy, but also became the cause of acute embarrassment.

On the way home I was tiptoeing down the escalator at the Tube station, which was jam-packed with commuters, and the next minute flat out down the bottom, lying prone on the station, wrapped around a hoarding advertising: a painless way of removing superfluous hair. My boots slipped and I beat everyone to the bottom. To rub salt into the wound, an old lady in her eighties helped pick me up. I don't think Alan ever had this problem.

Things had changed at home for the better: now I was a hero. My mother treated me like a conquering warrior, and the dinners got bigger and bigger. My dad even sorted out his W's from his B's. I heard him telling his mate that I was no longer a banker but had joined the West.

Another daring deed that went wrong because of my boots was when I jumped off a speeding bus. The bus route ran past the end of our turning and had bus stops 300 yards either side. You had the choice to get off at the first one or chance your arm and jump off before reaching the next, if conditions were right. Or, like everyone else, get off when the bus stops. Being unique, we always tried to save walking, and now I was airborne, speeding buses held no fear. So the drill was to come downstairs early and judge the speed as it passed our turning. If favourable, by crouching as low as possible at the rear of the platform hanging onto the pole, you could drop off, and as long as you got the legs going quick enough there was no problem. Normally if the bus was on time, the speed was reasonable and jumping was the standard routine. However, this night not only was the bus late, but also it was raining. I came downstairs thinking I will have to get off at the bus stop, but couldn't help but notice the scrutiny I was under from the clippie. She looked at me, looked outside, then back at me again, her eyes fixed first on my red beret, then my wings. Not a word was said but her expression said it all. I jumped!!

I remember seeing sparks, and, although my legs were doing 20 mph, my body was closer to 30 mph.

Back in Aldershot I was posted to Brigade HQ: this is where the soldiering begins, I thought. My first mistake was to ask an old sweat what the score was and he told me how cushy it was in Defence Platoon. "Don't bother to make your bed up, and no one inspects you on muster parade," he spoke with forked tongue. My second mistake was to believe him.

The muster parade was more intricate than the Opening of Parliament and the scrutiny from the sgt. major equal to anything I had experienced in my short career so far. I was checked for dirty beret, brasses, blanco, and boots. Leaves blew off the trees when the CSM roared; he was huge, the biggest thing I've seen without wheels on. My fate was sealed; I had to report to him later. We were dismissed to police the area while he went on to inspect the billet. Minutes later, I heard a scream of anguish and knew he had arrived at my bed space. All the new guys were introduced to the OC who asked various questions. My mate Joe was asked, "Where you from, private?" and Joe replied, "Depot, sir!" "I know that, where were you friggin' born?" "I don't honestly know, sir, I was very young at the time." The OC was trying to control his temper and create a good guy image to his new charges. He asked Scouse the old favourite, "Why did you join the army, Jones?" Expecting an intelligent reply, he completely lost it when Scouse replied, "My brother joined the paras six months ago and hated it, and I like what my brother don't." I was loving this banter and my grin was getting bigger and bigger, which didn't go unnoticed by the CSM who I had to see next.

He had a field day with me. "You dare show up on my parade wearing trousers that any self-respecting tramp would refuse to wear. Wearing a beret looking like the bottom of a baby's pram and find it amusing. Your belt looks like its been regurgitated, and I've seen better boots on a deep sea diver. The scruffiest stevedore from Malacca wouldn't be seen dead in that jersey, and your gaiters……" It went on and on. It was then that I realised I had made a grave mistake and I hated the army. What do I do next? I couldn't go home. One thing that was drilled into us from the very beginning was to use your airborne initiative. I certainly had to do this.

Delivering coal, emptying dustbins, and cleaning dixies filled the next six months of my life. At least when we emptied the bins we went to a tip where there was a good café. By a stroke of luck I got talking to a soldier who was on inter-tour leave from Malaya. He was in the SAS, a special unit that was resurrected in Malaya to carry out deep, penetrating patrols in the jungle against the CT, terrorists who Alan had told me all about months earlier in the Downham Tavern. This lad called Archie could have been related to Alan, as he was one of the biggest romancers I've ever met. His stories were better than Alan's but I was hooked: the SAS was for me.

I went to see the OC of my own free will and it made a difference not being marched in for a change. I told him I wanted to volunteer for the SAS and I could see the joy on his face spreading. It was infectious and even the CSM was smiling. Later he took me aside and clearly told me he never wanted to see me again. I said the feeling was mutual, and he even offered to help me pack. So grinning ear to ear like a dog with two dicks, I'm off again to Brecon.

It just goes to show:

WHO DARES GRINS

CHAPTER THREE

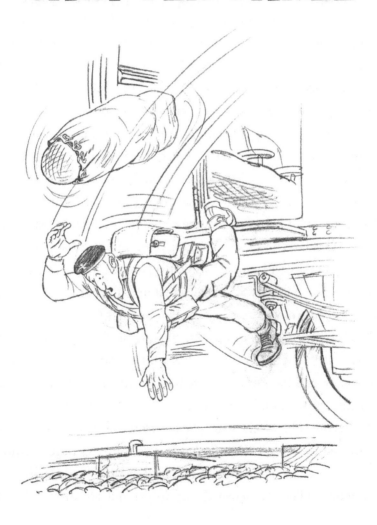

SELECTION

My joy at leaving Aldershot knew no bounds. I felt like Julie Andrews singing "The hills are alive with the sound of music" as they escaped from Nazi Germany. I had to travel in full-scale marching order, which is not very convenient. This was everything I owned or signed for, all my worldly possessions stowed in various pouches, pockets and packs. My greatcoat weighed a ton and was wrapped around my large pack. Hanging from this was a poncho gas mask and camouflaged net. My small pack contained clothing with a set of mess tins in the side pockets. Inside each mess tin were boot brushes, KFS and a button stick. In my ammunition pouches I carried spare socks, underwear and a *Daily Mirror*. As I walked everything creaked, jangled and grated, creating a cacophony of sound protesting against its configuration. My kitbag contained all of my combat kit, clothing and equipment, topped off by a steel helmet. It weighed in the region of 80 lbs. Reminiscent of an overloaded tinker, I started my journey to Dering Lines in Brecon where the SAS selection course was held. It was a Saturday morning, my favourite day of the week. No one could tell me what to expect, as the regiment was cloaked in secrecy. Nothing could be worse than Aldershot, so, with an open mind, laden down with kitbag hoisted above my large pack, I staggered to new horizons, keeping in rhythm to the noises that my kit was making: the old grin was back.

I had to change trains in Cardiff, crossing platforms against a torrent of humanity. It was international day, with England playing Wales. For every step forward I was knocked two back. I battled through, thinking this was all part of selection. I knew I had to change trains at a small station called Talybont, but wasn't told that the platform was so short that the train stopped to let the passengers for the front two carriages alight, then shunted forward and let the passengers in the rear two carriages disembark. Like a good soldier I anticipated our arrival and got dressed in all my paraphernalia. When the train stopped I opened the door and stepped out. It was like being back at jump school: there was nothing under my feet, just space. I was horizontal by the time I hit the track, and the initial impact, although heavy, was absorbed somewhat by my pouches. But eighty pounds of steel-tipped kitbag caught up with me with unerring accuracy, causing all the damage, forcing my head down deeper in the cinders. I lay there assessing my injuries, thinking how lucky I was to be Para-trained. That fall could have killed a civvy, and at least this time there was no old lady to help me up. I had a fat lip and a grazed nose that matched the colour of my beret.

I arrived at Brecon looking strictly second-hand and was met by a well-built guy wearing a sandy beret. "You look like you've had an interesting journey, mate: come and jump in the wagon." He took my kitbag and threw it in the back of the Land Rover with ease. This was the first time I had ever sat in the front of any military vehicle and the first time in a Land Rover. This may not sound very significant, but to me it was a momentous occasion. It had a pronounced effect on me: it was more like a welcoming home gesture than an introduction. Here was an old soldier calling me mate, wearing a parka. These were as rare as hen's teeth. He was in his thirties, sporting a large moustache that covered most of his lower face, and was wearing rubber-soled boots that I would have died for. He was wearing puttees that held his OG trousers neatly above his boots that were dubbined, not polished. This was how I always imagined soldiers to look like. First impressions are important and I was so impressed. This man made me feel wanted and I respect him to this day. I was accommodated in a spider with thirty others, making up a total of 120 for the course.

On the Sunday we went for a run first thing and spent the rest of the day getting kit issued: this was better than Christmas. I was issued a poncho that was waterproof that actually covered all the body. In the Paras we only had a gas cape that barely covered your top half. Next to come was a sleeping bag nicknamed 'the green maggot': things couldn't get any better. The nights I shivered under a lightweight blanket on Salisbury Plain don't bear thinking about. I was near to orgasm when given a windproof smock. This was made from cotton and, although you got soaked underneath, it kept you warm in much the same way as a wetsuit does in the sea. As long as you keep walking, your body retains the heat generated, and the windproof prevents heat loss caused by the wind. Unlike the Denison smock we wore in the paras, this dried out quickly, whereas the smock just got heavier and took weeks to dry. Jersey cobbly wobbly came next. This was a heavy-duty woollen jersey, reinforced at the shoulders and elbows. I was ready for anything now and itching to get going. Everyone got a prismatic compass, but not many of us knew how to use them. Usually only officers had these. All this kit was stowed in an 'A framed' bergan. There are better backpacks available today, but this was the dogs kahunas then.

A briefing was given that evening explaining what was required of us, and again I was impressed with the manner with which we were assembled and addressed. There was no shouting, bullying or abusing. It was like Heaven with the gates shut: a completely different atmosphere compared to Aldershot. I was with a great bunch of lads, drawn from all branches of the army. Making friends was easy, as we were all curious and needed each other to overcome the following weeks. We soon found out that, although we came from a variety of backgrounds, we all had two things in common. We were all fed up with our own units and looked forward to some real soldiering.

The Para Brigade and the infantry made up the majority of the course, but most corps were represented. The average age was probably twenty-six; I was still a fresh eighteen-year-old, but now dressed to kill. It started raining that night and didn't stop for the next fortnight.

Selection was very physical and initially an individual effort. To wheedle

100 plus down to a more manageable number for continuation training, we were subjected to long marches carrying heavy weights over the Brecon Beacons. Each day the distance got longer and the weight heavier, and you were encouraged to go as fast as possible. Cliff Richard had the hit record at the time which was very inappropriately called "Travelling Light". What lyrics: I could eat alphabet soup and vomit better than these. He has a lot to answer for. My missus loves him, and surprisingly he is the same age as me. All the kids ask me why we don't look the same. They say, "He looks so young while you look so old." All I can say is, "He isn't married to your mother."

There were no parades, no early calls, just a roll call. You were told what truck you were on and what maps required. If you didn't make the transport it was taken for granted that you had quit. You could jack in at any time: it was a self-selecting process. As long as you kept going and achieved the times set for each exercise you stood a chance of passing. No one knew the times allowed: this ensured you went as fast as possible. Even if you were the first in, it didn't necessarily mean that you had passed.

It was always an early start, around four o'clock most mornings. The first person we saw was Scouse, the cook. What a sight for sore eyes first thing in the morning. All the stoves were coke-fired and his first job was to get these lit. He was always covered head-to-toe in soot. His whites were black and his face permanently camouflaged. Everything he cooked was swimming in fat, just what we needed to keep out the cold. You could have as many runny eggs as you wished and as much bacon that you could get on your plate. Not many men came to breakfast, preferring to stay in bed for that little bit of extra sleep. I used to go to bed fully dressed and only had to get up and put my boots on. I didn't tie these till I was in the cookhouse. Jacky had an electric razor which six of us shared, and we could do this while eating.

We were given a haversack lunch each day which never varied. One spam, one cheese, one plain butter sandwich, and one boiled egg. If we stayed out longer than twelve hours, a bar of chocolate was included. We took it in turns to make these haversacks, preparing them of an evening. We got this down to a fine art. One man dealt the bread onto the table like a Mississippi gambler, while another brushed on the marge that was melted on the stove. Someone else lobbed on the spam or cheese, and another packed them complete with egg. Although not very appetising they were wolfed down, and there were never any complaints. For a laugh to set someone up, we sometimes left out the spam and cheese and put in a cardboard replica with 'this is a steak sandwich' written with marker pen on it.

Our instructors were excellent. They were very experienced and gave great advice, although this was not always appreciated at the time. They built you up and offered encouragement when needed. No one wore rank, and imagine my surprise when I discovered the guy who picked me up from the station was a sergeant. To put this in perspective: when my mate got made up in the Paras we celebrated with a few beers and got involved in a large punch-up downtown. In the morning the CSM got a grip of Joe and ripped his stripe off, saying what a disgrace he was to the Regiment. Joe protested his innocence, explaining that some crap hats started the fight and denounced the Paras. The CSM was unmoved. "It's not the fighting I'm upset about, it's you drinking with privates that I find despicable."

The instructors (DS) manned the checkpoints and RVs, hustling you on to the next one. It was no good looking for any sympathy, as you were told it comes between shit and syphilis in the dictionary.

I vividly remember the first day when we were turned loose over the Beacons. Dropped off individually, we were given RVs to make. This entailed going over Pen y Fan a couple of times. When you could see through the rain the scenery was magnificent, but unfortunately I couldn't relate it to my map or know where I was on it. When you could identify a summit it simplified matters, but when the mist came down I was lost. I covered twice as much ground as anyone else and failed to make some checkpoints. That night I was advised to take the compass from the bottom of my bergan and use it. That's how I learnt to navigate. Each day I got more confident and started getting a feel for the ground, using time and distance with magnetic bearings. Map-reading is fine when you have an accurate map, but places in the world where the Regiment often operated were unmapped. So to get you accustomed to this, we were introduced to a sketch map. There is very little topographical information on a sketch map, making you rely solely on compass bearings. This ingrained into me the importance of the compass. The only way to maintain orientation in any weather night or day is by using the compass. Remember this old Chinese proverb:

YOU CAN GO NORTH WITH A TOUCH OF EAST

YOU CAN GO SOUTH WITH A TOUCH OF WEST

YOU CANNOT GO NORTH WITH A TOUCH OF SOUTH

In the Paras my confidence was destroyed by my platoon officer. He took us out one night on a recce on Salisbury Plain. He was the only one with map and compass, and we blindly followed him. After two hours meandering we knew we were lost. On one rest halt one of the lads had a crap and, being on compo rations all week, it was enormous and half-blocked the track. Our plight was confirmed when we passed it for the second or turd time. We eventually stopped and watched the sun coming up on a nice patch of level grass. Believe it or not, we had finished up on a golf course. This had to be Tidworth that was at least twenty miles off our route. His debriefing went something like, "Of course we were on a course, although we were off course."

I was lucky to have good feet and started selection wearing my best boots. A pound on the feet is equivalent to ten on the back, so I was handicapped like Arkle. They didn't stay best boots for long, but were my only boots for some time. They were indestructible: you couldn't wear them out. They were eventually replaced by a rubber-soled pair months later. They really came into their own at the end of selection, when the powers that be thought it a good idea to break Barbara Moore's record. She was no spring chicken and covered a hundred miles in twenty-four hours. This was on roads, so after the mountains it seemed a snip. But it was hard on the feet. I was lucky, but some of the lads never recovered, with blisters that turned septic and never healed. Of course we had to do it carrying rifles and a fifty-pound bergan. On selection we were not allowed to use any roads or tracks, so we were not used to the continuous impact of a hard surface. Later, I did suffer two broken metatarsals which I blame on this folly, but no blisters.

There were lots of injuries keeping the medics and doctor busy. It's so easy to turn an ankle or tear ligaments. The MI room was open all hours so the lads could receive treatment. They were frightened to tell the doc too much in case they got withdrawn from the course. A typical diagnosis went something like this:

Where does it hurt?

Here and there.

When does it hurt?

Now and again.

Let me put this on.

When can I walk again?

Sooner or later.

The weight carried puts a huge strain on the body, and bergan sores were common. These are caused by the continuous chaffing of the backpack to unprotected flesh. The best way of avoiding these was to pack the frame of the bergan with a poncho, keeping the frame away from the body. It also helps to pack it correctly. Heavy, bulky items should be carried as high as possible, relieving pressure on the lower back. Increasing the width of the shoulder straps also helps to distribute the load. I found it beneficial to take some of the weight of the pack on my belt gear. By resting the pack on my water bottles it took weight of my shoulders. Modern packs incorporate this with a waist belt. I must have been born before my time. Regardless of how you carry the kit, you still have to get it from A to B as fast as possible. The last exercise on test week is Endurance. This is a 55-kilometre march with 55 lbs on your back. It's over the highest peaks in the Beacons and 20 hours are allowed for this. The weight of the pack was strictly monitored. Each day you were told the weight and bricks were used as ballast. These had 'TW' (Training Wing) painted on them so they couldn't be jettisoned. There was random testing at some RVs. Scales were produced and Heaven help anyone who was light. They were given a rock as compensation signed by the instructor that had to be produced at the end of the march.

One thing they don't do now which we did was a weight march. We were laden up with support weapons and ammo, and organised in groups of six. Every man carried eighty pounds plus and shared the thirty-two-pound Browning machine gun and the eighteen-pound tripod, as well as their personal weapon.

At the end of the day we were exhausted, but had to dry out kit and clothing for the morning before we turned in. It rained every day during test week, and it was always a race to get to the drying room first and get the best spot. So reaching the final RV early ensured you got on the first truck back to camp, and stood a chance of having dry kit in the morning. This didn't always work out to plan, and many a morning we were soaked before we started. The last truck was hours behind the first one, having to wait for stragglers, making it very difficult for those on-board to adequately prepare for the next day. The food was cold, all the hot water gone, and no space left in the drying room. We were always starving and the size of our meals took some believing. It was a workout on its own lifting the laden plates to the table.

Weapons had to be cleaned and this was usually done on the trucks going back to camp. These were old FN rifles, but they had to be spotless, and severe penalties were handed out to transgressors. One of the penalties was manning the telephone exchange: more about this later.

Some lads recall that the worst part of selection was travelling in the four-tonners. These trucks never had a complete canopy on. It was always torn, unlaced or missing. In the back it was freezing, so we used to get in our sleeping bags. The drivers were practising for Brands Hatch and threw the trucks around with gay abandon. We were packed tightly, spread over the bench seats and floor, but still got tossed around. We didn't have the strength to complain; at least we got back to camp quickly. Years later, a Yank was heard to say, "No wonder you've so many good racing drivers: you're always practising."

Each day the course got smaller and smaller. Initially most were voluntary withdrawals, or those medically unfit to carry on. As the course progressed, men were withdrawn if the standard wasn't reached. They were RTU'd (returned to unit). No way was I going back: I loved it here. From one hundred and twenty personnel that started, at the end of test week we were down to sixteen.

Test week, that actually lasted ten days, was mainly physical. It was designed to test stamina to the limit and selected those who never gave in, regardless of the situation. It was an individual effort: you were not allowed to follow anyone. In the beginning everyone was encouraged to keep going, but as the numbers diminished we were invited to drop out. It was mind games that you had to overcome. You would reach what you thought was the last RV only to be told there was another three clicks away. It was your choice either to get on the transport there, or go to the final RV. Naturally, if you wanted to pass you carried on and were called back after covering a hundred yards or so.

No two days were ever the same, but they all started pretty much alike. Jick's alarm clock would penetrate the subconscious, bringing you back to reality from a deep dream where the sun was always shining. Gradually the snoring and the smells would waken the senses, helping to orientate the mind as to where you are at 3.30 on a typically freezing Welsh morning. You could stay in bed for another month and still feel tired, but you had to move. As soon as you did, the aches and pains returned with a vengeance. Normally you didn't notice the smell, accepting it as normal, but it was unique to a coke-heated basha full of sweaty, encrusted clothing drying around the stove. Jick was always the first one up and got the fire going again. It was topped up last thing at night and only needed the damper opening and a quick poke. Sounds like a 'bishop and the actress joke'. Once or twice the fire went out, so it was wet kit at the start, and condensation froze on the windows, lowering the temperature to subarctic proportions. Hopefully you took the time to stuff your boots with newspaper the night before, helping them dry out. Although you should never place leather close to any heat source, we used to ignore this and many boots cracked and curled. You had to make sure to remove all traces of newspaper before putting them on, as on one occasion I was halfway up Pen y Fan when forced to stop because of great discomfort. On removing the offending boot I discovered half a page still stuffed up in the toecap. I think my toes were doing the crossword puzzle.

Fully dressed, it was off to the drying room and retrieve all items such as webbing, bergan or sleeping bag, which were left overnight to dry. There was only room around the stove for boots and some clothing, until we were thinned out. Off to the cookhouse and load up with as much grease as possible. Pints of tea were swallowed between mouthfuls of egg, bacon, fried bread and beans, remembering to pick up a haversack before going to the arms khote which was next to the guardroom where we mustered. We took it in turns to sign out and hand in weapons, and pick up haversacks for anyone who didn't make breakfast. This really helped when pushed for time, which we always were. When your name was called out you got on a truck, and when this was full, away you went to a drop-off point. This was always miles from the beaten track down a narrow path that only the instructors knew. When the truck stopped, one man jumped off and was shown where they were on the map. A blade of grass was used for this, never a finger. A grid reference of the first RV point was given, and once you convinced the staff you knew where you were going, they would drive on to the next release point. Sometimes it was beneficial to get off early; other times it was favourite to leave it as long as possible.

It always paid to study the map and select a route before plodding on. Hours could be saved by choosing the best route. When orientated it was head down and keep going. It rained consistently on my course and you were wet through in minutes but comfortable as long as you were on the move. Stops were kept to a minimum, but it was wise to stop and adjust the pack if it was uncomfortable, or if a sock was slipping down. The secret to prevent this was to wear nylon socks next to the skin, and the army-issued wool pair on top. This prevented them slipping which caused pressure ridges which damaged the feet. You always seemed to be going uphill and heading against the wind. Usually it was still dark when we were dropped off, and as the light improved, features were recognised and this helped to confirm your position. Other figures could be seen on the skyline scurrying to their RVs. It was no good following, as they were on different routes. It was a great relief to make the first RV where you were checked out by the DS (Directing Staff) to see if you could continue and given the next checkpoint. As little time as possible was spent here. You cleared the RV before plotting your next route. On some checkpoints on the longer tabs, tea and food were given. On Endurance I vaguely remember getting a tot of rum. This was G10 rum, probably the strongest spirit on earth. Under its influence you could amputate your own leg and not realise it till you tried to stand up.

It was fatal to sit down as the body cooled off so quickly. Muscles starting cramping and ligaments and tendons tightened. It was easier to run downhill zigzagging under control, with the legs wide apart. On the flat we jogged and attacked the climbs with as much energy as could be mustered. You promised yourself a rest when you reached a certain rock, but kept on going till you reached the summit where again you promised yourself another rest but rarely took it.

When the weather closed in or at night, the compass was out all the time. When marching on a compass bearing, the brain thinks it is going in a circle. It takes time to get confidence in the compass but it never lies. Trying to maintain a straight line without one is nigh on impossible. What you think is a straight line is in fact a big arc.

Rain was uncomfortable but wind was the killer. It was relentless, attacking all parts of the body, stripping it of heat. It played havoc with the bergan, often forcing you off-balance. When tired you fell over more frequently, and battling against the wind quickly uses up energy. You always looked for shelter when stopping, normally a rock or a dip in the ground, anything to get out of the wind.

Decisions had to be made on what route to take. You could either contour, which is tiring, or climb straight up to the ridge. A lot depended on your condition, the terrain, and the weather. Good map-readers picked the best route, and I was upset not to be the first man in. I knew I was faster than most but lacked the map-reading skills. I soon learnt. It was a great feeling to be amongst the first in at the final RV. You had time to make a brew and clean your weapon before there were enough men to fill up the truck and return to base.

The next phase of selection was continuation training, where compatibility, mental strength and intelligence were tested. Working behind enemy lines in small groups is very demanding, so everyone must get on.

After test week, continuation was a doddle. There were still night navigation exercises which were very demanding but interspaced with weapon training, range work and small unit tactics. We were introduced to foreign weapons and this impressed me no end. We also did a demolition course that broke every rule in the book. It was fantastic and whetted my appetite. Years later, I was to run the Regimental demolition cadre which was one of the best courses in the army. My interest in explosives was aroused in that watercourse that ran through Cwm Gwdi ranges, where charges were placed and exploded. At the end of the day any explosive or devices left were placed in a hole and detonated. The resulting shock wave rerouted the stream and brought a ceiling down in a cottage a mile away.

We formed into a tight-knit group and the lads I passed selection with became my best friends: you never forget them. In later years we became each other's best man when we got married. Only five of us passed selection and we were all Paras. Three more went on to join the Signal Squadron, and Dutch, who passed selection, was one of the few men to fail his Para course. Jick, Rob, Jackie and Stan were the paras. Ralph, Geordie and Jim were the signallers.

In many ways I found selection easier than basic training. All the hardships and physical discomfort shared with a great bunch of blokes welded us together, making us inseparable. I can think of no other process that comes close to achieving this lifelong bond.

Special mention must be made to the sergeant major who ran selection. Paddy was one of life's good guys. He asserted his authority with humour, and achieved a rare quality: respect. He went out of his way to help anyone who needed it and encouraged rather than condemned. Manning the telephone exchange out of working hours was the only punishment dished out, and this led to quite a problem. One of the lads lived in Scotland in a remote village called Graillach that no one had ever heard of. He used to phone his wife regularly, putting the call through himself. When the phone bill was checked at the end of the month, the OC wanted to know who had run up the large amount phoning a place called Graillach. Obviously Jock was the prime suspect, but in his defence when accused of this he said, "If I catch the b'std who's phoning my wife I'll kill him."

We had an end-of-course party and he was the star turn. He knew more rugby songs than anyone present and wasn't too shabby at dancing. At the end of the evening one of the lads stripped off, and to cover his embarrassment Paddy shoved a dustbin over his head. It just goes to show:

WHO BARES BINS

CHAPTER FOUR

LIFE IN 'A' SQUADRON

After completing selection we had two weeks' leave before reporting back to Malvern where the Regiment was based. During this leave I bought a motorbike and sidecar, and used this to return to camp. It was an old Royal Enfield and cost me £18 in old money. It was an uneventful journey until I reached Oxford when a small explosion blew the dynamo through the sidecar. A small petrol leak accumulated on top of the magneto which the dynamo was bolted to. This must have grown into a large puddle before it got ignited by a stray spark from the magneto. It missed my leg by inches and had sufficient velocity to penetrate into the sidecar. I could still drive the bike but it meant I had no lights. I was deployed to the Middle East two weeks later, and left that combination behind a shop in Malvern. As far as I am aware it is still there to this day.

Meerbrook camp was an old American Army hospital located about five miles outside of Malvern. After reporting in and assigned accommodation, the first familiar face I saw was Jick who had returned off leave early. We actually walked to town for a pint. Malvern is built on the side of a hill, and you are going either up or down, never on the flat. At least it was mainly downhill back to camp.

We were welcomed by the colonel whose nickname was 'the cupboard'. In the last war he hid in a cupboard for fourteen days to avoid capture. We were told not to expect any rank, promotion or medals. Just being part of the finest regiment in the British Army should be reward enough. We were told in no uncertain terms that we were on a probationary period, and until we proved ourselves, were a liability rather than an asset. We were handed our sandy berets at last and wore them with pride. All five of us were posted to 2 Troop A Squadron. We celebrated this achievement many times in the next fortnight. Our arrival in the Squadron hardly raised an eyebrow and we were ignored by most of the troop. This was normal practice, apparently, and it encouraged us to look and listen. The regiment had just returned from Malaya where they were resurrected in 1950 after being disbanded at the end of the last war. Some of the yarns had became folklore, and as we felt our way to become part of the troop, these fascinating stories were retold. I must stress these are unconfirmed stories. My indoctrination had begun.

During one operation a patrol had a contact and killed a terrorist who they believed to be a ringleader. Having no camera, they needed to have evidence for identification, so they cut the head off. This was wrapped in cloth and carried by the patrol commander. Things went wrong when they returned to base. The patrol commander suffered an attack of malaria and was taken to hospital in a feverish stupor. He kept gibbering about his bergan, so the driver, thinking he was doing a good turn, delivered it to his married quarter. Like a dutiful wife who was used to his filthy kit after an operation, she opened the pack to wash it, especially the dirty bundle on top. She got a nasty surprise when she unwrapped this, and certainly wasn't expecting a Chinese takeaway. Most soldiers took their wives perfume.

Even harder to swallow was another story of a contact where the lead scout shot a CT, and gave chase to three others. They had been in the Ulu for months and their kit was falling apart. The second member of the patrol was renowned as the best scrounger in the regiment, and allegedly overtook the lead scout, taking up the chase wearing the dead man's boots.

These are the stories I was brought up on, and I longed for the day when I could tell my own tales.

No one wore rank, and to any outsider a soldier could be anything from a trooper to a colonel. This was very advantageous at times and led to some interesting situations. I once attended a course with Dusty who looked very distinguished with a well-clipped moustache. We got a taxi from the station to the barracks where we were going to learn all about malaria at the Army School of Health, back in good old Aldershot. For some reason the driver dropped us at the officers' mess and we were surprised to be greeted by a captain who actually picked up Dusty's suitcase and carried it up the steps of the mess. They were deep in conversation and I followed behind, and couldn't help hearing the change of tone in the captain's voice. It got louder and very agitated. I clearly heard the scream, "TROOPERS!" and had to take evasive action to avoid Dusty's suitcase that came flying down the steps followed by Dusty.

Another time, years later, my patrol was waiting to be weighed in before insertion into the jungle. We had the honour of the colonel's presence. The RAF corporal called us forward one by one to manifest us for the flight. "Rank?" he asked. "Trooper" was the reply. "Next, rank?" "Trooper." And so it went on. The cpl was getting cocky with all the seniority power he wielded. When he got to the last man, who happened to be the colonel, he said, "I suppose you're a trooper also." He was gobsmacked and brought back to earth with a bang when the answer to his question he was, "No, I am a colonel and getting paid for the privilege."

It was noticeable that no two soldiers were dressed the same. Although we were all issued with the same kit, it wasn't worn at the same time. It's amazing the number of combinations made possible by mixing and matching jungle kit with desert issue with items that were begged, borrowed or stolen.

Even muster parade was fun. The SSM called the role and used the old guys' nicknames if they didn't answer. Drill was not a strong point, so we lined up in open order and were called to attention. It went something like this. "Excuse ranks, listen in. Smith." "Sir." "Brown." "Sir." "Williams." Deadly silence. "Williams." No answer. "Anyone seen Debussy?" On one occasion the SSM gave one of the lads a hefty dig in the ribs for answering for his absent mate. "I respect you for sticking up for a mate, but I don't like you thinking I'm an idiot."

I realised I was in the company of men who did not let this lax atmosphere in any way lower their professional standards. They had to be treated with respect in order to give respect. Looking back, I now realise that Basic Training was the best possible preparation for selection and inclusion to the Regiment. It wasn't very pleasant – medicine rarely is – but it thoroughly prepared me for anything that I was likely to encounter in the armed forces. It taught me discipline, loyalty and respect. Without these virtues I could easily have gone off the rails. The reason I did so well in the Regiment was due to that training. It prepared me to handle self-discipline, which is the hardest discipline of all. It's only once you have this that you can advise or train others. It was a tried and tested system that no one escaped or bettered. The saying 'Train Hard and Fight Easy' is very valid, and it all starts with basic training. No one beat the system and this discipline is so ingrained, like the lettering in seaside rock. Once there, it lasts a lifetime.

I hardly got used to my new surroundings or comrades before we flew out to Oman in the Persian Gulf. It was an oil-rich state that was getting over a coup from the year before. Communist-inspired rebels attempted to seize power from the Sultan, and the Regiment were deployed in a masterly fashion to put down the revolt. They scaled Jebel Akhdar at night and completely surprised the rebel stronghold on top of what they thought was an impregnable position. It was all very hush-hush, with few people ever hearing about it. We were being deployed to enforce the peace and record topographical information. There were still minor skirmishes between those loyal to the rebels and local security forces.

Anyone familiar with the armed forces will be aware of 'crabs'. These small body lice cling to any hairy region of the body, but especially favour the genital area. 'A Squadron' adopted the crab as its mascot, calling it 'Gripus Titus'. Everywhere we went we left behind this motif. The airport was suitably adorned with little red crabs drawn in the unlikeliest of places. No toilet seat or cupboard door escaped: one even appeared on the control tower.

Oman was very hot and dusty, which did little to make our tented camp comfortable. The only tent used was the mess tent, as we preferred to sleep outside on camp beds. Working dress was a pair of shorts and boots. We were camped just outside a village called Ibris, which was the nearest source of water, and every day a bowser would go and fill up, keeping the camp supplied. We only spent a short time here getting acclimatised, zeroing weapons, and servicing trucks. We did the odd patrol to test the radios and shake down all the kit needed for the next four months. There was a very prominent rock a few miles away and one of the lads couldn't resist climbing it and drawing on 'Gripus Titus', which could be seen for miles.

We were deployed in one-ton Austin trucks. Each troop had four of these loaded with sufficient stores to last a month. We set off on all points of the compass to map and gain intelligence of the whole of Oman. Like washing an elephant, a huge undertaking.

Each truck would follow the leader till we reached a specific area where we would split up and carry out area searches. There was only me and Eddie on my truck and Ali the interpreter, whom we called 'Lips'. We took it in turns to drive: Eddie had only just passed his driving test and I didn't even have a licence. The terrain was very harsh on the vehicles, and with inexperienced drivers lots of breakdowns happened. By the end of four months we knew every inch of that vehicle and could drive it blindfolded over any terrain. We soon got through the vehicle spares which we carried, half-shafts and springs being the common causes of breakdowns. These were resupplied by air, free dropped with no parachutes.

We were living on ten-man compo packs which were nearly all A menu, making our choice of meals limited. Ali was a strict Muslim and couldn't eat certain foods. The main meal was mutton, Scotch-style. After the first week we were fed up with this. We curried it, baked it, fried it. Took out the barley, put in potato powder, left out the carrots. No matter what we did, it still tasted the same. Curry was the only answer. This was my introduction to curry. It was always a competition to see who could make the hottest. Having Ali on our truck put us well in the lead. It took a lot of getting used to, but now I can take it intravenously. For the first fortnight my Khyber looked like a Japanese sunset: no wonder the locals washed their backsides.

We covered many miles and would go weeks without seeing another human. One day we came across a seismic camp at a place called Habrut. This was just a drilling rig surrounded by half a dozen Portakabins. I went back there years later and was amazed to find a small town thriving. This was the first location to produce oil in the country and we happened to drive into this camp when they had just received a resupply for winning a competition for the most holes drilled. Although they had not found oil yet, they were confident it was there. The reward for this was beer. We thought we were witnessing a mirage when we first saw the camp shimmering in the heat on the horizon. We were handed cold beers and sat down in proper chairs for a chicken salad followed by fresh fruit. That evening we had a film show: it was Bruce Woodcock fighting Joe Baksi. There was a carpet laid in the mess tent that would not have looked out of place in a stately home: these guys sure knew how to rough it. What really impressed me was the refrigerators that ran on paraffin. To me it was a marvel of modern technology: how could a heat source turn something cold?

The seismic crew really made us welcome as they hadn't seen any new faces for months. We just tipped up out of the wilderness and were treated like heroes. Their mechanics helped service our vehicles, and welded a gun mount on the cab that would take a .30 Browning. Another truck got a seat welded on the roof for the comfort of the passengers. You can imagine what state we were in the following morning. Brummie accused someone of spewing on him during the night. The lad retaliated, saying, "You want to find that bloke: he also shit your trousers."

Another thing that impressed me was the lads doing astronavigation. They would set up the theodolite every evening and plot the stars to give us a geographical fix. The mathematics involved were complicated. Sometimes we were placed 200 miles out in the Indian Ocean. The first Sputnik was flying around the earth, and the same guy who asked the drilling crew what they were drilling for, was led to believe he could see it through the theodolite. He thought that petrol, diesel, paraffin and oil were in separated layers at different depths. He would spend hours searching the heavens, only to be told he had just missed it and it would be visible in another hour. I was glad that he was the butt of their pranks and not me. One of his appointments before coming to the troop was provost sergeant!!!

The desert is a very harsh place: everything in it has to be tough to survive. A good example of this is the acacia. To protect itself from unwanted diners, it arms itself with very sharp thorns. Of a night hours were passed digging these out of each other. We only wore shorts, even when recceing on foot, so the odd scratch was inevitable. We were all jealous of the truck with the newly welded seat until one day, when negotiating a difficult steep descent, the driver lost it and careered off-track through a stand of acacia. The two reclining sunbathers were impaled and many hours were spent that night digging for thorns. If any part was left in, it turned septic.

Another memorable scene was early one morning when Dave, the driver of the second truck, decided to check his vehicle. This was called first parade and all fluid levels, tyre pressures and wheel nuts are checked, and any signs of leaks or wear are recorded. His crew were still trying to snatch a few more winks and ignoring his loud rendition of "Oh what a beautiful morning", which he sang with great gusto every morning without fail. The truck was facing downhill and Dave finished his check straddling the front bumper with the bonnet up. He got the fright of his life when he pressed the solenoid to start the engine and it was in gear. Because it was facing downhill it took off, gathering speed and dragging scrim nets and ponchos with it. His crew took evasive action, knocking over mess tins full of boiling water in their haste to roll away. His singing surprisingly stopped as he sped spreadeagled over the bonnet, heading for a patch of dreaded acacia. He entered the trees at 20 mph with skin and shorts, and exited at 30 mph with a lot of both missing. He finally came to rest at the bottom of the hill.

We stopped camel trains that we came across and searched them for mines and explosives. It was like turning the clock back centuries: little had changed. They carried salt and spices across great tracts of desert using no navigational aids except what nature provided. Using the sun and the stars and thousands of years of experience they graced the earth. Here we were with all our technology still plotting our position in the Indian Ocean.

We found the most accurate way of navigating was by using time and distance. Keeping an eye on the speedo to work out an average speed and constantly checking the compass for direction, we got fairly accurate. If you haven't an accurate map to relate this to, it's hard to establish with certainty exactly where you are. Our maps were very vague, taken from air photographs: nothing had been surveyed. We filled in all the missing bits like village names, ground conditions, tracks and unmarked wells.

We roamed the Empty Quarter and crossed a large area of salt sea. This was just like a choppy sea that had been frozen. It was so hard on the trucks negotiating three-foot-high waves of solid salt. Progress was slow and uncomfortable. Nothing survived here: it was desolate wasteland. The name Empty Quarter says it all. Just a featureless expanse looking the same in all directions, making navigation difficult. After many days of seeing nothing we were pleasantly surprised to see a pinnacle of rock sticking up on the horizon. We thought we would get there and have a brew. It was best part of fifty miles away and took most of the day to get there: distances are very deceiving in the desert. One truck went one way and the second one the other, and they met head-on at the back of the feature. For the crack they wrote out an accident report, the only one ever recorded from the Empty Quarter.

No matter where you go in the desert, as soon as you stop there are flies. What they survived on before you pitch up is one of Mother Nature's miracles.

Up in the Niswah area we cordoned and searched villages. This is where the coup started the previous year. We also climbed Jebel Akhdar, all 11,000 feet of it. The villages on the Jebel were amazing. They irrigated their land carrying water in falages. The Persians had built these hundreds of years ago, and they still work to this day. These water channels were built of rock and clay and contoured the Jebel, carrying water to where it was needed. They supported wildlife such as frogs, fish and birds, which were a welcome sight after the barren regions we had just come from.

In the villages our medic treated the locals, and I became his assistant. He dealt with some difficult cases and I learnt a lot from him. Every member of the troop had a prime skill and I was impressed by their expertise. I had so much to learn.

I learnt one very important lesson on this trip. At the end of thousands of miles' travelling we returned to Ibris with four months' growth and ingrained dirt. We were greeted by the SSM and told the beer tent was open and a truck was available to take anyone up to the oasis for a bath. I looked at Eddie for guidance and followed him into the beer tent. We sat there drinking ice-cold beer and hadn't finished the first one before we heard an explosion. The bath truck had hit a mine. They say that cleanliness is next to godliness, and fortunately no one was seriously injured. But they were nearer godliness than they intended. Eddie said if you ever get to decide between a bath or a beer, take the beer every time. What a philosopher: what good advice. The driver of the bath truck was involved in taking the trucks back to Muscat. He stayed in the middle of the convoy but still managed to run over another mine. He survived without a scratch and this endorses the theory that you will only go if you're meant to.

This trip gave me an excellent insight as to what the Regiment was all about. I had so much to learn, and in the coming months volunteered for every course going.

We returned to Malvern and went on leave from here, but after leave had to report back to Bradbury Lines in Hereford, which was to be our new home.

After an excellent leave flourishing my duty-free watch and suntan at every opportunity, I set off for Hereford. I had bought a Norton Dominator and was going to return in style. All was well until I reached Hereford. I didn't know where the camp was, so stopped to ask a guy for directions. He was carrying a large suitcase and, luckily for me, he was a soldier returning to camp. He offered to show me the way and climbed on the pillion, settling the suitcase across his knees and telling me to 'screw the nut'. I was getting tired by this time and looking forward to a bath. I was halfway across a junction when he said, "Left." I leant the bike over and made the turn. We were fast approaching another junction when he said, "Right." I should have carried on and made a U-turn but I attempted to make the turn. I remember hitting the kerb and becoming airborne. In mid-flight I looked over my shoulder and my passenger was in formation, flying slightly higher than me and still clutching his suitcase. He looked like Mary Poppins. When I landed and cleared my head, he was gone and I have never seen him to this day. I still didn't know where the camp was, and spent the next hour recovering bits of bike and luggage.

Hereford was a great place to be stationed. A small city split by the River Wye, it boasted more pubs than houses, at least that what it felt like. Dependent on agriculture and tourism, it has the largest cider brewery in the world. Unlike Aldershot, we were the only soldiers. There was an RAF camp five miles out of town, but we rarely saw anyone from there. When the locals heard we were coming they were concerned. We were replacing a boys' artillery unit, and they were bad enough. Now they had to put up with some hairy-arsed Special Forces. It couldn't have worked out better. 1960 saw the worst floods for years and we helped rescue stranded animals, workers and farmers, and took food to outlying communities. We ferried people over the Wye which was nineteen feet higher than normal. This cemented our relationship with Hereford and many lads married local girls. We named these 'white faces' after the breed of cattle. One memorable night we took tea to a convent. Climbing up to the second floor and hanging onto fresh air, I passed a flask to a nun. "Has it got sugar in?" she asked. "Yes, love, it's got everything," I answered, hanging onto nothing. "We don't take sugar." I forgot where I was and swore. As we were leaving she shouted, "May God go with you!" My mate replied, "I hope so, I can't swim." We were to receive the Freedom of the City and Hereford became our ancestral home.

Cider is a risky drink to overindulge in. It's so sweet you don't realise its effect until you try to stand up. You get drunk from the waist down, and, although you still have all your faculties, your legs have a mind of their own. One pub we liked was a scrumpy house that served up a strong cider that aggravated your thirst, rather than quenching it, causing you to drink more. Jick, Rob and I had become inseparable and became known as 'The Three Musketeers'. We went everywhere together and never stopped laughing. We enjoyed darts and always started the evening with a few games.

After a few pints of 'rough' we played darts, and big Rob needed double top for the game. He was so laid back he looked like a scene from a slow-motion movie. He was so economical with energy that he only breathed in. He ambled up to the oche, took deliberate aim, then turned and rushed to the door. To see him move so fast was a rare treat. He returned shortly after, fully composed but walking funny, and got his double top. He then calmly walked up to the bar and asked, "Have you got the key to the toilet?" Cider definitely loosens the bowels, and Rob touched cloth in a big way.

It was through playing darts that we met a character called Jack Thomas. Jack was an ex-matelot from Wales with a beautiful tenor voice. Jack and his wife Molly became a second set of parents to me, and I can honestly say that I have never met a family like them. More about the Thomases later.

We hadn't been home long before going to Norway for winter warfare training. Bardufoss, which is four hundred miles inside the Arctic Circle, was, as you can imagine, freezing. Yet here we were in temperatures of -30 wearing the same kit as we wore in the desert but with a few additions like long johns, string vest and a parka. Our same boots were suitably modified with three wood screws screwed into the heel to take a ski binding. To top off this elegant attire we each had a pair of yellow-lensed welder's goggles, woollen gloves, and a cap comforter. The Norwegians had never seen anything like it. We looked more like a penal battalion than Britain's finest. We were a good source of amusement for them, as they had very little entertainment at these latitudes.

After the first day they issued us with their kit, otherwise I think the whole squadron would have perished. Skiing was hard work and every day we were on the nursery slopes practising. Our instructors had never seen anyone take so much punishment and come back for more. We fell forwards, sideways, backwards and over cliffs, and ran into trees, fences, buildings and other skiers. After a week there was a great improvement but we still fell forwards, backwards etc., only now we were faster. I would stake a large sum of money that anyone wouldn't laugh at a line of rookies like us attempting to turn around wearing idiot planks. The locals found it hilarious and turned out in droves to watch us. Coming down a slope flat out one minute and to dead stop the next happened to me when I caught one ski under a wire stay holding up a fence. Only my right leg stopped, but every other part continued for several yards. It's a wonder I'm still not walking in circles. I was like a fast jet landing on an aircraft carrier.

Typically SAS, at the end of the second week we were towing pulks cross-country. These were small sledges, with one man between fixed shafts, and another in front attached by a harness. We soon were carrying bergans with weapons and getting more adventurous. We had an American Green Beret with us who had skied before and laughed at our downfalls, which were many. Revenge was sweet when he was in the shafts and fell negotiating a steep slope. The weight of the pulk forced his head down in the snow, and his weapon that was carried across the body hanging from the neck pinned his arms effectively so he couldn't move. He was like a channel swimmer turning his head to breathe and shouting for help as we stood by in hysterics. If we hadn't helped he would still be there to this day.

People always ask, "How do you go to the toilet in the Arctic?" With all the different layers of kit and bulky gloves it is difficult, but it's exactly the same as anywhere else but carried out faster. Our OC was a tremendous character and gave us one of the biggest laughs on the trip. He decided to have a crap while still on skis on a steep slope. He faced up the slope, dug in his poles and dropped his trousers. This alone is some feat as you have to remove gloves, drop salopettes, undo belt, unzip fly, drop long johns, ensure nothing is dangling, and brace yourself. He carried out all these tasks but forgot to brace himself. He started slipping backwards picking up speed, crouched with his bare arse at the mercy of the wind, which played tunes around his nether regions. He stopped first thirty feet lower than his sticks, with his trousers full of powdery snow. He takes off one ski to try to empty this out, allowing it to slide further down the slope. His free leg just sinks in the snow so he can't climb back to his poles, or go down the slope to recover his ski. Our laughter didn't help matters and he didn't appreciate the flashes from all the cameras. His rosy-red cheeks shone like Belisha beacons lighting up a dull day, and while talking about cracks here's another episode.

The whole troop got towed behind a tracked vehicle using a ski stick wrapped around a long line. Frozen riverbeds became the highways in winter and we were dragged miles along these. When one man fell, we all fell. Naturally we inquired about the thickness of the ice and were reassured when told it was metres thick. We doubted this when cracks appeared, spreading out like a spider's web beneath us. Sixteen men abandoned the ice in double-quick time.

Our finale in Norway was sleeping out for four days in snow holes. Being winter, it was dark twenty-four hours a day, which took a lot of getting used to. The evening temperatures plummeted to below forty, and it was a pleasure to get up to get the circulation going. Give me the desert anytime.

We had ten casualties on this trip, mostly broken legs. They were all plastered up and had their own transport from the airport. This was an ancient coach that Boadicea used to visit the Iceni. Cyril, the driver, thought it would go downhill faster if he knocked it out of gear. This was correct but he didn't realise the brakes were not used to such speed. He crashed the coach halfway down Birdlip Hill, running out of road on a bend, finishing up straddled across a hedge. The lads evacuated the coach as best they could, and a passing truck stopped to assist. The driver was amazed as the plastered patients limped and crawled to safety. He wondered how they were treated so quickly, thinking they were the victims of this crash.

I failed my first driving test through no fault of my own. We had a week practising, instructed by one of the lads. He sat next to you with the work ticket in his hand. This was a large, flat canvas pouch which held the vehicle's documents. It was quite heavy, having a plywood base. Wally used this to bash you over the head every time you made a mistake. Often not only would you be fighting for control of the vehicle, but had to defend yourself from Wally's assault also. The severity of this attack matched the misdemeanour made. I think Health and Safety would not approve of this teaching technique.

There were two learners in each Land Rover, taking it in turns to drive. At the end of one day we were returning to camp, and it was my turn to sit in the back. I was a smoker at the time and had run out of cigarettes and was praying for a drag. We were just going over the Wye bridge when we had to break hard. A cyclist, concentrating more on drawing on his ciggy than on the traffic, ran into the back of us. As he opened his mouth to shout abuse, his Woodbine inscribed a perfect arc, landing at my feet in the back of the Land Rover. My prayer was answered.

On my test I wasn't so lucky. The MTO who examined us was a stickler for the law. From the moment I got in the cab he started criticising. Adjust this, move that, take that off, put this on. Wally hadn't showed us any of this. So with my confidence shot to ribbons I attempted to overtake a truck going up Dinmore Hill. Changing down into second without grating the gears was nigh on impossible. So, to save the change I accelerated to pass this juggernaut which was coming up to a sharp bend. I can still hear him screaming. When he finally composed himself some minutes later, he ordered me back to camp. When we got there he said, "You've failed, do you know why?" I couldn't resist saying, "No." The screaming started again. So from overtaking it leads me on to undertaking.

On an exercise in Castlemartin we were carrying out boat training. Boat troops were paddling canoes while we were in rubber boats with outboards. The sea was horrendous, and even in the shelter of the bay where we launched it was rough. A wave ran up my sleeve and came out of my neck. Anything to do with water always ensured you got wet and very cold. We attempted a beach landing down the coast, but had to abandon it because of the sea state. Unfortunately, the canoeists were forced out to sea and one boat capsized. Two men drowned that night: one of them was Ralph who was on selection with me. The funerals were very touching and full of respect; however, they were not without humour. I was part of the honour guard lining the porch of the church. Opposite me was Knocker who was a giggler. Every time I caught his eye he would shake with suppressed laughter. Our new OC was not the smartest man in town and turned up with his wife looking like something that the cat dragged in. I whispered from the corner of my mouth, "Look at the state of this." He was deaf but still managed to hear this comment and took a long, hard stare at me. Knocker laughed that much that his bayonet, that couldn't have been fixed correctly, came off and finished up stuck in the oak floor, quivering at his feet.

If we were not abroad we were on courses. These were either held in camp or with other units. Whenever we came across the 'Green Machine' there was trouble, so if possible we tried to avoid these external courses.

Survival is a very important part of Special Forces training. Anyone who might find themselves in enemy territory must be trained to escape capture and live off the land. We had certainly done our fair share of this.

Every regiment has an allocation of ammunition, fuel and rations. When these become exhausted and the budget is tight, survival courses become very popular, as they cost little to run. You were dropped off and expected to live off the land till picked up a week later. Although very popular with the guys controlling the purse strings, they were not very popular with the lads. A survival course is like a good hiding, nice when it stops.

Our arms' storeman kept racing pigeons at the back of the camp. He would spend hours at his loft releasing and recovering them. He would shake a container of corn to encourage them back to roost. If they were returning from a race he would clock them in, which was a lengthy process. It was a nuisance sometimes waiting for Sailor to secure his pigeons before he would issue weapons. Likewise, trying to hand them in was equally difficult. We were always in a hurry: time was precious. We were going on an escape and evasion course up in Yorkshire. Imagine our delight when he asked us to drop off some pigeons. As the name implies, escape and evasion involves getting chased all over the countryside with no equipment. You are always cold, tired and starving, and here was Sailor handing us a haversack lunch. The birds were divided up before we got to the start line, and they were never seen in the skies of Hereford again.

For the next fortnight Sailor was like Edmundo Ros shaking his corn container, but to no avail. He interrogated us all as to where we released his precious birds, and all we could say was, "Coo."

All this training came in handy and we learnt that when you are hungry enough you will eat anything. This story is the result of putting this theory into practice.

When we were on a course we only got twenty minutes for NAAFI break, just time enough to grab a pie and a cup of tea, so we were always in a hurry. We would pile into the canteen and bang on the shutters, alerting the staff to our presence. The shutters never went up a second before ten o'clock. The bolts would be drawn and we would heave the shutter up till it hit the stops, and years of accumulated dirt would cascade down, covering the cups and food neatly lined up on the counter. The regular staff were used to our antics, serving us efficiently. The trouble started when Speedy stood in for a regular who was on holiday.

Speedy was a large woman with no sense of urgency. Any woman is entitled to be ugly but she was abusing this privilege. The first thing she did when we opened up the shutter was to stroke the ginger tom that always lay curled up on the counter. So now we have not only dust and grit in our tea, but cat hair as well. The cat was definitely moulting, as his hair was everywhere. This particular day when the shutter was eagerly raised, Speedy was propped in a chair with a nurse in attendance. "Come on, Speedy" was the cry, and the nurse, never having seen anything like this before, said, "If she doesn't get this injection she could die." A big cheer went up and someone said, "I thought she was already dead the way she moves."

One night after a party some of the lads were hungry; they arrived late and missed the buffet. Worse the wear for Guinness, they looked around for something to eat and spied Speedy's pet languishing on the counter. Everyone hated that cat and it didn't take long before the cat was strangled, stripped and curried. The empty skin with head still attached was left on the counter in its usual place. In the morning when the shutter was raised, Speedy carried out her ritualistic grooming for a good minute before she realised the cat was empty. All the lads stood in line licking their hands and washing their faces making catlike sounds. Speedy fainted, and so did I when marched up in front of the colonel accused of this offence.

Not having a vast wardrobe, we used to borrow each other's kit; this often led to cases of mistaken identity. One night while wearing Jackie's jumper, I did a runner from the Chinese restaurant. When Jackie went in there days later he was offended when presented with a large bill. Other problems arose when we fell out. One night while I was wearing Rob's shoes and Jick's shirt, we fell out over something trivial and they demanded their kit back. I finished up like a Cheyenne Dog Soldier, walking back to camp wrapped up in newspaper and a bit of canvas that I found in the park.

Jackie had the most kit but he was the biggest and couldn't wear a lot of our stuff without losing weight. So it goes to show:

WHO SHARES SLIMS

CHAPTER FIVE

FREE FALL

Everyone in the regiment was parachute-trained, having completed at least eight jumps for their wings. For this we were awarded twenty-eight shillings a week, or four shillings a day (40p). All the lads would openly admit to being terrified at jumping; it was regarded as a necessary evil. To qualify for Para pay we had to jump at least four times a year. This doesn't sound like much but it's very time-consuming. Before any jump we had to do 'synthetic': this is refresher training conducted by the RAF. We had an attachment permanently based with us who would take us on parachute rolls, canopy control, aircraft drills, and emergency procedures. It was a light-hearted affair with lots of laughs.

Parachuting is governed by the weather, and many jumps are cancelled because of this. Strong winds are the limiting factor, anything over ten knots considered too dangerous. We all know how fickle the weather is in this country, and the times we paraded only to be stood down were many. It was always an early morning start because we had to travel to the airfields miles away. It was rare to get the jump in as planned: there were always complications. Another limiting factor was the aircraft. These were notorious for breaking down. If the weather was right, parachutes available, the aircraft would go u.s. (unserviceable). In demolitions we always wanted an accurate time delay. The RAF provided the best time delay ever invented.

Small, fixed-wing aircraft like the Twin Pioneer did come to Hereford for parachuting, landing at suitable drop zones. This was more convenient, allowing a wet-weather programme to be run in case the jump was cancelled, and courses were not interrupted, as they could carry on till the aircraft arrived. Helicopters were in their infancy at this time, but years later we did use these.

Everyone's favourite was the balloon on the racecourse. A special detachment from the RAF used to come with all the paraphernalia to inflate the balloon, staying for several days. It was only two miles from camp and attracted great interest. The married pads and local population turned out in force to watch this, especially during school holidays. We acted bravely in front of the crowd, acting macho and pretending to enjoy the carnival atmosphere.

Most exercises began with a parachute entry. This was always at night, carrying equipment. It's when you stand in the door waiting to jump into the unknown, wearing eighty pounds of parachutes, carrying an eighty-pound bergan, weapons and belt kit, that you think 'Is all this worth forty pence a day?' We certainly didn't do it for the money.

Two troop was to become Free Fall troop and the RAF was responsible for this training. Free fall was very new in this country with only a handful of people with any experience. It was pretty well the blind leading the blind, and looking back, I still get nightmares over some of the things we did. Even Alan hadn't done this.

I was one of twelve who attended the third course run at Abingdon where I had done my static line course with the paras. I was equally nervous but lucky to be in the company of some top-class guys. The RAF treated us well. They had to really: how else would they get us to leap out of fast-moving aircraft at great heights unattached with no safety net?

Regardless of rank, we all slept in the same basha. This in itself was amusing, as Charlie used to talk in his sleep in one voice and answer himself in another. He could keep a conversation going all night.

We wore a one-piece, camouflaged suit that was very convenient, as you could wear anything underneath it. Our boots were issued DMS (direct-moulded sole), but we had these modified with a thick sponge sole, making us two inches taller. Jim was pulled up by the RSM about this unauthorised footwear. He spun him a tale of how they reduced impact from twenty thousand feet and without them his feet would be crushed. I don't think he bought this explanation so we had to tread lightly. (Years later, I trained the Jamaica Defence Force, and they thought DMS stood for 'dems my shoes'.)

The training was good fun and different. Our instructors, vastly experienced in parachuting, but were novices at free fall, having just been trained on the first course. They knew exactly how we felt and treated us accordingly.

One of the hardest aspects of f/f was getting a stable exit. Hours were spent on the nutcracker to achieve this. A parachute harness was secured to the roof of the hangar and the instructor would hold a piece of wood up vertically to simulate the door of an aircraft. A forceful exit was required to beat the slipstream, so a lot of enthusiasm was required. The student in the harness would step forward crablike with a leading shoulder and launch himself when he touched the wood. Then, adopting a froglike position, he would swing away in the harness, looking up with an arched back. It wasn't called the nutcracker by accident. If the leg straps on the harness were loose, the lunch box was crushed. Adding to the discomfort was the arched back. This had to be exaggerated to prevent you flipping over and going unstable.

We had a visit early on in training from the local Women's Institute. They took a great deal of interest in our activities. Determined to put on a good show, Dusty volunteered for the nutcracker. We had never seen him exert so much energy and aggression. He threw himself with gay abandon into space, swinging higher than anyone thought possible, with a smile to match. But when he reached the transition point for the return swing, an agonised scream from a tortured body got everyone's attention inside and outside the hangar. The women responded in various ways. The majority couldn't suppress their laughter and, like all of the course, erupted. Others were sympathetic and tried to hide smiles, and two of the oldest had to sit down before they collapsed. The trouble was it took several more oscillations before we could rescue him. Seeing Dusty dangling in agony must have turned one old dear on. She asked for his phone number: must have been a swinger. He went sick with swollen testicles that were twice their normal size, and black. Dusty told the doc to take away the pain but leave the swelling.

A different parachute is used which is steerable. It takes a lot of experience to determine the direction of the wind and guide the parachute, to set up for a safe landing. Initially it's the exit that's scary, but after a few descents you realise that it's not the exit that hurts but the landing. Running with the wind if you are short of the DZ, or holding the wind to decrease your descent for landing, had to be practised, but only experience will give you this skill. Theory is all very well, but putting it into practice is the key.

The outside exit trainer was used and modified to frighten us even more. The fifty-foot-high tower had a cable attached that ran to another pole about fifty metres away. Instead of jumping out of the door normally as per static line, we dived out face-down suspended by rubber bungees bouncing down the cable, holding a free fall position. It was nigh on impossible not to fold in half, and it's no wonder that now we all suffer from dodgy backs.

To test our confidence we were taken up in the balloon to two thousand feet, wearing a normal PX parachute. All of the static line was pulled out before we were encouraged to dive out of the basket. This was a real eye-opener, giving us a taste of what's to come.

Two aircraft types were used, the Hastings and the Beverley. The Hastings was a four-engined aircraft with a tailwheel. The doors were staggered, with the starboard one being ahead of the port door. They were curved following the contours of the fuselage, so height and width were restricted. Soot and dollops of oil used to fly off the engines, and at night sparks and flames were seen.

The Beverley was a monster and held the world record for heavy drop, which was ten ton. It had a boom which held twenty men, and downstairs in the main hold fifty men could be carried in four rows of seats. A demonstration was given by the instructors. We were all in the boom which had an aperture. All twelve of us lay down around this and watched the instructors falling away as they exited downstairs. Some blew kisses as they fell. We were at ten thousand feet and they quickly merged into the ground. No one spoke but I know I was so impressed. It was soon to be our turn.

When we started jumping, on take-off the basic course would be downstairs with us up in the boom. The aircraft would climb to one thousand feet and the recruits would jump in sticks of simultaneous fives. When the last stick had jumped, the aircraft would climb up to jump altitude, then we would come downstairs to jump from the doors.

Our very first jump was a nervous affair: climbing down from the boom was bad enough, as there is little to hang onto and the aircraft is pitching about. Wearing both parachutes is uncomfortable and the leg straps hinder movement. On top of our reserves we carried two altimeters and a stopwatch mounted on an aluminium board. Before run-in the pilot gives an altitude check so we can calibrate the altimeters. Everyone taps the glass excessively to ensure the hands are still working. The reserve was the size of a cocktail cabinet which was prone to smack you in the mouth when the main chute deployed. When ordered to check equipment, everyone stands up, and from head to toe everything is checked. You check the pins of the man's parachute next to you. When the ripcord is pulled these pins allow the canopy to deploy. So it's important to make sure these are not bent and are free-moving.

When the red light comes on, the stick comes to 'action stations'. Taking up a position facing forward, the goggles are pulled down. Green light on 'GO'. Three men at a time, well spaced, make their exit. Some fancy footwork was required that would not disgrace *Come Dancing*, to get you in the correct position for exit. Outside shoulder leading, inside arm to touch the door, press the stopwatch, and thrust. Nothing in training comes close to resembling the effect of the slipstream. Its important to exit forcibly, oblique to the door, allowing the slipstream to straighten you up. A group of instructors were up in the boom, watching through the hatch and monitoring your performance. The position which we were trained to adopt on exit was not the easiest. The arms were folded in, shoulder high, with one hand on the ripcord and the other clutching the harness. This was amended later to a full spread which aids stability. Our first jump was a three-second delay which was counted and checked with the stopwatch. Thousand and one thousand and two thousand and three, pull. Just typing this gets the juices flowing. Look up, check canopy, determine drift. Steer towards impact point, turn out of wind, feet and knees together. We knew no different and followed instructions diligently. You have little recollection of the first jump, and at debrief a lot of argument arises from what you think you did as to what you actually did. The instructors would ask you what you thought you did, listening with unsuppressed smiles. They would then tell you what actually happened, which in most cases was the complete opposite of what you described. Some of the lads recalled a perfect exit, whereas in fact they somersaulted without realising.

If the basic course jumped before us, they gave us a hero's reception on the ground. They would help us roll up our parachutes and help carry them to the transport. On our fourth jump while we were airborne, the winds got up, forcing the basic course to cancel their drop, but because of our superior canopies we could still jump. After climbing to jump altitude we came down from the boom onto the main deck which was full of adoring paratroopers, making us feel like popstars. When the doors were opened you could cut the tension and anticipation with a knife.

Trying to act the part with as much swagger as we could muster, we awaited the green light. I was in the second stick so I could watch the first jump. We call it 'disco legs'. This phenomenon occurs when control of the legs is lost and they get a will of their own. It happens a lot in mountain climbing, but now it was happening in the back of the Beverley. Watching Em doing a war dance before falling out of the door is engraved in my mind. He lost all coordination and vanished like a puppet with all the strings cut.

What lost us a great deal of credibility was when Geordie felt the effect of his birthday celebration at altitude. We sat there fully kitted up wearing equipment when he suffered the effect of the Guinness and vindaloo which he had in abundance the night before. He expressed the need of urgency, dramatically holding his stomach and crossing his legs. He desperately wanted to have a pony. I told him that it was impossible as we were on finals.

He pleaded his case and we came to a compromise. The Yanks had just walked on the moon and their astronauts wore diapers. They were cleaned up when they got back to earth. So we told Geordie to fill his boots, so to speak, and pretend he was an astronaut. He could clean himself up when he got back to earth and no one would be any the wiser. Like a good soldier he carried out the motion and even had a contented look on his face as he exited, but on the ground this expression turned to one of woe. He must have spun in free fall as he had shit coming out of his cuffs, collar and boots. A recruit went to help him, but turned away in disgust, shouting to his mates, "This twat's shit himself." Yes, we lost a lot of credibility here. (Geordie died in a parachute accident in the Musandam Peninsula years later.)

The smell inside the aircraft changes as it gains height. On the ground it smells strongly of hydraulic fluid and avgas, but this is replaced when troops enplane, replacing this with sweaty body odours. As the aircraft climbs, seventy sets of bowels start responding to the thinning air and increased pressure. It doesn't have to be turbulent to start the first man vomiting. This is highly contagious and spreads rapidly throughout the aircraft. The sweet, sickly smell attacks the senses and triggers a chain reaction. In no time at all half the aircraft are regurgitating their breakfast. Brown paper bags were carried for this emergency, but they should have been three times larger.

Although the victim held it as close as possible, in most cases they missed. The odd bag that was filled often was spilt or trodden on. With this heady atmosphere it was a relief to get the doors opened, and a big incentive to jump to escape from this flying sewer.

Jim fell foul of the RSM again. "Why are you still wearing those boots?" he enquired. Jim told him the usual spiel about comfort and safety. Unimpressed, the RSM said, "See if they're still comfortable after running around the airfield a few times," and sent Jim off on a couple of laps of the perimeter track.

One of the lads had really bad acne on his face. When he jumped you could hear him whistling. Eddie became the star on the trampoline, which we used in training, as it was good for agility work. We had a jump cancelled, so returned to the hangar and were told to strip off for a session on the trampoline. We were wearing a variety of clothing under our jumpsuits which wasn't appreciated by the visiting dignitaries who were accompanied by their wives. As well as a crater face, Eddie had short, fat, hairy legs and was wearing shorts. The technique for mounting the trampoline was to do a forward roll which Eddie did, but his head went between the springs and he finished up with his legs kicking in the air with his head held firmly. His choice of language wasn't appreciated by the visitors either, but the sight of those legs cycling in mid-air made everyone else laugh.

Once we mastered clean fatigue it was time to jump with kit. This made the exits more difficult, but as long as the kit was fitted correctly, stability was easier. The next step after this was night descents. No one looked forward to these, and when we heard that the aircraft was a Hastings, the old sphincter started complaining. The starboard door is close to the wing and you think you can reach it with a good leap. In reality you don't even come close, but it takes a lot of convincing to prove this.

Weston-on-the-Green was a massive drop zone, but we still managed to miss this on occasion. There was a pig farm nearby, attracting parachutists like moths to a flame. Pigs are not the cleanest of animals and the experience of landing there was never forgotten.

After twenty descents we could jump at night with full equipment, but where we landed was a bit of a gamble. We were trained just to fall stable, and depended on the release point to get us onto target. We needed to learn tracking which is adopting a body position that enables you to move across the sky, making up ground. Straightening out the body with a reverse arch was contradictory to our training, where a full arch ensured stability. To get this experience we went to France and America. They were the experts along with the Russians, but we couldn't go there.

Every Frenchman you meet insists he loves parachuting, and is very passionate about this, even claiming it's better than sex. This subject was often discussed in great detail while waiting for aircraft and hanging about drop zones. 'Powerful Pierre' was our French instructor who told explicit stories of his expertise in the bedroom. He told the story of when making love to his wife after removing her little pink panties with his teeth, he had her hovering six inches above the sheets. Fred, not to be outdone, said, "That's nothing: after I make love to my wife I wipe my dick on the curtains and she goes straight through the roof."

America was a very good place to learn free fall. They had the weather and unlimited resources in parachutes and aircraft. Their policy was to start jumping from altitudes of ten thousand feet. This enables a parachutist to go unstable on exit, but with time to sort this out before pulling. The worst scenario is tumbling while trying to deploy the main chute. We did it the other way round, jumping from low altitudes that gave you plenty of time to get into trouble but no time to get you out. Everything is big in America, including the doors and drop zones. Jumping from an aircraft with large doors or, better still, a rear ramp is so much easier than trying to get out of a Hastings while folded in half and terrified of hitting a wing. The drop zones were the size of Wales, but in good old SAS fashion we still missed these. They say we are two countries only separated by the language, which we discovered many times to be true. When we run into a DZ we always give the reciprocal bearing of the heading and head into wind, whereas the septic tanks give the true bearing, putting our release point downwind rather than into it.

On one night jump the wind was gusting, making conditions difficult, especially on landing. Two lads had difficulty in deflating their canopies and got dragged through a barbed wire entanglement. They use a bottle of Dettol each soothing their abrasions; it just goes to prove:

TWO TEAR SKINS

CHAPTER SIX

TRAINING AND MORE TRAINING

Every squadron has four troops who each have a specialist skill. These were boat, mountain, mobility, and free fall troop. At least now I have a troop skill, but to be any use in a four-man patrol I needed an individual skill. I had the choice of medic, demolitionist, signaller or linguist. Everyone was encouraged to do signals, as this was our bread and butter. Gathering intelligence is no good if you cannot report it. Being a signaller means you carry the set which weighs a hefty fifteen pounds, and batteries to keep it going don't come light, either. Another big drawback is when the patrol stops and everyone makes a brew, except the signaller who is busy putting up the set to make a call. When everyone is turning in, the signaller is encoding outgoing messages, and decoding incoming. Everyone is supposed to share this load, but it rarely works out equally.

When I first went to the jungle I was so impressed when the signaller put up an aerial and tapped a Morse key, resulting in an aircraft coming and dropping us a resupply. I thought this so clever and never dreamt that one day I would be doing it.

So off to the sigs centre I go, listening to dots and dashes for the next eight weeks. Some people never get the hang of it: they are incompatible like a dyslectic is to figures. You learn Morse in groups of five letters chosen at random. Sitting with earphones on, these are received till they become familiar, writing them down so they may be checked. When these five are learnt, another five are given. It takes time but it's surprising how soon the Morse code is learnt, including numbers which are easy to pick up. It's easy to get a mental blockage, and any outside noise is very distracting, causing you to lose your way. High levels of concentration are needed, which is very tiring, so frequent breaks were taken. We took our breaks down the bus station. It was an all-out race to see who could get there first in a variety of cars. There was only one bridge over the Wye at this time, and one set of traffic lights. Everyone had a shortcut and it depended on the traffic as to which one was quickest. Backstreets, garage forecourts and a builder's merchant's was used to drive through to avoid congestion. The bus station was a busy place full of travellers, drivers and conductors. Mary, the woman who ran the café, would come out and shout, "Two bacon rolls!" We would shout, "Over here!" even if we hadn't ordered them.

Once we had learnt how to receive Morse, we had to learn to send it. Practice proves perfect, and we spent hours on a key tapping out messages. Procedure must be learnt along with Q and Z codes. This was all classroom work and hard-going. Once we were introduced to the radios we could spread out around camp and run a signals' net. Me and Mac set up our base at the back of the bus station: it was a big change from the classroom.

Aerial theory was a black art and I don't think anyone quite understood this. Diapoles, end-fed, three-quarter wavelength were all taught. It was very technical, not the subject to be taught in the afternoon after a heavy lunch.

Everything had to be encrypted. This was a complicated procedure that involved the use of code books and a one-time pad. Letters were substituted for numbers and grouped in sets of five. Our patrol radio set ran on batteries, limiting its range. For longer distances we had a larger radio that used a hand-operated dynamo to power it. This dynamo was the best part of twenty pounds and no one wanted to be lumbered with this, but someone had to carry it. Give it to the new guy was the obvious solution. Someone had to crank it over while the operator sent his message. If the signaller was new it took ages. In the jungle it was built into a frame so it could be pedalled. A long signal like a resup was equivalent to the peddler completing the Tour de France. There was a connector that could be plugged into a power source. On a previous Signals' course the students were deployed all over the country using this set. They were told it could be powered from a telephone box. Some tried this and cut the phone cable and tried splicing this to the radio. This was not the way to do it. A connector was supplied that went into the light bulb fitting in the telephone box.

Morse was our main means of communicating, but there were occasions when we used voice. Everyone learnt voice procedure and some adopted a style of their own. A Scottish regiment were trialling a new radio in Edinburgh and they effed and blinded.

This broke into the TV network and *Blue Peter* was never the same for some households.

We did invent our own phonetic alphabet which always raised a smile even when under fire. The Sultan's air force was giving us ground support and our air controller referred to them as 'Sultans Shite hawks'. On another occasion a Hunter giving ground support in Aden told the controller, "I have you visual." He was answered, "Never mind that, can you see me?" We were told to be brief and precise, keeping airtime to a minimum. Officers tended to have verbal diarrhoea so were kept well away from the set. We had a code word 'Green Mould', which was used to initiate a quick move. The operator was a Geordie and he sent this. The recipient had interference so he said, "All after Green 'over' Mould." For some reason this sticks in my mind, and Geordie was nicknamed 'Green Mould' from that day hence.

To illustrate why we kept the Rupert off the set reminds me when I was troop signaller in Borneo. We were basha'd on a hilltop defended by the Gordon Highlanders. It was during the monsoon which caused a lot of atmospheric disturbance, making signalling difficult. I had the dog section on one side, and the pipe band on the other. When the band piped up, the dogs started howling, leaving me in the middle struggling with a weak signal. Our boss initiated a signal containing the sentence "apprehended two itinerant Chinese loggers". I told him the signaller wouldn't understand this, but he was adamant and ordered this to be sent. At the end of the day I was still on air: I think they only understood 'two'.

On the same trip I was sending a sitrep, when there was a loud explosion and I was thrown across the basha. I thought we had been hit by a rocket but found out later that lightning had struck the aerial. What made this more dramatic is that someone had taken my earth spike. Being made of copper, it probably finished up as a piece of jewellery or an ornament in a longhouse.

One perk for the signaller was that he was the first to know what was going on; also when the net was quiet, he could ask the operator the football results.

We were encouraged to take the sets out on weekends and get as much signal time in as possible. On the final exercise everyone paired up and went home; Ginge, the instructor, came home with me to Downham. From an upstairs bedroom we were control, with outstations in Scotland, Yorkshire and Wales. It lasted a week and confirmed everything we had learnt. I felt like a wartime spy operating the net, waiting for the bedroom door to be kicked in by searching Germans. Only my mother entered, bearing tea and food. She was only half-German, having just one hairy armpit.

Stan attended a demolition course and tried to photograph an exploding charge. As quick as his reactions were, they were not quick enough to prevent a house brick breaking his kneecap.

There was another trip to Norway which was in midsummer. So, instead of twenty-four hours of darkness we now had twenty-four hours of light.

The Norgies have an addiction for towing things behind vehicles, and this time we were on bikes. We were pulled by a truck through villages, up mountains, and around lakes. Imagine sixteen men strung out behind a vehicle hanging on for dear life. Bends are not exclusively dangerous to deep sea divers, they are very dangerous to bike-towed soldiers also. On a bend the last men are swung wide in danger of overtaking the truck. A soldier sat in the back of the vehicle looking out for our safety. As soon as a man fell he was supposed to tell the driver to stop. He had many distractions and sometimes failed to notice a faller. This resulted in being dragged over asphalt. His main distraction was still laughing from the last incident. If the frontman falls, everyone follows suit. Trying to sort out a heap of bikes with pedals through spokes and rope wrapped around gears takes a long time and the novelty soon wears off.

We trialled a new ration that was far from appetising, called Complan. Basically it was dried milk powder with additives. A pound and half per day gave you something like four thousand calories. After the first few days most of the lads couldn't eat more than a few ounces. We were weighed at the beginning of the trial and again at the end to establish any weight loss. The trial lasted fourteen days, involving long marches over mountainous terrain. You could eat it dry or mix it with water, but whichever way you tried it, it tasted the same: glorified baby milk. (Or fortified baby milk.) Every day we covered in excess of twenty-five kilometres. We had the pleasure of an American exchange captain with us called Elliot. He started off with a bergan full of goodies, but soon realised he had to jettison a lot to be able to keep up with us. Out went his airbed, axe, one-man tent, stove and spare clothing. He did keep his King Edward cigars. He had never been with people like us before and was desperate to fit in. He even grew a tash, which was against regulations back in the States. He practised swearing like us and eventually wore all of our clothing and boots, saying how much better they were than his own issue.

We were attacked by mosquitoes and flies continuously. Elliot reckoned the mossies were that big that they could stand flat-footed and mate with a turkey. The deer flies penetrated clothing, inflicting painful stings. We were glad to get back to camp for the weigh-in. Most lads lost a stone but I lost nothing. Elliot was given his first taste of G10 rum, and when he bent down to do up a bootlace went into a series of forward rolls.

We were challenged to a football match which was held in the local stadium. All the town turned out to watch, and we knew we were up against it when a band marched in with their team following. They were all dressed the same, which is another sign of a well-prepared team. In comparison, we were dressed in cut-off trousers, jungle boots, sweat vests, and any socks we could get our hands on (or feet in). We got thrashed. It was like playing Arsenal. I was the centre half and can't remember touching the ball.

Back home in Hereford the Regiment attracted a lot of visitors. There were politicians, high-ranking officers, some from foreign countries, and even royalty. A lot of time was wasted putting on displays for these dignitaries. They were unpopular with the men, and whichever squadron or troop was responsible for putting on the demo tried to economise in manpower as much as possible. On one occasion we were thin on the ground so each of us had multi-roles. Me and Drag started off on the armed Land Rover wearing desert kit. While the VIP was talking to me, Drag slipped away and climbed in a canoe dressed for boating. On another stand he was laid in a hammock in jungle kit, finishing up in a four-man patrol as a medic. Here they were asked questions and the first one for Drag was, "You look familiar. Where have I seen you before?"

A poncho used for these demos was sprayed with black paint, giving it a camouflaged effect. It was folded over to form a shelter and went unnoticed. But when it was spread out it spelt F… OFF. No one ever noticed but once you knew what was on it, it looked so obvious.

Another course I attended was troop medics. This was fourteen weeks' duration covering all aspects of trauma, fevers and illnesses we were likely to encounter throughout the world. Again there was a lot of classroom work but stacks of practical. The first two weeks on physiology and anatomy were hard-going, but after that it was interesting and very rewarding. The final four weeks were a hospital attachment working in the casualty department.

The trouble when you start covering the signs and symptoms of various illnesses is that it's easy to apply them to yourself, and it gets you thinking,

"I've got that."

We had lectures on gunshot wounds by the army's top surgeons up in the Millbank Hospital in London. This entailed an early morning start and we were all knackered. However interesting the lectures were, it was hard to stay awake and very embarrassing when a snorting snore was heard above the lecturer's voice. The slides shown were very gory and succeeded in grabbing most people's attention, leaving us all slightly nauseous. We were all in serious need of a brew. I think we were the first and last to attend these lectures.

Not feeling very hungry but dying of thirst, we went along a corridor to the NAAFI. In rows lined down each side of this corridor were large jars with specimens floating in formaldehyde. They were freakish babies distorted with large heads and extra digits and lumps. They swayed gently in the fluid as you walked by: not a pretty sight but you couldn't stop looking. In the canteen we ordered tea which was eventually served by a woman with gnarled hands who was bent over and walked with a limp. My mate said she had escaped from one of those jars.

Part of the course was tropical diseases, so for this we visited the Wellcome Museum in London. This was a research establishment and had a vast display of all tropical diseases known to man. It was an incredible display, with everything preserved in bottles. One specimen that really caught the imagination was 'Mossy Foot'. It was a sailor's foot from the 18th century completely covered in barnacles and moss. We used to sneak up on it, but it always managed to turn the stomach. We would be eating and someone would mention 'Mossy Foot'. Plates would be pushed aside as a sudden loss of appetite was caused by visions of this foot. It was a fungus disease encouraged by salt water and vitamin deficiencies. One specimen we did like was a case of elephantiasis. A bloke had swollen balls so large that he had to walk around with them in a wheelbarrow. I can imagine what a stir he would cause at the checkout in Tesco's.

We had lectures on midwifery which we laboured through, thinking that we would never need these skills. How wrong I was; in Borneo some years later this knowledge was priceless.

Before these intensive courses were set up, the medical training was very basic. Attachments to army hospitals were tried, but it was more bedpans and nursing than dealing with trauma. One place used was Houghton just outside Oxford. Paddy was there for a week, eager to get his hands on casualties. All he was allowed to do was wash and change patients. He kept on complaining and upset the matron who was a fearsome specimen of undecided gender. They argued continuously and at the end of the week, just as Paddy was returning to Hereford, he told her what he thought of her. His last words as he ran out of the door were, "I never want to see you again." He only got as far as the A40 when he ran into another car. He was taken back to Houghton in an ambulance and the first person he saw as he came round was the matron. "Hello, Mr Scott." Paddy was there another week and if he thought he had seen the worst side of matron he was mistaken.

It was a big step forward when we got permission to work in civilian hospitals.

You certainly see life in the casualty department of any hospital, and that's where we completed the last four weeks of the course. I was lucky to get the Boscombe Hospital near Poole which was particularly busy. We didn't get away to a good start, falling foul of matron over what we wanted to wear and what she wanted us to wear. We wanted white coats, but she insisted we wore white vests and trousers. This made sense really, as you had to change them regularly. But instead of looking like trainee doctors we looked like a bunch of inmates from the local asylum. There were four of us all hairy and heavily tattoo'd, and we didn't want to come out of the changing room. I was elected as spokesman to tell the matron we weren't going to wear these and she said, "You had better go back to Hereford, then." So she got her wicked way with us and we very self-consciously sneaked out of the changing room and tried to mingle with the patients.

Once our embarrassment was overcome we got down to some good work. We accompanied a doctor when he treated casualties, learning all the time. These casualties varied from road traffic victims, industrial accidents, suicides and drunken brawls. Saturday night was always busy when the pubs turned out, and Casualty was full of drunks. They were used to terrorising the staff and getting their own way. All this changed when we were on duty. One drunken bully was really taken back when offered outside by Paddy. We fought fire with fire, offering to double their wounds if they didn't toe the line. Most responded but we always had the last laugh when suturing and cleaning their wounds. You never upset medics: they can hurt.

In the second week we were invited to attend a post-mortem. Paddy said you wouldn't get him in a post office, so we declined this offer. We did witness our first operation where we had to dress up in full whites, Wellingtons and masks. We were told we could leave at any time if we felt uncomfortable. Looking at each other gave us the giggles, and at every opportunity we did a little skit. Mick Jagger had a hit at the time called "Wild Thing". We used to impersonate his hop and a skip singing "wild thing" and clapping at the same time. The nurses found it amusing as they prepared the patient for an operation involving the removal of piles. Every time we were asked to do something we would go into this routine. When the surgeon came in he scrubbed up in his own inimitable way, pulling on his rubber gloves amidst a cloud of talc. The first thing he did when examining the patient was to hit his head on a spotlamp. Rubbing his head, he went back to the sink and scrubbed up once more. This loosened our chuckle muscles and when he did it again after the nurse had repositioned the offending lamp we were on the verge of uncontrollability. Our masks were slowly disappearing as they were used as gags. When the anaesthetist applied the gas, the patient, being a heavy smoker, started shaking and coughing, nearly falling off the table. This was the last straw, or in my case the last draw, as I drew the last of my mask into my mouth. When Strikey did a "wild thing", that was it: I had to leave, followed by the others. I think it was wearing the Wellingtons that triggered us off. They are more suitable to agricultural activities like muck-spreading rather than the sterile conditions of an operating theatre.

One of the funniest stories about a hospital attachment was about a middle-aged couple who bought a house. The toilet was badly stained so the wife soaked it overnight with a healthy dose of Lysol. In the morning the old chap sat on the khazi reading the sports page, puffing on a Woodbine. When he finished he dropped the dog-end between his thighs which with his large posterior formed a good seal around the seat. The dog-end ignited the combustible gas which exploded with sufficient violence to blow him partly through the toilet door. His wife was hysterical and called for an ambulance. When they arrived they couldn't stop laughing at the sight of a bloke with his head rammed through the door with his rear still smoking, shouting abuse at his wife who was in advanced stages of hysteria. One medic carefully cut his head out, avoiding the splintered woodwork, while the other applied cream to his smouldering backside. They couldn't lay him on a stretcher because of his burns, so they had him balancing precariously in a kneeling position with his arse pointing skywards. He was still threatening to do all sorts to his missus and the ambulance men were still laughing as they tilted the stretcher to negotiate a doorway, causing the patient to topple off, breaking a leg.

Now we could answer questions like, if a kid swallows the front door key what would you do? Answer: go round the back. What's the treatment for a stove-in chest? Answer: remove stove and treat for heartburn. Does it hurt when you go like that? Yes. Well, don't go like that. Why are you squinting? I'm short-sighted. What's that in the sky? The sun. How far do you want to see?

Like a doctor all we needed now was patience (patients). This was the first of many medical courses, and the skills learnt gave me enormous pride and satisfaction when using them.

The regiment was the best in the world at counter-guerrilla warfare, but some of our basic skills were a little primitive. This was all to change when we had a visit to the States. We were the guests of Special Forces, Fort Bragg, N. Carolina. And their training facilities and techniques were second to none. Their medical course included shooting a dog and nursing it back to health. Not only was a great deal of knowledge given, but also a great medical kit as well.

Our demolition techniques hinged around the standard charge, which was a pound and a half of plastic explosive with time pencils. The Yanks gave us special formulas for advanced techniques that were more effective and saved explosive. We adapted a lot of their teachings which helped form the basis of our own very successful demolition cadre. Signal-wise we probably taught them lessons: our signalling was very good. The most boring lecture that I have ever endured was how they sent fingerprints by Morse. Work that one out: I couldn't. They had a language laboratory and ran courses teaching foreign languages, which was completely new to us. We had enough trouble trying to speak English. When we returned home this was instituted and everyone was encouraged to learn another language.

They laid on endless demonstrations and we learnt so much from them. It helped shape the Regiment to what it is today.

We got off to a bad start in the States. At the welcome party we all got down to some serious drinking, which led to us performing the regimental dance, 'Aye zaki zumba zumba zumba aye zaki zumba zumba zay'. As you sing this you must remove all clothing above the waist. For those who don't, it's ripped off. Well, the Yanks had never seen anything like this and stood there clapping and we started ripping their kit off. This led to a major punch-up which happened to coincide with the appearance of General Westmoreland, who came to greet us officially. He diplomatically said, "I see the lads are introducing each other," and left.

At our farewell party the reverse of this happened. The Yanks had been drinking all day and we didn't arrive till early evening. As soon as we entered the bar they started ripping our kit off with no prior warning. We had just bought our 'fruit of the loom' shirts, and to see them ripped off was too much to bear. So another massive punch-up took place, in the middle of which Westmoreland turned up accompanied by his wife. This time he said, "This is where I came in."

There were many fights in the four months that we were there, but the training made it worthwhile. Everyone learnt so much, certainly how to duck. There was a full-blooded Red Indian, who was a nuisance when he was drunk, who got filled in regularly. He complained to our sergeant major who gave us a gypsy's warning to leave him alone. He said we had to be more tolerant and turn the other cheek. Guess who filled him in at the squadron barbeque?

We became well acquainted with the Smoky Mountains and the Okefenokee Swamp in Florida. Sometimes we would work with our hosts against the American Airborne, and other times as enemy against them.

On the HQ building on Bragg was a huge sign that read STRATCO. This stood for 'Skilled Tough Ready Around The Clock'. Some reservists who were called up for the riots in Missouri wrote underneath "Shit, The Russians Are Coming".

We were introduced to volleyball and it wasn't long before we were competing with the Yanks. We challenged them to a game down at the NCOS club. There was a big turnout, and we took great pleasure in beating the Yanks at their own game.

I did a HALO course (high altitude low opening) which was excellent.

I learnt more in one jump than in the previous ten. We were dropped from fifteen thousand feet and encouraged to try things. Tracking, turns, back loops and recovering from spins were all taught by very experienced instructors. We jumped a variety of aircraft, including helicopters and a seaplane. This had a small door, and unstable exits were the only way to get out. It had a boatlike hull and the door was a metre high. You had to adopt a Quasimodo position to exit. Bend in half, lean forward, duck your head, then step up but remain compact.

After the famous end-of-course punch-up we went to the rigging loft to say our farewells to the Halo team guys. Everyone of them had a fat lip or a black eye or both. They said it was the best night they've ever had, and asked when was the next one.

They thought that this was a normal part of our everyday lives and many started enquiring how they could enlist. When we mentioned the difference in pay they rethought.

We flew back from the States in a Comet, which was the first jet aircraft to enter service. It was a beautiful-looking aircraft and really impressed the Yanks. It only had one drawback: it wasn't safe. We didn't know this at the time but they started falling out of the sky due to metal fatigue. They were later withdrawn and converted to Nimrods, anti-submarine aircraft.

Being back in Hereford again was like a homecoming: everyone had adopted the place and we were made to feel welcome. Jick, Rob and I started using The Golden Fleece, a pub opposite the town hall. It was frequented by councillors, Midland Red drivers and conductors, *Hereford Times* personnel, taxi drivers and anyone else with the price of a pint in their pocket. Everyone was so friendly, a big difference from Aldershot where one pub had a notice displayed saying, 'NO DOGS OR SOLDIERS ALLOWED'. The attraction for us was they had a darts team. We started playing for them every Monday night when we could, and soon got to know all the locals. It was here that

I met Jack Thomas. Jack was born in Wales and served in the Navy before settling down in Hereford where he married Molly, a local girl. They actually met in Coventry while working in a car factory together. Jack and Molly became my second set of parents, and most of my leave and spare time was spent in their house. I can honestly say I have never met a family like them: they were absolutely brilliant. Jack took us home and Molly fed us in their semi-detached house that always had a party atmosphere.

Nothing ever got Molly down. Every Saturday night, Jack would take half the pub home with him and every one got a bowl of soup. She never knew how many were invited to Sunday dinner but, however many turned up, they all got fed. Molly should have worked in intelligence as she knew what we were doing or where we were going before we did. All year round, regardless of the weather, she had a coal fire burning in the kitchen. Whenever I called, Molly would make toast using a wire fork in front of the fire.

It's a very distinct taste, one that I will never forget.

Jack was reading the newspaper one day and read out an article about a rentman who had gone missing in London. Years after his disappearance, the police raided a house responding to a robbery. In the kitchen they noticed a row of screw-top jars containing meat, which they sent away for a forensic examination. The meat turned out to be human flesh and belonged to the missing rentman. Molly said, "Fancy that, was he dead?" Jack's response is unprintable.

On a Friday night I took Jack to South Shields where he gave his daughter from his first marriage away. The wedding was a boozy affair starting when we arrived at three in the morning at his ex's house. His ex, daughter and friends were the worse for wear, drinking gin. I was the driver in need of sleep; instead I was handed a bottle of Newcastle Brown and we carried on drinking till Sunday. Jack fell asleep that night in an armchair by the fire which died out in the night. The only trouble was Jack had collapsed with his foot in the ashes and his nylon sock was melted to his foot, looking like something out of Quatermass. It reminded me of Mossy Foot from the Wellcome Museum. When he looked at it, he thought it best to have another drink before the pain started. It was a long drive back to Hereford so we stopped frequently to top Jack up. The only thing he had to eat all weekend was some peas which he had in his pockets still in their pods. Just outside of Birmingham we went in a pub and Jack limped up to the bar and ordered the beer. He takes a pea out of his pocket, shells it, flicks a pea at the barman, rips off the loudest fart I've ever heard and breaks into "Ave Maria" at the top of his powerful tenor's voice. The barman refused to serve him, and Jack in all innocence said, "Why?" When Jack showed him his foot, the barman relented and served us. What a man! As a youngster he auditioned for Ken Macintosh who said, "Hayden, you have a lovely voice but you're too ugly." His correct name was Hayden Brinley Thomas.

Occasionally in the cookhouse an encyclopedia salesman would show up and lay out his books, trying to make a sale. I was looking one day, checking on what I couldn't afford, when he asked me did I know a guy called Washington. I thought this was all part of his sales patter so I said, "Of course I do," thinking he meant George Washington. "Do you know where he is?" he asked. And I answered, "Dead." "Oh, that's just my luck, he still owes me for a set of books," he moaned. It is then that I realised he was looking for a guy in the Signals, not the President of the USA.

A favourite trick at mealtimes was to pour boiling water onto the plastic seats while people were still eating. Everyone carried their knife, fork and spoon with a pint mug to the cookhouse. A wash point consisting of three sinks was provided to wash our KFS and mugs when we finished eating. First sink to wash, second one to rinse, and the third containing boiling water to sterilise. We used to wash up and fill the pint pot with boiling water and would start on a line of occupied seats, tipping this water onto the back of the seat. You could do a line of six before the first man reacted, leaping up with wet pants. It seems very childish but it happened at every sitting. It was very uncomfortable if you were the victim and very embarrassing especially if you didn't have time to change.

They say that little things please little minds, but a little hot water burns big behinds.

The food was excellent, with many choices, and you could eat as much as you wanted. It was well cooked and presented, the cooks taking pride in their work. The regiment was notorious for hanging cooks. If they didn't come up to scratch they were dangled over the hotplate by a rope tied under their arms.

I don't think it was just coincidence that we always seemed to do river crossings in the winter. They were bad enough in the summer, but no one said it was going to be easy. We always had to take things to the extreme and freezing cold torrents were a tough challenge. The normal drill was to strip off and put everything in plastic bags inside the bergan that became your floatation aid. Four bergans lashed together could support an injured man or a non-swimmer. Breathing deeply in anticipation of the cold, we would tiptoe down the bank, entering the water pretending it wasn't cold. As the water reached the groin area, several physiological changes took place immediately: the skin turned blue and two small spheres migrated to warmer climes.

We lost as many men to water-related accidents as to enemy action, so we took this training very seriously. You must always have a safety boat in the water manned by good swimmers, staying downstream till needed. Although it's good to get a line across the water it can be dangerous at the same time. If a man gets washed under the line the safety boat cannot get to him because of the rope. So if you use a rope keep the safety boat stationed upstream.

Getting the rope across is always the problem. Either the strongest swimmer volunteers or the new guy is nominated. A climbing rope, once wet, gets very heavy and I've seen even the strongest of swimmers nearly coming to grief. It's all very well tying the rope around the swimmer's waist, but if this gets snagged he cannot continue and he can't be pulled back. We were always looking for better techniques and D Squadron came up with a new idea that they were keen to demonstrate. We lined up on the river bank on a cold, crisp winter's morning. Two lads stretched a thick, rubber bungee between them about twenty metres apart facing the river. A guy in the middle held a grapnel that was looped over the bungee and walked backwards, telling the other two to brace themselves. The idea was sound enough, just like launching an arrow from a bow, only this was a grapnel weighing about two pounds. When all three were quivering with the tension they generated, Chalky let go of the grapnel. Instead of it flying straight and true across the river, taking a line with it, it took a nasty lurch to the left and hit the bungee strainer on the head, knocking him down the bank into the river. It took longer to sort out the tangled ropes than it did to take the injured man to hospital.

Chalky, to make amends, demonstrated a boat made from a pair of trousers stuffed with grass, three inflated condoms and a water bottle. He perched on this using his hands to propel himself, and the further he got from the bank the lower he became in the water. "I'm not sinking, I'm not sinking," he kept repeating, but there was only one outcome. It went down really well.

On another occasion, Chalky, the ideas man, came up with a new method of scaling a security fence. He wasn't that old but looked about sixty; he had lived a dangerous life. He made a pair of hooks from two large nails which were drilled through pieces of broom handle. Through the toecap of his boots two more nails were hammered and bent, forming hooks. The idea was to scale the fence with these nails hooked in the chain link and, moving one at a time, scale the obstacle. His mates erected the fence for this demo and made a good job of it. They chose two floodlight posts in the car park about thirty feet high, and wired the fence between them; it looked formidable. Chalky starts by engaging one boot and reaching up high to engage the hand-held hooks. Then the next leg is engaged above the other and so on up the fence like Spider-Man. Chalky gets near the top carrying on a non-stop commentary when the whole panel comes unstitched from the posts, and backwards he goes, still climbing. Lain on his back in the car park, still going through the motions, he was a sight to behold. Someone shouts. "Hurry up, Chalky, you're illegally parked!"

Every time a new aircraft was introduced into service we had to do a parachute conversion course. This meant going to RAF Abingdon to learn all about the new aircraft. In this case it was a Twin Pioneer, a smaller, twin-engined aircraft that we used extensively in the Far East. The whole squadron plus HQ was involved, and it was one laugh after another. We were there for a week and the idea was to do as much parachuting as possible. In the large hangar we were split into troops and engaged in separate phases of training under the personal guidance of a Parachute Jump Instructor (PJI). He told us to take off our belts and berets and to follow him. This was a warm-up and he sprinted off dancing in and out of the apparatus, but no one followed him. He came back rather dejected and threatened us with violence if we didn't follow him. What finally got us moving was when he said, "Screw the nut, lads, my boss is watching." So we played his game of follow the leader, going up and down ramps under beams and over boxes. An older figure had problems running up a ramp and jumping off the end. The PJI said, "Call yourself a man." The answer he got was, "No, I call myself the colonel and you should bloody well remember that."

Moby Dick was a huge mock-up of the Beverley aircraft and was used for ground training. The boom had an aperture which we dropped through, landing on a coconut mat. For training purposes a dummy chute is worn and the static line is just tucked on top of the rig. You go through all the drills of fitting equipment, hooking up and dropping through the hatch. We played tricks on the Ruperts at every opportunity, and here was one too good to miss. Jick was behind the adjutant who was stick leader and tied his static line to his pack, rather than just tucking it in. When he jumped he was suspended by this dangling just short of the mat. Once the lads started moving it was hard to stop them, and they were surprised to see him on the way down jumping all over him.

The top of the mock-up was open and about thirty feet from the ground. We carried containers weighing fifty pounds that were attached by a leg strap to the parachute harness. When we finished our drills, to save carrying this downstairs Sailor decided to throw his over the top. What he forgot was he was still attached to it. Imagine his face when the line tightened, whipping Sailor to the very edge. He was lucky the container landed before he did. It didn't end there. He undid the release strap, which was under tension from the weight of the container, and it flew over the top, catching the PJI on the shoulder who was bawling and shouting, demanding to know what sort of lunatic had thrown his kit over the top.

I think the instructors were glad to see the back of us, but they also enjoyed our company in a perverse way. They had never seen aircraft empty so fast once the green light went on. An avalanche of bodies would crash out of the door in all positions and attitudes.

Not many of the lads had cars in those days, so we normally walked downtown, cutting through the park. After a good night out it was a pain walking home and it was against all principles to spend money on a taxi. Our usual trick was to recognise a mate's car and climb in the back and go to sleep, knowing that you would eventually finish up in camp. One night

I awoke in the back of a car and couldn't recognise the couple in the front. They were surprised as I was when I announced my presence. It was all explained and they did drop me back to camp.

Outside the Chinese restaurant was the best place for a lift, and it was here that we usually finished up. The Wing Hong was one of the earliest Chinese restaurants in the country and unique to Hereford. We really messed the staff about and it's a wonder they ever served us. Rover, a new member of the troop, used to terrorise the waiters and they would run and lock themselves in the kitchen when he appeared. There was an upstairs to the restaurant which was served by a dumb waiter from the ground-floor kitchen. True to form, one night, Rover turned up in his normal abusive manner. The waiters sought sanctuary in the kitchen, thinking they were safe; but Rover climbed into the dumb waiter, transporting himself to the kitchen. He magically appeared through the hatch, turning the industrious kitchen scene into one like a fox in the chicken coop. What little pay they got they certainly earned it.

One memorable evening I had been out with Jick and we pitched up at the Wing Hong for a scoff. After drinking as though it was going out of fashion, we were slightly the worse for wear. Jick could walk but couldn't talk; I could talk but couldn't walk. We ordered two mixed grills, not very Oriental but greasy enough to reach parts that some beers couldn't. Jick disappeared towards the toilets and I grabbed a few minutes' shut-eye before our meals were served. Still no sign of Jick, so I get stuck in and demolish my meal. I thought Jick had legged it so I went to pay and was outraged to be presented with a bill for two mixed grills. I insisted that I was on my own and had never seen this other guy who had left his meal. After a long, noisy protest a policeman arrived called Bob Taylor. This was our first introduction, but he was to become a very close friend. We played veterans' rugby together, averaging one hundred years between us in the second row. He was the old-school copper who would rather clip someone's earhole than book them.

He heard both stories and retrieved Jick who was fast asleep in the khazi. After another argument I paid for both meals and told Bob I wanted to make a complaint and had the meal wrapped up in newspaper for possible evidence. He took us down to the police station so we could make statements. On the way we pulled his whistle out, undid his epaulettes and made real nuisances of ourselves. He had to hold us up and we leant heavily on him. Jick had the loudest laugh that you've ever heard, and he never stopped even when we were inside the station. Bob laboriously wrote out our names in full. I was Johnathon Wolfgang Launcelot Wiseman, and Jick was Terence Clauss Gunter Jickells. After thirty minutes of writing legal spegal he wanted us to sign this complaint which was paying for the same meal twice, we said, "Drop the charge." Bob went apeshit. He did a little dance while running on the spot and told us in no uncertain terms that if he saw us again that night it was going to be painful. Jick was still laughing as we collected the evidence, still wrapped in newspaper, and staggered back to camp.

We took the shortcut across the park and Jick was taken short by the swings. He slunk into the bushes while I started a small fire to warm up the evidence. I had it burning nicely when Jick staggered back, walking like a Spanish waiter. Whatever plant or grass he used to wipe himself had been sprayed with weedkiller. He began a dance around the fire, gyrating wildly and letting out the odd squeal. Just as the sausages started sizzling a voice penetrated the smoke, "Not you two b.....ds again." It was our new friend Bob, calling to investigate a fire burning by the bowling green. We shared our supper with him, becoming friends from that night on.

Every so often, a senior rank had to go on a drill course. This was hated more than 'resistance to interrogation' courses. It was run by the Guards lasting for three weeks, during which time every drill movement in the book was learnt. Eight hours a day poncing up and down the square. The lucky participant had to wear bulled-up boots with studs. There was one pair in the Regiment kept in the stores for such an event. If you were a size ten you were laughing. Anything smaller, extra socks had to be worn; any larger, then a John Wayne walk was developed. Paddy made the mistake of telling them that the guards were a luxury the army couldn't afford. He failed. Another failure was an SSM who had two left feet. Try as he might, he got the words of command wrong and gave them on the wrong foot. The squad was told to ignore any commands that were not correct, and off the square and into the distance they went with big L running after them.

At the time we had a troop officer who was clumsy to say the least. He would fall over anything, including his own shadow. In the jungle he was a one-man show, a constant source of amusement. Once a year we had an admin inspection. This was carried out by the General Commanding. We always had a pre-inspection to ensure everyone had all of their kit which was laid out on our beds. My bed was nearest to the door and Capt B brought all of his kit with him, sharing my bed to display his kit. He would shout out 'bayonet frog' and everyone would hold one up. Anyone deficient used to borrow from another troop or hold up something resembling it, so this was a complete waste of time. As we displayed things we stuffed them back in the locker, and when we finished Capt B had very little kit left. While he was kept talking, the lads helped themselves, making up their own deficiencies at his expense. He accused us all of being thieving b.....ds and stormed out of the door. Unfortunately for him, the door was held shut by a chest expander. He tried to get through the door before pulling it back far enough, and was battered several times before he worked this out.

I went on leave with a lad from Campbeltown in Scotland. I only knew him as Jock, so when I shouted his name at Glasgow Station a thousand heads turned around.

His family were well-to-do and I discovered his proper name was Desmond. He was the unlikeliest Desmond that you could ever come across. His climb to fame was when he dived off the Wye bridge: instead of a splash there was a thud. Desmond hit the pier. Three lads ran to the boat club and jumped in a boat moored by the steps. They rowed for some time before realising they were still tied to the bank. It didn't really matter as Desmond was going nowhere, certainly not for the next few months. I visited him many times in hospital and he never lost his sense of humour. He told me that there was a funny bloke in the next bed with artificial legs. I asked him what's funny about that. He said, "He's got real feet." I was a skydiver and Desmond was a Wye diver.

Desmond and I paired up on a demolition exercise. For some reason I finished up carrying all of the food, and Desmond carried all of the explosives. After the first day we got split up, and for the next four days Desmond had nothing to eat, losing about a stone in weight.

It just goes to show.....

WHO PAIRS THINS

CHAPTER SEVEN

FAR EAST

Now, having a few skills under my belt, it was time to use them. Active service is the only way to confirm that the training is working. Our trip to Oman was active service and, apart from a brief respite from 1961 to 1963, the Regiment would be on active service till I retired in 1986.

During the sixties and seventies we spent a lot of time in the Far and Middle East, and, looking back, it was the most exciting time of my life. When I heard we were going to the jungle for the first time I was over the moon. I was brought up on all the exploits of the Regiment's activities in the jungle. I knew all the operations that they carried out and could even speak the odd word of Malay. Just mentioning some of these operations necessitated taking Paludrine to ward off malaria. The Regiment was resurrected for the Malayan Emergency in 1951 and all of our operational procedures evolved and were adopted from this campaign.

Out of all the environments on earth most people believe the jungle to be the harshest and worse place to live. In fact, once you gain a little knowledge and understanding, the jungle offers the best place for survival. But it's hard work learning to live with nature, rather than trying to fight it. Once you accept this, what you first thought was a hazard becomes an asset.

So Lofty Boy, born in the concrete jungle, heads off to the green hell with his imagination running riot. I am finally going in the Ulu.

My training op was up on the Thai border at a place called Grik, a mountainous area covered in tropical rainforest. We landed in Singapore after a two-day flight, and the first thing you notice is the humidity. Just changing aircraft caused the sweat to flow. We flew up country in twin pins and landed on a grass strip. It was a little cooler but the air was heavy with the smell of vegetation. We deployed the next day, taken by a truck to a river where boats were waiting for us. We travelled upstream for hours watching the landscape changing as the river narrowed, allowing the jungle to close in. Apart from the noise of the outboard, all my senses were directed to new sounds, sights and smells.

We stopped by a small spur that had a freshly cut track running up it and climbing away from the river. We followed this, entering the trees with bated breath, with a feeling of great satisfaction: here I am at last, I have arrived.

Nothing can prepare you for the sounds of a tropical rainforest. Screeches, howls, hoots, chirps and whistles all compete for attention, but you rarely see what's making all this noise. You quickly learn that everything that moves bites, and everything that doesn't is prickly. It's dark under the canopy and a lot cooler. There are large trees growing over two hundred feet tall with a girth to match. Their roots are shallow because of the hard ground, so they have to grow tall buttresses all around the trunk for stability, giving them the appearance of ballistic missiles. Hanging from these are a mass of vines and creepers which grow on the jungle floor but climb upwards, competing for light in the canopy high above.

We had a welcoming committee of leeches that stand on the track, swaying waiting to make your acquaintance. They fasten on any available limb, injecting an anticoagulant before drawing blood. It's not long before you are covered in them. They get through the smallest of holes and have finished up in some very exciting places. The worst thing to do is to pull them off while they're feeding: this leaves the head inside which causes a bad infection. Insect repellent is the best way to remove them.

In the dry season it rains once a day; in the monsoon it rains all day. About four o'clock in the afternoon you hear the rain coming across the trees drumming on the foliage. One raindrop is a yard long made up of a pint of water, soaking you instantly. If you're not wet by the rain, the gentlest of exertion causes streams of sweat to run, soaking you just as effectively. So dripping wet covered in leeches I get acquainted with my new surroundings where I would spend the best part of my life.

This training op was one of the hardest things I've ever done in my life. After ten days of range work, tactics and navigation, we had a two-day march to the road head. I was partnered up with Eddie and we set off climbing a seven thousand-foot ridge. This took all day and we finished near the top but without water. It was probably the only day since Noah was a kid that it never rained, so we had to drop down again to a water source. We were on our chinstraps, but it's amazing what a brew can do to help revitalise you. It was while we were sipping our second brew that we heard two others in the same predicament as us crashing around just below. It was Fitz and Charlie who had selected the same route and they, too, were suffering. Charlie was American Green Beret on an exchange tour with us. On this op he got malaria, leptospirosis and scrub typhus. From a strong, fifteen-stone soldier he went down to an eight-stone weakling. He was in such a critical condition that they flew his wife out to Singapore where he spent a long time in hospital. He was so impressed by the Regiment that when he went back to the States, he badgered the White House to raise an equivalent unit. For his trouble he was deployed to Vietnam, where he got wounded. He put on weight instantly, caused by the amount of lead and shrapnel picked up courtesy of the Viet Cong. While he was recovering from this, he set up camp in the Pentagon to get his own way to raise an American unit similar to ours. The powers that be finally relented and Delta Force was born. Their first mission was the release of hostages from Tehran which Charlie was in charge of.

We marched all of the next day and half of the following one, arriving late-afternoon just as the squadron was deploying. We found out that everyone else had used a logging track which skirted the ridge that we climbed, using a road to reach the RV. You may call this initiative, but I call it cheating. They had a good night's sleep and time to wash and prepare their kit. The four of us were given twenty minutes to pack fourteen days' rations and rejoin our

113

troop. If you can picture everything you need for fourteen days packed in a bergan, you realise what a large load this makes. Food, fuel, ammo, sleeping kit, dry clothing, insect repellent, torch, spare batteries, candles and book. Bob had broken down my rations into two piles, one to take and one to leave. While we are talking about piles, haemorrhoids are common in the regiment, caused by carrying such heavy loads. The only way to adjust the weight was to leave rations out. One meal a day was the routine, with a snack at midday. I took advice and packed what Bob suggested. He must have had the smallest appetite in the Regiment; I came to this conclusion some days later. That night we basha'd by a river and starting climbing in the morning back up the ridge that caused so much grief two days before. We climbed even higher ridges which became easier as the bergan got lighter. My bergan got too light, too soon. After six days I was nearly out of rations.

Charlie had started with next to nothing, promising to give up smoking, cooking and eating; he nearly gave up breathing. He slept on the floor and got bitten by everything with teeth and sucked by everything without. He never took Paludrine or sterilised his water, and kept on asking where the jeep trails were. On the seventh day he was casevaced to hospital. At least he had a blanket that I inherited. In our haste to leave I didn't have time to retrieve my sleeping bag or dry kit that was drying in the Dhobi wallahs. Of a night I would wrap myself up in the poncho and lie under someone's hammock in my wet kit. It was freezing because of the altitude, and I lay there shivering, waiting for first light that never came quick enough. Poor old Charlie slimmed down to eight stone. I thanked him for the blanket and for half a candle; that's all I could salvage from him. I can picture him now staggering to the chopper with his eyes looking out of his ears.

I was starving hungry but at least I was warm at night now. I started sitting with the abos who we used as guides and trackers. They collected a variety of plants, insects and anything that crept, crawled, swam or flew. This is where my thirst for survival knowledge started. They shared the odd grub but I was never in danger of putting on weight. I was shown the nibong tree which has an edible core. The trunk is twelve inches in diameter, very rough and hard. One was pointed out to me so I attacked it with venom. It was on a steep slope, so when it was cut through it slid down about two hundred feet, coming to rest in a stream. Not knowing which part was edible, I carried the whole tree back up, all thirty feet of it, to seek advice. The nibong is a palm tree and it's only the inner pith of the top two feet which is edible. Cutting through many layers, I finished up with something resembling a large stick of celery. I probably expended a couple of thousand calories obtaining this which would only yield about two hundred cals at the most. This was the first time in my life that I was really hungry. I made a promise to myself that I would never be as hungry again. One of the lads had potatoes and I retrieved the peelings before they hit the floor. Someone else had a pack of hard tack that had gone green, which I took with equal relish. I had run out of hexi blocks, so what little I had to cook was done on an open fire.

All the old hands had curry powder, garlic and onions, and the smell of this cooking drove me wild. The golden rule is you carry everything you need. Everyone has just enough for themselves: there is no spare. It was a lesson that I was never to forget. Sometimes weight was so critical that you shared a book with the patrol. You started with the first twenty pages and handed them on when finished with.

On the thirteenth day a site was selected for an airdrop (DZ). It was hard work clearing the area, but it was time well spent. The next day all my Christmases came at once. Parachutes blossomed from the sky laden with food, clothing and supplies. Every fourteen days we got one day's fresh ration. This included steak, bread and sausages. I sat down and ate for six hours. Not only did I have food but also a parachute from which I could make a hammock and sleeping bag, and we also got new shirts, trousers, jungle boots and a towel. You stood more chance winning the lottery than getting the correct size jungle boots. There were three brands: Dunlop, Bata and Bell. Dunlop you had to order a size smaller; Bata a size larger; and Bell your correct size. This always got messed up in the coding when sending the resupply signal. Dunlops lasted a few days, Bata a little longer, and Bells two weeks if you were lucky.

We had another fourteen days of rations issued and this time I didn't throw much away. What I didn't want to carry I ate. Everything that was surplus to requirements was burnt. This was a dangerous practice, as tins exploded, sending boiling jam everywhere, leaving a nasty rash on exposed skin. A lot of rations were thrown away and I braved the fire to retrieve tins of condensed milk and Mars bars.

The colonel spoke to me after this op and asked if it was true that I ate seventeen Mars bars on the DZ. I told him I couldn't verify this as I was eating tins of condensed milk at the same time.

My confidential report for that year included a statement saying I must learn to eat less. I took offence at this, as I thought I was going to die of starvation. How can you learn to eat less? You can't, you just go without. You can learn to eat more: that's where the skill comes in.

I found the pace of the troop easy to keep up with, so decided to carry more. My bergan must have weighed a hundredweight. I had a sack of spuds on one side and a sack of onions on the other, and enough rice to feed the Brigade of Gurkhas.

My introduction to the jungle was a cruel one, but I learnt so much and never got caught out again. This lifestyle suited me down to the ground. No washing, no shaving, moving every day. Learning to live with nature and not trying to fight it, and acknowledging that you are the intruder, not the flies, hornets, reptiles, leeches, ants and spiky plants, is the key. Jungle training became part of selection and a lot of people could not adapt to the demands imposed and returned to their units. It was the jungle that made the Regiment what it is today.

After this four-month training op, my next jungle venture was in Borneo. We were inserted along the border with Indonesia in four-man patrols to gather intelligence and topographical information. To do this we had to win the confidence and trust of the locals, which we did by living with them. I went to a kampong called Mepi in the Second Division of Sarawak where we set up a hearts and minds campaign, giving them medical aid. This tribe were Ibans, the headhunters of Borneo. The youngsters and some of the elders had never seen a white man before. They were short, smooth-skinned, and the men heavily tattooed. We were over six feet and hairy. They thought we were gods and we got on famously.

On the first day of surgery we had a queue a hundred yards long. Most of them were just inquisitive, but there were genuine patients as well. I was amazed at how receptive they were to modern drugs. One man, badly emaciated, staggered in and waved a stick under my nose looking like it had been dipped in cranberry sauce. It was amoebic dysentery, which he had had for weeks. I started him on a course of Sulphaguanidine tablets, and by the end of the week he came in with a stick with a large turd impaled on it, waving it under my nose with great delight. I was pleased for him, but could have done without the evidence of his recovery. He showed his gratitude and gave me a live chicken.

I smelt another patient before I could see him. A man was carried in on a stretcher with his right foot wrapped in rags. The smell of putrefying flesh gave early warning of a bad injury. He was carried for five days after getting his foot cut by a boat propeller. If it was left for any longer he would have lost the leg and possibly died from septicaemia. I cut away some dead flesh and cleaned the wound; it was too late for stitches. I started him on a course of antibiotics, injecting him daily. At the end of the week he could stand on it, and after two weeks he had a healthy red scar. He also gave me a chicken. It wasn't long before I had a large flock of chickens: it was their way of saying thanks. Minor cases gave me eggs.

Our OC visited our location and carried the first Armalite rifle issued to the British Army. He cradled it with loving care, knowing how much we envied it; we were as green as our OG. There was a lot of hype connected with this weapon, claiming that, because of its high velocity, any hit on the body set up a massive hydraulic shock wave that would kill the victim. We wanted a demonstration of this weapon and the OC, whom we nicknamed Dolly, obliged. He selected a large clump of foliage suspended in a tree about fifty yards away. Casually he put a couple of rounds through the clump and moved forward to check the results. We moved back the other way, realising that the clump was in fact a hornets' nest and they don't like being disturbed, and certainly take offence at being shot at. As good as the Armalite's performance was, it wasn't a patch on the hornets. In formation they attacked Dolly and all the loving care for the weapon went out of the window. Hornets always go for the face, and personally I think their sting causes a loss of memory, because Dolly forgot to run. He stood there protecting his face with only one hand before dropping the weapon to use both. Realising now that he was under attack, he tried to run but forgot how to. His legs were pumping up and down but he wasn't moving. The way his arms were moving, I think he was trying to fly. When he finally got up a burst of speed he forgot his precious Armalite, overtaking us and heading for the river. That night he made us a curry which we ate by candlelight. His face was badly swollen, looking grotesque in the flickering light; it was only our laughter that prevented it becoming like a scene from a Hitchcock thriller. I soon accumulated a flock of chickens, and to identify them from the locals birds I painted on badges of rank using gentian violet from the medical pack.

One morning a woman came running up the track screaming "Ula, ula!" We went to her aid and followed her down to the river. She had found a python about twenty feet long, with three distinctive lumps in the middle, curled up by her dugout. It had entered the kampong at night, swallowed three chickens and curled up for a sleep. Before we could film it, the locals chopped the head off and gutted it. The chickens were two cpls and a sergeant, mine. That night we had a feast of snake and chicken stew.

We ate everything that the locals did, and most of their food was tasty. On one occasion as I was nearing the bottom of my bowl of stew, I uncovered a little hand complete with fingernails that was curled as if offering to shake hands. The first thing I did was to check the longhouse for missing kids, but the Penghulu assured me that it was a monkey.

I was down to my last thermometer when an Iban turned up lathered in sweat, telling me he was sick. It's unusual to see the locals sweating so I took his pulse and temperature. On his belt he carried a bamboo tube with his tobacco in. One of the lads asked him for a smoke and when he opened his mouth to speak my last thermometer fell out and smashed. I was a bit upset and told him that there was nothing wrong with him. He rambled on about his wife being sick, not him. It was all a bit garbled with him chuntering in Malay and me shouting in Anglo-Saxon. Finally I find out that his wife is giving birth and has a problem. Normally the older women are the midwives and they never ask for help unless there are difficulties. Now I am faced with a moral dilemma. Do I get involved and find it's too difficult to handle, or do I ignore it and lose face? I thought there was no harm in looking and I could make a decision then. I asked him how far it was to his kampong and he answered, "Ta berapa jau," not very far, and they use their lips to emphasis the distance. A little pucker in the general direction is anything up to a mile. A more pronounced pucker that's held for a few seconds can be half a day's march. The most accurate way of recording distance is by giving the time it takes. On a map it may only be a short distance, but if you know it takes an hour it gives you some idea of the difficulties like swamp, secondary growth or any steep climbs that you may encounter.

My man assured me his longhouse was only forty minutes away, so I told him to lead the way as it was now mid-afternoon, and raining heavily. He set a cracking pace with me hard on his heels. I'm carrying belt kit, weapon and med pack; he's carrying his tobacco and blowpipe. As we drop down a steep bank I slip, and my swinging leg kicks him up the backside. He takes this as a sign of anger and me punishing him for breaking the thermometer, so he speeds up, not wanting to be kicked again. I'm running now to keep up and the forty minutes turns into a two-hour sprint. No wonder he was sweating when I first met him. It was mostly uphill, being right on the border, and when we arrived I was the one in need of medical assistance. My legs were like jelly and now I'm suddenly aware of why I am there. Soaked through, covered in leeches, with red dots before my eyes, I try to look confident. Longhouses are built on stilts about eight feet high. They are reached by climbing up a log that has notches cut into it. Climbing this was like ascending the north face of the Eiger: I didn't know what to expect or what the outcome would be. I was guided to a dark room, poorly lit and full of family members. I asked for more light, a bit of space, and a mug of tea. His wife had given birth to a daughter who was fine but she had trouble clearing the placenta. Casting my mind back to the medic course, I knew you must never pull on this. I gave her a muscle relaxant and sat down drinking tea. Her husband, who looked as fresh as a daisy, massaged her stomach. Whether my presence had anything to do with it I will never know, but the placenta cleared and the party began. I stayed the night, staggering back in the morning; it was certainly easier going back downhill.

This village was the first one attacked when confrontation started with Indonesia about two months later.

There is a plant in the jungle that justifies a special mention, called atap. It's a creeper that's covered in spikes resembling fish hooks. It grabs hold of everything and, being strong, never lets go easily. The only way of disengaging from it is to back off and ease the hooks out of flesh or clothing. We called it 'nancy sikit' or 'wait a while'. It grew everywhere, slowing progress, hooking onto clothing, bergans and flesh. It is nature's barbed wire. Officers were not suited to the jungle and never quite managed to handle atap. When entangled there was only one winner.

We did have some good officers but these were rare; most had an infliction like a stutter, bad eyesight or deafness. One troop officer we had was a great bloke but clumsy; he would fall over putting his boots on. One day we were following a track that went down to a stream; it was very steep and slippery. Halfway down there was a difficult stretch so we used a pole for support and passed it back up when we crossed it. One of the lads didn't use it and left it stuck in the middle of the track. Boyo comes along slipping and sliding, and lunges out for the pole. Anyone could see that it wasn't a permanent growth and Boyo puts all his faith in this to stop himself falling. He was the first one to reach the river and finished lodged in a forked tree overhanging some rapids. It took hours untangling him and cutting him free.

You must have a sense of humour because sometimes it's all you have. I've been up to my neck in swamp, covered in leeches, starving, and exhausted, and looked at my mate and we started laughing. Why? You want to scream, but having the ability to laugh at yourself is a pressure release valve: without it you would explode.

In the jungle you use all your senses. At first you think the eyes are most important, but you quickly realise that you hear things before you see them. Smells carry long distances in the dense air, and a keen sense of smell is invaluable. You get accustomed to the smell, feel and the sight of your surroundings and any intrusion stands out. It's important to keep the eyes moving, checking for obstacles, as there are so many things waiting to trip the unwary. Never tread on fallen logs and watch out for atap. Try to avoid all the vines and creepers that lay across the track and occasionally look up.

I attended a Malay course in Nee Soon, Singapore, with six others from the Regiment. On the first day I was in class, when I was told to report to the camp commandant. I thought he was going to welcome me to Nee Soon and wish me a happy stay. How wrong I was. I was marched in front of him by an aggressive sergeant major who couldn't keep in step with me. We got wedged in the doorway which didn't help. The commandant started raving and ranting about the state of the barrack room, and his manner didn't improve when I told him he had the wrong person. Sharing this block were Aussies, Kiwis and Marines, all on different courses. I told him I was Lofty from Hereford on a Malay course. Apparently he had put me in charge of the room and it was my responsibility to get it ready for inspection. So now he's threatening me for not reading orders, failing to clean, wearing civvies, and I've only been there a day. He ordered us to parade in uniform at one o'clock and have the room ready for inspection at two. Three of us were A Sqn who would make up the advance party in Brunei when the course was finished, and three from D Sqn who were halfway through a tour in Kuching. The excuse I gave for wearing civvies was that we only had our operational kit with us and it was not the smartest.

We turned up at one o'clock wearing an assortment of clothing that they had never been seen before. It was too much for the CO and his sidekick: they weren't ready for this. We used to cut the sleeves of our jackets and sew a large pocket on the front to carry the code books. The stitches were large and crude made from the inside of para cord. Our trousers were skintight and covered with splashes of black paint for camouflage. We had them tailored like this so when it was wet they didn't make a noise. On our feet were an assortment of hockey, jungle and DMS boots. Some favoured hose tops soaked in mossie rep to keep the leeches out, but Wally favoured a pair of ex-GI-issued gaiters that came up to his knees. Our headdress was either a bandana or a mutilated jungle hat. Around our waists, keeping all this elegance together, were heavy drop belts that were used to keep loads together in resupply. We knocked them bandy, they were speechless. The outcome of this fashion show was we were ordered to stay in civvies.

We went back to the basha and tidied up, waiting for the inspection that never materialised, so like good soldiers we went to bed. There is nothing like Egyptian PT to keep the mind receptive, and after a little revision I dropped off.

I was just about to service the heroine in my dream when a large bang on the bed end brought me back to reality. "Get out of bed," I'm ordered. My sleep-laden eyes gradually focus on the group of people at the foot of the bed. I'm lying there with the sheet pulled up to my chin like a blushing virgin wondering what to do. "Get out of bed," I'm ordered again. I oblige and stand there with nothing on in all my glory at attention. The intruders were most surprised and were more embarrassed than me. Not only was the camp commandant with his hangers-on present, but also his Malay counterpart with his staff. It was like the Lord Mayor's Show in my bed space. What didn't help me was to see Joe, who slept opposite, giggling with the sheets pulled over his head. What do you do when surrounded by perverts? GRIN. I was ordered back into bed and it's the first time ever that I got a rifting while lying horizontal.

This was the start of a series of brushes with authority. Learning Malay was easy, but putting up with these creeps made life difficult. They insisted on regular inspections, but when Joe collected a handful of bedbugs and presented them to the CO, these inspections stopped.

There was a young captain on the course from the infantry, who was a keen cricketer. He was an all-rounder who could bat, bowl and keep wicket, and wasn't bad in the slips, either. He wanted to get a team up to play the garrison. So between us we rustled up a team and turned up wearing whatever we could find. Cut-down OG trousers, T-shirt and jungle boots were favoured by all except the captain, who was in whites. The garrison eleven turned out in immaculate laundered whites, and started throwing a ball around and stretching. We sat on the ground throwing the sun crème around and started scratching, The CO was their captain, the sergeant major was the wicketkeeper, and the provost sergeant was their fast bowler.

We won the toss and elected to bat. We were all back in the pavilion twenty minutes later with 28 runs on the scoreboard. Just as their openers walked to the wicket it started raining, so we all ran off for cover. Normally at this time of year it was a short, sharp shower, but this one was persistent, prolonged and pouring. So we headed to the nearest bar and never went back. The sun did come out later and the opposition was most disappointed when only the captain returned. Well, he was an all-rounder after all. So my next charge is for unsporting-like conduct, leaving my post without permission, or in this case a wicket, and stealing army property. I had the ball in my pocket when we walked off, and I think it was old misery guts's way of asking for his ball back.

When we finished the course the D Sqn lads had a flight that night to Kuching. Our flight to Brunei was five days later, and none of us wanted to hang around Nee Soon any longer. I got talking to a Kiwi officer who said we could go with his Sqn that was leaving at three in the morning going to Kuching. I plied him with more beer and told the lads to pack. We took off on time and it was a great relief to be leaving, but after one hour in the sky the aircraft developed a problem and had to return to Singapore. Waiting on the ground were two military policemen who took the three of us into custody. We finished up back in Nee Soon in front of the CO. He demanded to know how we got on that aircraft and Wally replied with a classic. He said,

"Up the steps." For this little escapade we had to parade at the guardroom four times a day for the next five days.

We finally got to Brunei where our HQ was based at a place called 'rumah hantu' (haunted house). There were many rumours why it was called that, but I never saw any ghosts. Some of the lads claimed to have seen all sorts of apparitions, but I put this down to the G10 rum.

The Indonesians attacked the oilfields of Seria and we were deployed on the border to prevent any more incursions. We camped on a busy cross-border track that was used by the tribes on the Indonesian side to go to Limbang, a trading port. They herded cattle to sell and returned with cooking pots, blankets and the like. They told us of all troop movements or military activity over the border. At least a dozen families a day used to make this an annual trip, but suddenly all movement ceased. We started patrolling and didn't see anyone for weeks. We never wore shreddies in the jungle and, being wet most of the time, this caused problems. Fred's dick was rubbed raw and I treated it with a liberal coating of antiseptic ointment that I let him administer. To keep it dry we placed it in a plastic sugar bag held on by piece of para cord. By the way, it was only a two-ounce sugar bag from a ration pack. Having not seen a living soul for ages we were surprised to bump into a group returning over the border. Fred's dancing around giving it "Selamat pagis" and wondering why the girls are giggling. You can imagine how rumours start. When they got home they probably told everyone that the Orang Putehs (white men) walk about with their todgers wrapped in plastic, hanging outside of their trousers.

On another tour we lived with the Muruts on the Sungei Barum in the fourth division, Sarawak. We didn't get away to a very good start. The headman had spotted one of the lads with a shotgun and invited him to go hunting with him. Traditionally, when they hunted for wild pig they would go out with a pack of dogs. They would turn them loose and sit on a high feature till they heard the dogs barking. They would do this when they confronted a pig, and would try to confine it in a stream or gully. On hearing his dogs, the hunter would find them and stab the pig with his spear. This is easier said than done, and very dangerous. Some of the wild boars are huge with sharp tusks. They are more than a match for any dog, and it's only the number of dogs that keep the pig contained. They encircle it, snapping at its rear and darting in and out. Occasionally they get badly gored, and hunters have been killed while attempting to spear the pig. The dogs had a strict pecking order and were led by a pack leader. This dominant dog was priceless, taking years to train.

On this occasion the dogs did their bit and contained a large sow in a stream bed. Nobby and the headman tracked them down, finding the dogs were keeping the pig occupied. Nobby's shotgun was a pump-action, short-barrelled Remington loaded with number 6SG shells. It was an ideal weapon for the lead scout, giving a good spread of shot that would knock anything over at short range. Nobby fired at the same time as the pack leader decided to attack the pig and got blown in half. The other dogs backed off at the sound of gunfire and the sow trotted off into the Ulu. The Penghulu was devastated and knelt down, collecting up all the bits that once was his favourite dog.

Things got worse when one of the lads said he had played with the kids showing them how to make bows and arrows from this springy wood he had found just outside the longhouse. The hairs on my neck stood up and I asked him did this wood have a white sap. When he said yes, I knew he had cut down some young rubber trees that the locals had planted. What else could go wrong? They say bad luck comes in threes, and the third incident was caused by the same lad who bought a blowpipe from one of the locals. He was caught using chickens as targets. He reckoned he accidentally hit the chicken in the neck which managed to fly and fall at the feet of its owner. It was all very embarrassing and compensation had to be paid. When the fourth incident happened, I knew this was just the start of another set of three.

They say lightning never strikes twice in the same place. This is nonsense: it certainly does. We had to clear a site for a helipad and hired some local labour to help. Arthur was showing off his scar that was caused by a parang when he was cutting a DZ a year earlier. It was across the back of his hand and had required twelve stitches. It's a dangerous practice to have two men cutting the same tree, but because of their size, sometimes it's a necessity. He gave a great re-enactment, placing his hand on a tree and giving a running commentary, and as he said, "I had my hand like this when," with that a parang swung and he was caught again on the same hand by his mate. They say you learn more from your mistakes, but the golden rule is never make the same mistake again. This time tendons were cut and he had to be casevaced.

My favourite place in Borneo was Bario in the Kelabit Highlands. We lived in a schoolhouse perched on a hill looking down on an airstrip. The Kelabits are a lovely people and we got on well with them. There were six outlying villages that we visited regularly. Bario was the main longhouse where the Penghulu lived, and it was about a six-hour journey to the furthest longhouse situated on the border. Every longhouse gave us a great welcome, feeding us and laying on entertainment in the form of tribal dances.

The threat of invasion from Indonesia was getting stronger all the time so we fortified our little hill. Pungees made from bamboo are very sharp, and we planted these all around the hill. We laid claymore mines that could be fired remotely and strung barbed wire everywhere. We thought we were impregnable, as nothing could get through our obstacles. We were very disillusioned when we saw local women planting pineapples amongst our pungee stakes.

I was out one day with a local when he shot a monkey. This was a welcomed addition to their diet which was mainly rice, with a little fish or chicken, and whatever greens that they could forage. As we turned the body over we discovered a baby clinging on for dear life. I raised this baby and it became a good pet. We called him Charlie after one of the lads who looked like his mother. It used to live in a hood that I sewed on my shirt and it went everywhere with me. You can imagine what I smelt like, and when we heard that the Defence Secretary was visiting us, our boss started panicking. We all had beards with shoulder-length hair and he threatened us with death to smarten ourselves up. We made it clear that we didn't want to shave to meet the VIP, and volunteered to go out on patrol. He was having none of this so we started sulking. No one likes shaving halfway through a tour and we resented this intrusion.

Even on the morning of the visit we were still unshaven and Flapjack was hysterical, running around in his new OG, tripping up the steps in frustration. No one wanted to be the first to shave, so we waited till we heard the aircraft before we moved. Flapjack ran off down the hill to meet the VIP, threatening us with torture. As soon as he went, we sprang into action and shaved and changed. When you try to rush shaving off a beard it's inevitable that you cut yourself. The three of us had multiple nicks which we stemmed with bits of tissue.

When Flapjack returned with the VIP, he was so relieved to see us lined up and changed, but the paper beauty spots failed to impress him. Our faces looked like a burst bag of confetti.

Eddie was introduced first and was a man of few words. The boss said Eddie was a medic with vast experience. The VIP asked, "How do you become a medic?" "Did a course," was the answer. Then Flapjack jumped in to liven up this boring conversation and said, "Yes, but he is an advanced medic." Not overimpressed, the VIP said, "How did you become an advanced medic?" Eddie replied, "Did another course." Eddie was asked various questions, and gave the briefest of answers, making conversation difficult. When he was introduced to Jimmy, who was the demolitionist, the VIP changed his tactics and asked him why he had became a demolitionist. He was taken back when Jimmy said, "I couldn't get on the medic course." I was trying to anticipate what questions I would be asked, trying to think up some smart answers. I had Charlie on my shoulder and thought it would be great if he could answer for me.

Not wanting him to be left out, I stuck a piece of tissue on Charlie's face, so he blended in. All the entourage oohed and aahed when they saw him, lightening the atmosphere. The minister was chuffed when the monkey jumped on his shoulder and I don't know if it was his aftershave or his personality; but Charlie got an erection and, hanging onto his sideboard and eyebrow, started rogering his left earhole. Every time I hear the song "Love Is in the Air" (hair) it reminds me of this incident.

The Minister of Defence didn't realise what was happening and was pleased with all the attention he was receiving. All the hangers-on and Flapjack were mortified, not knowing whether to knock the monkey off or ignore it. Good job there were plenty of tissues handy.

We used to take an airdrop once a week and took advantage of this to build up the suntan. Lying on the DZ wearing just a pair of shorts, we used to read till we heard the aircraft. This day was like any other but I was to have a lucky escape. I lit a flare to indicate the wind direction and the aircraft started dropping supplies. Being an airstrip, we used to refuel smaller aircraft and choppers, and had a stockpile of fuel. This was dropped in fifty-gallon burmoils, four to a chute. One of these fractured on landing, spilling its contents that came into contact with the flare. Whoosh, up went the barrel in a sheet of flame, igniting the other three with it. I finished up medium rare with no hair.

I spent a lot of time in Bario and watched the build-up to confrontation. The infantry came in to defend the airstrip, including our position. We stood by to go over the border and bring back a headman who was reported to be spying for the Indonesians. To do this I was given a bottle of knockout drops (Mickey Finn). I was assured that a small drop would knock out an elephant, and if taken with alcohol was doubly lethal. This op was cancelled but I still had the drops and was dying to use them.

I got the opportunity one night when we threw a party and invited some of the infantry to it. They had a guitar player and we sang long into the night. Their captain's name was Shaw who kept his men on their toes and told them to be extra-vigilant, especially when on guard. That night he was challenged as he was going to the party and it went something like this. "Halt, who goes there?" "Captain Shaw." "Are you sure you're Shaw?" "Yes, I'm sure I'm Shaw." "Yes, but we're not sure you're Shaw." And so it went on. When the captain said it was time to leave the party, his men didn't want to go. So I thought it a good idea to slip him a Mickey. I started with a little and saw no effect. I insisted he have just one more drink and gave him a larger dose. Still no reaction; in fact he was the only man still standing. I often think what would have happened if we had used these drops as intended.

Once a week on airdrop day we would make a rum punch. This was a lethal concoction that tasted so innocent. It was made by boiling all the sweets from the ration packs, with lemonade powder, and any fruit that we could obtain. Pineapples and bananas were always available and these were chopped up and included. G10 rum was added to this base, giving the punch a kick.

The monkey and chickens used to eat the leftover fruit from the bottom of the pot and would stagger around under the influence. We were given a lot of chickens and they free-ranged around the hilltop. Every now and then we would fancy a chicken curry and attempt to capture one. These could fly like eagles and would take off, landing down the hill amongst our defences. The best way to capture one, if it wasn't drunk, was to shoot it. It had to be a head shot, otherwise there wasn't very much left of the bird.

Our boss, Flapjack, decided to cheer us up one day, although he didn't realise this at the time. We took it in turns to burn off the tin pit, which was a deep hole covered by logs where we dumped all of our rubbish. There was a small aperture which we used to drop the rubbish through that we kept closed to keep the flies out. Flapjack turns up with a jerrycan of petrol and pours it through this aperture. We told him to strip all the logs off, but he knew best. We thought that if he wanted to commit harikari that's up to him, so we left him to it. He must have used the best part of a jerrycan and placed this by his side. He stood on the logs and dropped a match through the hole. The fireball rose to fifty feet, followed by the logs, Flapjack and the jerrycan. The explosion came next, followed by a shock wave that blew down the atap walls of our basha. We stood on the veranda and watched him perform a graceful backward loop engulfed in flames and the contents of the shit pit. When he landed, the smaller logs were still falling and by some miracle missed him. The jerrycan, however, being the lightest, went the highest, and just when Flapjack started relaxing, counting his blessings, the can landed alongside him, blazing fiercely. He was singed, seared and shaken, covered in hot jam and old tea bags. Never let children play with matches.

He didn't have a lot of hair to start with, so it goes to show:

FEW HAIRS SINGED

CHAPTER EIGHT

MIDDLE EAST

The majority of the lads loved the jungle and hated the desert. There are many reasons for this which I'll try to explain. The jungle offered good cover both from the elements and prying eyes, whereas the desert is open with very little cover and the sun beats down relentlessly. There are a few trees and small shrubs scattered around, but concealment is difficult. In primary jungle the visibility is only a matter of yards, which is the complete opposite of the desert where you can see for miles. It gets dark at six and remains dark till six in the morning, with nothing moving at night in the jungle, apart from a few animals, so a good night's sleep is guaranteed. In the desert all movement is done at night and sleep is grabbed when convenient during the day. Sometimes this is not possible and without adequate sleep, health deteriorates. A tropical rainforest is aptly named, as water is plentiful, unlike the desert that is dry with no surface water. We could operate for fourteen days before resupply in the jungle, but only for five days in the desert. Minimum water ration in the desert is one gallon a day; this weighs ten pounds. So a five-day op meant fifty pounds of water before you start thinking about anything else like ammunition and food etc. It was a pleasure living with the Ibans, Kelabits and Muruts of the Far East: we could trust these people with our lives. The different tribes we came across in the Middle East varied greatly, but on the whole were difficult. They were suspicious of all strangers and couldn't even get on with each other. One group of tribes we came across were the most argumentative people in the world, even worse than my dad.

In the desert there is no respite: you are under pressure twenty-four hours a day. Whoever dominates the high ground dominates the battle. It's a peculiar thing, but battles are always fought uphill and on the edge of four maps.

Hunger is bad enough but thirst is ten times worse. Because of the open terrain there was nowhere to run or hide, so a lot of ammunition had to be carried so you could defend your position if compromised. We used some voice communications in the desert to communicate with the infantry, and so extra radios and batteries had to be included. This all adds up, and it's difficult to keep the bergan below a hundred pounds.

The deserts where we operated, like Aden, Oman and the Trucial States, were mountainous. Climbing these at night loaded like pack mules was very arduous, and the amount of energy and body fluid expended was astronomic.

Aden was the cesspit of the world; God was having a bad day when he made this country. It was the location that made it a strategic port in the Gulf that controlled the Red Sea that led to the Suez Canal. In the days of steamships it was a vital refuelling port. It did produce some oil, but to me the country was not worth fighting for.

My first visit here was in the early 1960s and, although it was a great experience, I didn't really enjoy it. It was like getting a good hiding: it's nice when it stops. As soon as you land you know that you are in a hostile environment. The heat attacks you, making breathing difficult, and a strong smell of sewage invades the nose. We landed at midday when the temperature was over a hundred degrees F, heating up all surfaces reflecting off the tarmac, threatening your skin with incineration. Only good sunglasses could protect the eyes from the intense light, another item that I didn't have. Flies flew in squadron strength and always managed to land in an eye or a mouth. Brushing them off only encouraged them, and they went away and returned with their mates.

Communist-supported terrorists attacked oil installations and tourists in the town, and up country they attacked the security forces, blew up roads and government installations. The Russians would dearly love to have a base here, acquiring an airfield and a port in the Gulf. All I thought it was good for was the duty-free, which was the cheapest in the world.

We had two roles here, one up country and one in the town. The one in town was interesting and a typical SAS role. We had guys dressed as Arabs following others acting like naïve tourists. These targets were trying to lure out the terrorists for the pseuds to deal with. The tourists were off the ships that called in regularly. Also there were a lot of families who lived in the town from RAF Khormaksar, along with Europeans working in the oil industry. There were a lot of shootings, and grenade-throwing incidents which severely destabilised the country.

The lads who dressed up looked the part. They had to be dark-skinned and most spoke Arabic. They were armed with 9mm pistols that were concealed under their robes. The blue-eyed, fair-skinned lads became the targets – guess what I was. The training for this type of operation was intense. Firing a pistol from a concealed holster was new to the army, let alone the Regiment, and we had to learn quickly. The only body armour available at the time was made by Wilkinson. It was made of small titanium plates that overlapped and clanked like a tank as you moved. It weighed a ton and couldn't be disguised under a shirt.

Aden town was called Crater after the volcanic activity that created it. Rising steeply from the sea was the rim of this crater, which we used to run up on a daily basis. At a place called Shamsam there were eight hundred and seventy-nine steps that led up to an old lighthouse. We ran a mile along the beach, climbed the stairs and back again all before breakfast.

Sheikh Othman was a slum district of Crater where a lot of terrorists lived. We used to sneak round this at night. We were told to stay at least twenty metres from any buildings or walls as the locals would throw bricks, stones, bottles or anything else they could get their hands on. One night the patrol commander, who had a loud, squeaky voice, held a discussion as to how far twenty metres was. We still dealt in feet and inches, not knowing what a metre was. Someone said it was about fifty feet, so Pete walked up to this wall and started pacing. He got to forty-nine when a bottle came over the wall and hit him straight on top of his head.

Our base was at Falaise to the west of Crater. The journey from here to the town passed a place called Silent Valley, where the military cemetery was. Without doubt this is the most depressing place I've ever been to in my life. Craggy rocks surrounded a flat area which was devoid of plants, birds or any living creatures. I had to promise myself that I would never be buried there. I attended several funerals here and each time experienced a feeling of bleakness. The place was well named, having a haunting aura about it. There are no good places to die, but this one was to be avoided.

There was a road that went from Aden up country to Dhala which was just short of the border with Yemen. Halfway up was Habelyn where we had a fortified position and an airfield. This road was mined regularly and was the only link to these positions.

We travelled this route regularly and dropped off to lay ambushes, hoping to catch the minelayers at work. Lying up in the heat of the day and ambushing at night is laborious.

With water so scarce, it's amazing that the ration we carried was dehydrated. This is not as daft as it seems, as we carried our water separately and had the option of cooking with it or not. It was all down to weight. A normal ration with tins of stew etc. was too heavy, and because we carried all of our rubbish back to base, impractical. Five days on meat blocks is not very appetising, and it does nothing for the bowels.

We were laid up one day and had the pleasure of the colonel's company. Whenever he visited the Squadron he inevitably was put with Two Troop. We lay there festering under our scrim net, and Jimmy had what I can only describe as clinkers. This is a very sore condition affecting the rectum. Because of the diet, heat and curry powder, this made us very loose. Army-issue toilet paper was not the softest and was banned on ops. We found the best use of this was for tracing paper. It certainly left traces in your pants. What Jimmy did next really impressed the CO. He put a small drop of water on his face veil and pulled it to and fro between his legs. The CO was speechless and watched Jimmy's ablutions, wondering what was coming next. When Jimmy retied it round his neck he fingered his own with suspicion. When it came to make the curry the CO insisted that he would make it, but Jimmy wouldn't hear of it. He took both their meat blocks and crumbled them into a mess tin. Needless to say, he didn't eat much of the curry.

Two days later it was my turn to impress. Visualise five men hidden amongst rocks covered by a scrim net all huddled together. There was only room for two to lie down at any one time. I had a good dose of the trots and had to relieve myself in the only available place in our laying-up position (LUP). It was a shallow depression, and after I did the business I lowered a flat rock to cover it. The rock crumbled and fell causing a splash. The CO who was freshly shaven, suddenly was covered in freckles, with the rest of us getting a little extra colour in the beard.

We were always dropped off at night either by truck or by helicopter. Before first light we had to get as far away from our drop-off point as possible. Then we had to select a laying-up position where ideally we could observe our target. Often this would be a village where we suspected terrorists operated from. It meant climbing mountains that would be difficult in daylight with no kit. To do this at night with the weight we were carrying was inconceivable. We always left a sign and the locals had such sharp eyes that often we were compromised. Sometimes this was used as a ploy. The group would be extracted, leaving behind a well-hidden patrol with the water they had carried in.

There is not a lot of entertainment in the desert, so the locals found it good fun to shoot at any strangers. You always knew if you were compromised because you would be shot at. One tribesman could hold up a whole Marine Commando. They knew the land and could navigate through it without leaving signs. They could encircle a position before you realised it, and knew how to dominate the ground.

Six of us were dropped off one night to observe a village high in the mountains. The pilot did a great job hovering to let us out, and flew a deception plan, hovering over different features in the area to confuse the locals. We clung to the side of a mountain and couldn't go up or down. We had to wait till first light to select a route away from our drop-off point. We finished up in a saddle with a goat track running through it so we felt really vulnerable. I was on first stag while the others slept. One of the lads started talking in his sleep and then screaming. I leapt on him and put my hands around his throat. The screams continued, so I squeezed harder. It was then I realised I had the wrong bloke and let go of Jimmy to jump on Mick. As soon as I let go, Jimmy started screaming. To wake up with a pair of hands around your throat to the sound of screams must be terrifying, and Jimmy let me know how much. The only thing to do was to brew up and call for extraction; I think we woke up the whole district.

Regardless of training it's very hard to remain silent when you are hurt, but I did witness a man screaming in silence. He was the signaller sending the sitrep while his mate made the curry. Without thinking when the curry was ready he placed the mess tin on the signaller's thigh. The signaller was so engrossed in sending that he didn't notice it till it started burning the delicate flesh on the inside of the thigh. His face screwed up in agony and his mouth opened wide, but no sound came out. He must have learnt this from Alan.

We went to great lengths to keep our presence a secret. When we deployed through Habelyn, we didn't want the hired locals to report our movements. To ensure this we had a senior rank to act as our liaison officer, who became a master of disguise. We nicknamed him 'Smersh'. He started off wearing a Signals' beret but was asked to send a signal so he changed the badge to a REME one. When a truck broke down he was called upon to fix it, so he changed once more, becoming a medic with the RAMC. When the position took casualties, he was asked why he wasn't attending the wounded. He was fed up of being rumbled, so he settled for a Carabineers badge, a unit that had been disbanded for several years. The very first time he wore it, an old sweat who enlisted with the carabineers quizzed Smersh. So much for blending in the background and not drawing any attention, he stuck out like a vegetarian at a cannibals' BBQ.

The Marines had a sergeants' mess tent where you could buy beer. One of the lads was having a drink one night wearing shorts. The Marines are sticklers for dress codes, and he was told by the senior rank that he couldn't wear shorts in the mess. So he just took them off and carried on drinking.

Insertion was always a problem, mainly due to the heavy kit we had to carry. We tried free fall entries onto the Dhala road which were exciting but not very fruitful. Flying at night through the mountains was always a risk. The choppers we used at the time were heavily overloaded, and having no night vision aids, mistakes were made. On several occasions we were dropped off on unscaleable peaks and had to be lifted off again. It's easier to climb up than it is to climb down. Climbing up, you can see all the hand- and footholds with a choice of routes. Going down, you don't know what's below. It could be a sheer drop and, once committed, you can't go up or down. It's a dangerous venture without any kit, and the reason mountaineers rope together is to stop the sensible one going home.

Probably the most publicised operation in Aden was the Radfan. Three Troop were inserted to mark a drop zone for the Paras. They were compromised by a shepherd boy as they lay up during the day, and were quickly surrounded by tribesmen. With continuous air and artillery support they held out till last light, when they decided to break out. Unfortunately, two men were killed and their heads were displayed in Sana, a town just across the border.

The road was always a dangerous option because of the mines. We used a Stalwart truck which could survive an anti-tank mine blast, as long as you sat in the middle on a layer of sandbags. Mick was a driver in the RCT before he came on selection. He told us a story when he was demonstrating the amphibious qualities of the Stalwart in Germany. He spent all week preparing the vehicle, sealing different components and waterproofing others. The idea was to enter a lake and drive past a pier where all the dignitaries sat. They stood down for the weekend and all he had to do on Monday morning was to fit two plugs which he left on the dashboard. These were left out to allow the vehicle to drain, getting rid of the excess water. They were vital for the floatation of the vehicle. When he arrived on Monday morning he noticed the rear tyre was flat and had to change it. Everything is big on this truck, and changing a wheel is a two-man job. They finally fixed the problem and Mick jumped in the cab and entered the water, trying to make up lost time. All was well till he spotted the drain plugs still on the dashboard: too late now, he was committed. As he passed the VIPs who were all lined up, the water was up to the wing mirrors and rising fast. Mick decided to go down with the ship like a good captain should.

If the tide was out, the beach was a good alternative to the road, and this was used if you were going to Mukhella on the coast. The same Rupert that blew himself up in the jungle was map-reading in the front of a pinkie which is an open-topped jeep bristling with guns. They were driving along the beach at forty miles per hour, when he told the driver to stop. He put aside the map and stepped out. They were still doing 40 mph: the driver hadn't responded. Flapjack bounced along the beach at 40 mph, coming to rest 50 yards later spitting sand and venom.

Just before we pulled out of Aden, trouble was expected, so we had a quick move which was sensitive. We mingled with other passengers at Heathrow in small groups wearing a variety of clothing. Kilts, hockey boots, macs and jeans were all part of our cover. This was blown when a message came over the tannoy: "Will the SAS party please report to gate seven?"

At the other end we were met by the QM in full uniform wearing beret and belt: so much for secrecy. We were whisked away to a block of married quarters that we used as our HQ. All of the families had long gone and this was the best accommodation we ever had. We didn't stay long here. After zeroing the weapons and a few days' acclimatisation, we flew north.

We finished up on the border in the far north, amongst the most rugged terrain I've ever seen. The people who lived there were equally rugged, and the fiercest I've ever come across. They jealously guarded their territory and hated outsiders. We did our warm-up training in Wales where it was wet and cold, with the landscape green and undulating. This location was completely the opposite. Sheer, barren mountains rising to six thousand feet, with steep valleys trapping the heat like a furnace. We picked the highest feature for tactical reasons, which put us closer to the sun with no shade.

Every male in the area carried a weapon, and shooting each other was a national pastime. Now that we turned up, they had fresh targets.

We patrolled out from our sanctuary regularly, the first part being easy. We were fresh, fully hydrated, carrying plenty of water, going downhill, all before the sun come up. By the end of the day we were at our limit of endurance. The heat was overwhelming and the rock absorbed the heat, acting like storage heaters. The climb back up was excruciating. We tried to save a little water and have a brew halfway up, and this was always the best brew that I've ever tasted.

It's funny how adrenalin works. One day halfway up the climb, seeing red dots before the eyes, and staggering like a drunk, shots rang out. All signs of fatigue disappeared. We couldn't determine where the shots came from and got back to camp in record time. We found out later that a village was celebrating a wedding where they fire a lot of shots in the air. Another troop thought they were under fire and called an air strike in. It must have been some wedding reception when the hunters bombed and strafed the newly-weds. Did the ground move for you, darling?

When calling in for air support, a flare is fired to indicate the location. A new type of flare came into service and Jim was unsure of its performance. He thought it was hand-held and pulled the pin and held on. The flare burnt intensely and a blob of molten metal dropped out of the bottom onto Jim's bare wrist. He is still hollering.

So a lesson learnt:

NEW FLARE STINGS

CHAPTER NINE

HEREFORD

Hereford was a great place to return to: it felt like home. The best sight when returning was from the top of the Callow where you got the first look of Hereford. It was only then that you realised you were finally home. A lot of lads married local girls and I was always invited round to test their wives' cooking. I was always a big eater and could eat anything. I was the guinea pig, the official food taster. No matter if the meal was burnt, raw or rancid, I would finish it. I always gave favourable comments because I wanted to be invited back. I came unstuck once when liver was served. It was overcooked and rubbery so I tried to feed it to their dog. He sat by me under the table but he didn't like liver, either. He smelt it, licked it, tried to chew it, then left it. I couldn't leave it on the floor so I recovered it. When Julie asked me what's wrong with the liver I said, "Nothing," and swallowed it in big lumps. Next day I had a wet nose and a barking cough.

We watched this dog grooming itself and was envious when he started licking his tackle. My mate said, "I wish I could do that," and Julie said, "Give him a biscuit and he might let you."

The QM had a small Pekingese that went everywhere with him, and would curl up in a basket in his office. One of the lads had an Alsatian and he took it with him into the QM's office. This upset the Peke who jumped out of his basket in a frenzy, trying to defend his territory. The QM shouted, "Get that dog out of here!" so Dusty picks up the Peke and throws it out of the window.

There was a steakhouse in town that offered a free meal if you could eat it all. The only snag being the steak weighed five pounds. I fancied my chances at this and was in strict training. I demolished a three-pounder that was massive with chips, tomatoes and extra mushrooms, washed down by six pints of Guinness. All this training was in vain as one night my mate caused a scene in the restaurant and they wouldn't serve us. The governor set the dog on us which we managed to throw out, so he got the darts team from the public bar. They may have been good at throwing darts but couldn't throw punches, and we threw them out as well. Didn't they realise they were tackling a twenty-five-year globetrotting veteran with jungle and desert experience?

We had to be careful as any offences committed could result in an RTU (return to unit). This was the harshest punishment of all, which we all wanted to avoid; no way was I going back to the Paras. So this threat kept us on the straight and narrow.

I bought a brand new Volkswagen Beetle in 1965 for the princely sum of £550. Inside of a fortnight it looked like a stock car, with every panel and wing dented. That car stood up to so much abuse. I hit the rear wing turning into the bus station on day one. The front nearside followed suit on a lamp-post a day later. The right front wing was crumpled while I was in the picturehouse, so no fault of mine, and the other rear wing suffered the same fate when I tried reversing out of a car park. I collected a carpet for a mate and put it in the boot which is in the front on a Beetle. When I was delivering it to the married quarters a truck rolled back at the lights and squashed the front end. I couldn't open the boot, much to the annoyance of my mate's wife, and eventually had to force it. So the bonnet was knackered. The engine compartment was well and truly flattened when I drove backward at speed and hit a steel stanchion in a hotel car park. I had a girlfriend in the front at the time, and when I hit the obstacle she disappeared over the back of the seat and got wedged down in the back. I think we had been rowing, so I left her there. All I could see in my mirror was two stocking-topped thighs pedalling in the air. She wasn't best pleased when I stopped a few miles later and she demanded to be let out. I tried to placate her by telling her she had nice legs for a fat woman, but to no avail. She was quite a large girl and was wearing a dress that you could hold a wedding reception in. She slammed the door with vigour, causing the left sun visor to break off, and as I pulled away I heard the sound of ripping material. Her dress was caught in the door.

I think her struggling to get free weakened the seat runners, and when she pulled herself up she actually broke the driver's side. My party piece was to put the driver's seat in the back and drive it from the back seat. I could reach the pedals with my feet and steer it using my knees. I would come up to a junction, and lie back with my arms folded, looking out of the side window, giving the impression that there wasn't a driver.

I serviced the car and changed all the wheels around to even out tyre wear. I tightened the near front wheel first, then worked back around the car. When I got to the open driver's door I jumped in for a test-drive. Big mistake. I was bumping down a country lane when the front off side wheel accelerated on its own and climbed a tree. I had forgotten to tighten this little rascal.

I got a lot of the repairs done by a mate called Harold who owned a garage. He was fond of VWs, and mine brought back nostalgic memories for him. Harold was a big man, weighing twenty stone or more, with a slip of a girlfriend topping the scales at a modest sixteen stones. They went canoodling in a remote lay-by and climbed in the back. Their combined weight of half a ton was too much for the metal-framed seat that was stuffed with horsehair. The frame buckled and shorted out on the battery that was located underneath. Harold was on the vinegar strokes when he first smelt burning and put it down to passion encouraging him to new heights. His girlfriend thrashed about, trying to escape the heat that was building up below her, giving Harold a false impression of her emotions. He felt quite proud of himself and when smoke started coming up between her legs. The flames were the giveaway that something was wrong, and they had to abandon the car. It burnt out with most of their clothes still inside. This is very embarrassing when the local vicar is the first on the scene. Some people get enflamed with back seat drivers.

Four of us started the Strongbow Skydivers, which was a free fall team sponsored by Bulmers cider. We jumped into county shows, sports events and any outdoor festivals that had enough space for a landing zone. This was one of the first display teams in the country and demand was high. We jumped for money and, looking back, took a lot of chances. All four of us held the highest certification that allowed us to pull and be under the canopy by 1500 feet. On many occasions this was flouted. At the Warwick Water Festival we flew in at 1100 feet and threw a streamer that disappeared in the smoke and heat haze of the chip vans below. The wind was too strong but we jumped anyway. It's alright if everything works as it should, but Murphy's Law always plays a part. It was a hop and a pop for three of us, but more of a rip and a dip for Andy. His main chute ripped on deployment and he had to cut it away, resulting in him landing in the Avon that ran alongside the DZ. Tony said he knew we were low on run-in as he could smell the hamburgers in the aircraft.

We did a water jump at a stately home using an ornamental lake to land in. It was midsummer, so just trainers and cossies were worn. Our chutes were Para-Commanders, an advanced design for the time but difficult to control. One of the newer members, who didn't like being told what to do, assured us he could manage. He was still at 500 feet when he ran out of lake and sailed on into the trees to become impaled on blackthorn.

Joe was dying to do a display and pleaded his case to jump at RAF Odiham. Airfields make good DZs, as they are large and free of obstacles. So Joe was given a chance and told to keep well away from any aircraft, particularly if they had engines running. He should have been told to keep away from any buildings as well, because on the day he steered away from a parked heli and went straight through a plate-glass window of a hangar. He landed on the floor inside an office – without a scratch. A guy was making tea and Joe casually said, "Just dropped in for a brew." Before the startled tea maker could answer, the canopy which was still outside the building inflated and dragged Joe back through the window the way he came. Only now it was ringed by broken glass and cut Joe to ribbons.

He was going on leave the next day, so to save going to hospital he got one of the lads to suture his wounds. The worst one was a large gash on his thigh. The next day he went with his wife and four kids to Tenby in South Wales and went paddling in the sea. The tide goes out a long way and the family was so absorbed looking for crabs and shrimps that they failed to notice the incoming tide. They looked shorewards and were horrified to see that the tide had cut them off and the little shallow island they were standing on was diminishing by the minute. Joe's wife and kids were non-swimmers and climbed up Joe as the water got higher. Joe certainly felt the water when it reached his wounds. He had his wife on his shoulders, the eldest boy on his back, and a kid in each arm, with the youngest hanging around his neck. Joe thought it undignified to scream but his family made up for this. The water was up to his waist when a fishing boat rescued them. We made a song up for Joe based on a Johnny Cash number. It went like this: "How high's the water, Mama, four kids high and rising."

We got involved in running combat survival courses for the army. These were very realistic, and as long as you were doing the hunting and not being hunted, were a lot of fun. It was for senior ranks and officers from all of NATO. It started with a week in the classroom learning basics, a week of practical training, building up to the final week which was an exercise where they evaded, got captured and finally were interrogated.

A lot of outside lecturers were invited to give talks on their experiences. There was never a dull moment and not many people knew what was coming next.

The regiment borrowed a snake and used it in some of the lectures. The instructor asked the class, "What is the best way to kill a snake?" A young naval pilot piped up: "Grab it by the tail and crack it like a whip." "Come up here, son," the instructor invites as he opens a sack and gets out a nine-foot reticulated python. Young Nelson nearly faints as hissing Sid is placed around his neck. You either love snakes or hate them. We were taught that every snake is deadly. This way you won't be tempted to pick one up, and leave them strictly alone. A good analogy is, more people are killed in the tropics by coconuts falling on their heads than by snakes.

I must tell the story about my mate who kept a pet snake. While on leave he went to a dance and decided to give his snake a treat as well. So he wrapped it around his waist and went tripping the light fantastic. He was dancing a slow waltz with a girl whose husband was playing trumpet in the band. Geoff was out to impress and held his partner close. When the trumpeter started playing a solo the snake came alive and uncoiled, probably thinking he was hearing a snake charmer. The girl felt this movement and thought her luck had changed till she looked down and saw this reptile poking out of Geoff's shirt. She let out a tremendous scream before collapsing in a heap of lace petticoats. The trumpeter thought Geoff had assaulted his wife and jumped off the stage, setting about him. This allowed the snake to escape and thrash about the polished dance floor which was crowded at the time but didn't stay that way for long.

When the students went out on their final exercise we were used as a hunter force. I teamed up with Dave and we drove round the exercise area in his car dressed in civvies.

Dave was the worst driver that I have ever been with. He had an old Morris that took ten miles to reach fifty miles an hour. Once at speed he wouldn't slow down regardless of what was in front of him. I told him he had better put the lights on; he said they were. Instead of a penetrating beam, a feeble glow plopped out. When it started raining his wipers completed one full sweep every five minutes. The car was so cold and draughty that a polar bear would perish. I asked him where the heater was so I could switch it on and not distract him. He said it was in his shed at home; he hadn't had time to fix it yet. I was shivering with both cold and fear: what a journey. Although I told him that we were five miles from our destination, we still overshot the lay-by. He had no reverse gear and I had to push him back. He told me later about his brakes. He had tried replacing the front shoes himself, but had bought the wrong ones which wouldn't fit, so he left them out. I wondered why the car was pulling to the left when he tried slowing down.

I was cramped in the car and was so relieved to get out and have a stretch. We had time to kill so I stretched out on the back of a trailer of a parked truck. Dave had put years on my life and I was exhausted. I didn't wake up till the artic was moving; I could have finished up in Birmingham. We drove around the area and caught a prisoner who was skulking by a farm. We trussed him in the back and took him to the holding pen which was in Dering Lines. In the camp they had put barbed wire barricades across the roads and the roundabout was sealed off, only allowing one route. Dave reached this and got confused. He missed the exit and tried to take the next one, but it was sealed with barbed wire. He buried the car in this entanglement and I had to climb out of the window through a tangled mass and push him back on the correct route. What a farce. It got worse when it came to handing over the prisoner! Dave had tied each arm to the back doors, so when the guard opened the right door he could only pull him so far. When they tried the left door, the same happened. When they tried it at the same time from both doors, the prisoner thought he was on the rack. Finally Dave's quick release knots had to be cut and we eagerly left to escape further embarrassment. Dave got to the roundabout, missed the turning, took the next one, and buried us in the wire once more. I will relate more of Dave's driving exploits later when we were in Kenya.

On the first course that was run the interrogation centre was in a boys' camp on the coast in Mid-Wales. The timing couldn't have been worse. The boys were passing out, and proud parents had come from all parts of the country to see their little heroes. They had been assured that the army treats its soldiers well, and feeds and clothes them to the highest standards. One of the lads broke out of the interrogation centre which was located at the back of the camp. He was dressed only in a pair of drawers Dracula and sporting a week of encrusted filth, sprinted for his life straight across the parade ground, through the marching band, before disappearing amongst the huts. To make matters worse, he was pursued by angry guards who chased him shouting obscenities about what they were going to do with him when they caught him. Not very good for recruiting.

Drawers Dracula were jungle-issued cotton pants correctly called 'drawers cellular'. We also called them 'drawers peculiar', so this may help paint a picture of what the escapee looked like.

We had French Paras as the hunter force on this course, and we were always amused at the way the captain briefed his troops. We nicknamed him 'Powerful Pierre'. He would line his men up and strut up and down the ranks, gibbering away in his camouflaged kit and red beret. He would stop in front of a man with feet apart, toes turned in, with hands on hips, chest inflated. His voice would raise and he either patted the man on the shoulder or slapped his chest, depending on the answer given. His antics attracted an audience and we watched this ritual daily while finishing our breakfast brew. One day he was strutting his stuff, really playing to the crowd, when he stepped back and disappeared down an old sheep-dip. This was a metre-deep pit filled with stagnant water covered by green scum which camouflaged it nicely. As he submerged, a cloud of black fly alighted and their wings helped to dissipate the smell of putrefaction towards us. We fell off the gate we sat on and his men were creased with laughter. But as soon as he surfaced they struggled to conceal their emotion. Water was streaming from his many pockets for ages as he patrolled the ranks looking for any signs of mirth.

We had a good trip to Corsica where we worked with their equivalent troops, the Parachutists du Shock. They were deployed in Algeria at the time and were switched on. We had a party in the sergeants' mess which was a tough place as even the arms of the chairs had tattoos. One character really stood out as the party animal leading the dancing and singing. In the morning we were doing a water jump, and surprise, surprise, the pilot of the Nord Noratlas was the song and dance man. The French were very professional in everything they did. Two jumps before breakfast were possible because they flew their own aircraft and were not dependent on the RAF. All the chutes were packed in the camp, which had its own airfield. They led a tough life: there were no frills attached to them. The worst aspect of training was drinking the wine that they served up at mealtimes; it was like vinegar. Breakfast was just a brew and a slab of bread that was harder than the mattresses we slept on. They had meat only three times a week, and on Wednesdays they would slaughter a pig in the kitchen. Seeing a pig hoisted up, squealing for all its worth, was not a pretty sight but just part of normal life to them. The more agitated the pig became, the tenderer the meat. To encourage this they sharpened the knife in front of the pig. Horse meat was one of the meats served which didn't go down too well with some of the lads. I was used to this: we had it as kids and called it 'gallop'.

I did another demolition course while I was there which I thought was pretty basic. The highlight was when we stopped for lunch and washed the bread and cheese down with wine. One of the lads disappeared and it was as well that they checked the range before blowing some charges. They found the lad asleep cuddling a length of railway line that had a few pounds of plastic on.

They had excellent training facilities and it was all on their doorstep.

They organised their troops in much the same way as ourselves. Based on an airfield and flying their own aircraft was ideal for the free-fallers. The weather was good so they could jump all year round, either in the sea or onto the camp. Their amphibious training centre was based on the sea, and they could dive in clear water from a variety of boats that they used. Corsica was mountainous, so good climbing was available: they had the lot.

We were there at the same time as the Foreign Legion Parachute Regiment was on the island. They had mutinied and didn't want to pull out of Algeria. For punishment they were stripped of their camouflage uniforms, their Red Beret, and not allowed to sing their marching songs.

A very memorable event I did there was an escape-and-evasion exercise. We were strip-searched and given battledress, our own boots, and an empty wine bottle. The idea was to be dropped off on a mountain road and head north to the coast, a distance of fifty miles. Everyone in the exercise area was alerted to our presence and encouraged to report us to the authorities. The army, Air Force and police were all part of the hunter force. Local papers carried news of this, and local radio stations reminded everyone to be vigilant and look out for these Anglais.

I was partnered by big Jackie and our ploy was to hang back and let the cordons move north before we did. We were encouraged to hide escape kit on our bodies and we tore a map in half, secreting it the best way possible. Mine was discovered in the search: I had it under my privates. Jackie got through with his map by wrapping it up in masking tape and shoving it up his you know what.

Four days were allowed for this exercise, so when we were dropped off we went south for an hour and laid up for two days. Jackie recovered the map but wouldn't unwrap it: this was left to me. Imagine my disappointment to find that his half of the map was of the wrong area. Some good came out of this: it stopped me biting my nails. On the third day we stripped off and jogged through the mountains, covering the distance in twenty hours. We didn't see a soul till we reached the coast. The final RV was in a nudist camp, but this was closed down for the winter. We sat on a track feeling really smug and said no matter what happens now we can't go another yard. We had been running all day and this was our first break. We heard a jeep engine and both leapt up at the same time and sprinted for cover. Where this energy came from was a mystery.

A lot was learnt in Corsica and some of their ideas were adopted by the Regiment.

They were very practical and the best that I had seen.

I attended a cadre run by the Regiment and got made up to the dizzy heights of lance corporal. This meant an extra eleven shillings a week to squander. They say there is a field marshal's baton in every soldier's backpack: I wonder.

We were always busy on either courses or exercises, fitting them in between trips to the Far and Middle East. Some courses were better than others. Foreign Weapons was always a good course, and Water Duties where you learn all about sterilising water: not so popular. One of my favourites was the Donkey Wallopers course. This was a three-week course in Aldershot learning how to use donkeys, mules and horses for transport. We were issued First World War jodhpurs and puttees that were sixteen feet long. We had to get up twenty minutes early to put these on. They wrapped around the top of the boots till just below the knee. You could break a leg and not know it till you took the puttees off at night.

This course was run in Aldershot by the RASC who still had horses. We would get up at five each morning and clean out the stables and feed the horses. Then, after our own breakfast we would exercise and groom them. You quickly learn that horses take a lot of cleaning and a lot of exercise. There's nothing like the smell of stables to clear the head early morning, and the amount of tack that we had to clean was impressive.

The best part was the riding. This started in an indoor school where we were shown how to mount, steer and find the brakes. It was a continuous laugh. Someone was falling off every minute. When we got more proficient we graduated to outdoors and rode over the tank tracks. There were twelve of us on the course, a mixture of A and D Squadrons. Slosh, an old-timer, looked every inch the gentleman sitting astride his horse, ramrod straight, sporting a huge handlebar moustache. Clancy and Bill were the complete opposite, hanging onto anything they could to stay on.

After we groomed the horses and cleaned all the tack we would load them with stores and take them for a long walk. This was the aim of the course: to learn how to carry loads on animals. The army had got rid of all its mules and donkeys, keeping just this unit of horses. In the Middle East, the Regiment had used donkeys in a campaign but hired the wrong ones. There are jebel donkeys that are at home in the mountains, being small and nimble, and the plains donkey which is larger but only good in flat desert. The lads hired the cheapest (typical squaddies) and got the larger plains donkeys. The reason they are bigger is they eat more. Food has to be carried, which is part of their payload. The lads were carrying more than the animals and halfway up the jebel they slaughtered them.

Camels were also used at times, and before my time elephants were used in the Far East.

When we were out riding, anything that upset a horse used to set up a chain reaction and all the horses would react. We used to ride down Barossa Road where the 2nd and 3rd battalions of paras were stationed. We would look down on these peasants and give them the odd salute and royal wave. One day a dog took a dislike to the instructor's horse that sent it skittering, but he still had it under control. Our horses reared up, galloped, and did a bomb burst amongst the barrack blocks. Most of us opted to abandon horse when this happened, but a big snag was our rubber-soled boots. Being knobbly it wasn't easy to get them out of the stirrups, leaving you in danger of getting dragged behind the fleeing beast. You best chance then was for the stirrup leather to break, because as you kicked out to clear your foot, it spurred the horse to greater speeds. To restore our dignity we used alternate routes after this. It was probably a stray dog that attacked us, but we swore blind that it was a set-up.

Another time we were riding in an area that was located under the flight path of Farnborough Airfield. We were in a circle trotting and cantering, feeling very pleased with our progress. Without warning, a jet took off and stayed at treetop level for miles. The noise frightened us, let alone the animals. Everyone, including the two instructors, was thrown off and some of the horses never stopped running till they reached the stables three miles away.

We were shown how to mount correctly. Pulling your weight up without using the stirrups was difficult, but that was how we had to do it. One day we were all outside grooming and cleaning when a horse was led out and a rider mounted a set of stone steps before throwing his leg over his steed. We couldn't help but jeer him, calling him a big pansy. He shouted to his aide to round us up and started giving us the bollocking of our lives. He was the Provost Marshal of Aldershot and was not used to this behaviour. We couldn't stop laughing, which didn't help matters. No one was wearing a beret so he didn't have a clue as to who we were. He asked our instructor why we were dressed in so many different outfits, and he just shrugged his shoulders. He grabbed hold of Jock and asked him why he was wearing a parka, and demanded to know where he was from. Jock said, "It's cold and I'm from Scotland." He turned to Slosh for some common sense and asked him what he was laughing at. Slosh said, "You used the mounting steps." The Provost must have been hard of hearing and said, "What do you mean, you were amused with the cheque." Slosh was also mutton Geoff said, "There's nothing wrong with my neck." We melted away, leaving them to it.

Johnny was a torment and always messing with the horses. He would undo a buckle when you weren't looking or loosen the cinch that held the saddle firm. My horse had to fasten its teeth on something when I tightened the girth; normally it would bite the stable door or hitching rail. Johnny was bending over, cleaning the hooves of his horse, when I pulled on the girth to tighten it. My horse fastened onto Johnny's buttock and wouldn't let go till I stopped pulling. I held it there for a good minute before relaxing my hold. Johnny showed me his bruise: it was quite something. Not quite breaking the skin, but big, black and purple. Johnny was a great guy and died young. He loved the outdoors and I'm sure he's organising a big safari for us when we finally all meet up.

This was a great course: we all learnt so much, and it was fun. The RSM, who was our instructor, was one of the most knowledgeable men I've ever met on his specialist subject. He answered every question we asked. What he didn't know about horses you could fit in your saddlebags.

I went with Johnny to a dance in Worcester where he lived. I had a brand new suit on and Rob's chukka boots which I borrowed from him. Desmond the Wye diver was with us and we drove over in Johnny's van. At the dance I met Johnny's uncle who turned out to be a wild man. I was getting some funny looks and put it down to my sartorial elegance. Desmond the lover started chatting up someone's girlfriend and a fight started. Before I could move, Johnny's brother was amongst them, knocking over everyone in his path. Desmond went down to the first punch, but Johnny's performance made up for this loss. I carried on drinking at the bar and it was all over as quickly as it had started. Johnny and his uncle had cleared the dance hall between them. Everyone had given me a wide berth which got me wondering, and it wasn't till we were on the way home that Johnny said his uncle had told all the dance that I was the heavyweight champion of the army.

It was some scrap and they still talk about it to this day. On the way home I finished up driving, although I can't remember when we changed over. Coming down Fromes Hill, I started weaving from side to side. On the side of the hill were piles of grit which they spread when it froze. I ran up one of these piles and started the car rolling. I think we managed four complete revolutions before coming to a halt. I remember Johnny disappearing past me on the second roll. The van had a canvas roof and Johnny was ejected through this. Desmond was in the back cuddling two jerrycans of petrol. When the car came to rest against a tree, the door was burst open and my foot was caught under the door. It was well and truly trapped, I couldn't budge it. Johnny finally finds us after his brief expedition in space, and is holding up a lighter to check on our condition. I could smell the petrol, and before Johnny could speak, I was out of the car standing behind him. Rob's chukka boot was just about cut in half still trapped by the door. Desmond was groaning about his back, and we got rid of the jerrycans and pulled him out of the wreckage. I will never know how I got my foot free: we had to lift the van before I could recover Rob's boot. Johnny had landed on a pile of gravel and this was rammed up his nostrils. I can still picture him delicately picking his nose.

Another good course was testing prison defences. The Home Office spent a lot of money on new security fences and we were invited to try and defeat them.

Six of us went to a prison just outside London where we could look at a variety of new fences and obstacles all designed to keep the prisoners secure. I thought it would just be my luck to be spotted by a neighbour from Downham and spread the news that I was really in the nick, not the army.

We were issued prison clothing and could use anything that the prisoners had access to. Most of the obstacles had sensors and alarms on, so speed was essential. Once you triggered an alarm, the guards would be alerted, so about five minutes was all you had to scale, tunnel or go through the obstacle.

We started off on fences. These were made of variable meshes too small to get a finger grip in. We improvised hooks from nails and wire to scale these. They were trialling a new type of barbed wire called razor wire. Like the name implies, it was razor-sharp. Instead of the conventional barbed wire, which you could lay on with padded clothing with no discomfort, this stuff cut you to ribbons and held you firmly. All the obstacles had this on top. Trying to climb through this was costly. You left most of your clothes behind and a fair amount of skin as well. On several attempts we had to be cut out, making the boffins very happy. Their laughter used to get right up our backs and their smart comments were more hurtful than the razor wire barbs.

We came up with a simple solution to defeat this obstacle in the time allowed.

By cutting two-inch strips off our trouser legs and joining them together like you would with rubber bands, we made a strong climbing rope. Tying this to a bundle of clothing and throwing it up to snag the wire gave us an anchor point. By pulling down on this, it dislodged the wire, forming it into a staircase which you could climb with ease.

There was an inclined wall covered in grease which made climbing impossible. We defeated this with our grapnel and improvised rope. The grease got everywhere but gripping the rope with the teeth you could hang on and rest. Jimmy got to the top but left his bottom set halfway up. They also smeared walls with glue and tar which made climbing very sticky. Jim got stuck at the top of one of these with his teeth, but it just goes to show:

GLUE SNARES JIM

CHAPTER TEN

BACK TO THE JUNGLE

Things were warming up in Borneo, making each tour more demanding than the last. It was decided to raise an indigenous force that would help protect the borders and give early warning of hostile activities. So the Border Scouts were raised, and I had the privilege of training the first bunch. Our first recruits were Ibans, the warrior tribe of Borneo, the original headhunters. We had a base west of Kuching, the capital of Sarawak, on an isolated hill. A logging track went part of the way, then an old animal track had to be used that went all the way to our camp. Each day the logging track got nearer to our camp. It was good that we could walk out if we had to and not have to rely solely on helicopters.

Our scouts had all the jungle skills required but we had to teach them tactics, leadership and discipline. They were all hunters and excellent shots, but lacked the safety aspects of firearms. They needed organising into groups where they all knew their specific roles and could be self-supporting. We tried them in boots but they became clumsier than us wearing these, so they reverted to bare feet. We tried to be as much like them as possible, but found walking barefoot very difficult. It was alright when walking very slowly with no pack, but as soon as we reached rocky ground our feet suffered. It had taken them centuries of evolution to develop their hard, flat feet; we couldn't achieve this in a few months.

Our camp was built on top of a jungle-covered hill and the bashas were on stilts. They were arranged in a circle with the doorway facing inwards about two feet high, and the basha would go out over the edge of the hill supported on legs about ten feet high. Every morning we had a stand-to at first light and the scouts would drop through a hatch in the floor and go to their trenches. There was one hatch in the middle, and one at the far end. This one was a good drop of at least eight feet, and the agile scouts didn't find it difficult. One morning me and Jimmy were at stand-to in our trench and watched the OC prowling around checking that everyone was in position. He went in the scouts' basha and at the farthest end he saw someone still in bed. He sneaked up on the prone body and was about to make his presence known when he disappeared through the open hatch. He didn't stop rolling for ages. The underside of the basha had been cleared of all foliage but was bristling with the little sharp ends left behind; and when he climbed back up the hill he looked distinctly the worse for wear. He didn't think anyone had seen him and over breakfast we kept quiet as long as we could, but he picked up our jovial mood. We asked him if he had been on any good trips lately. He had to laugh and said, "He who laughs last laughs longest." In the coming months we reminded him of this many times. He never found the culprit: the scouts all insisted it must have been the way the bedding was arranged.

Our boss was a good bloke and his claim to fame was he played the bagpipes in the British Embassy while it was under attack in Jakarta. We told him he was the reason they attacked the Embassy in the first place. He would get his chanter out regularly and practise the scales and other unrecognisable things. The scouts cut thin bamboo stems and made flutes from them which they played their traditional songs on. As soon as the boss piped up they would accompany him, driving him to distraction. He had the temerity to criticise them, like Dawn French calling Twiggy fat.

He had a lot of publicity over the Embassy affair and received a sack of fan mail. We divided the letters up between us and started corresponding to our new fans. We only wrote to the women and they sent us magazines, books and chewing gum. We all made a lot of promises that we had no intention of keeping.

We had a petrol-engined generator that we used to recharge our batteries. It kept cutting out, so I decide to strip it down. I didn't have many tools and when I was removing the valves I got my thumb stuck. I depressed the valve spring using my thumbs, and as I removed the collets, only one came out and the spring turned sideways, trapping my thumb in the cylinder head. Everyone had a go at releasing me, but to no avail. The only solution was to remove the cylinder head and walk out to where the loggers had a camp with a workshop. It felt strange walking through the jungle with a cylinder head in one hand and a rifle in the other. I got released by the loggers and had a nasty cut around the front knuckle of my left thumb. I wrapped this up in a big dolly to keep it clean.

Several days after this incident I decided to take vengeance out on the rats that raided our food store. We kept a lot of rice in sacks and the rats would come in of a night and feed at our expense. By shining a torch you could catch the rats eating and curb their appetite with a parang. Three of us set about them with a will and slashed to the left, right and centre. It was only when we became knackered that we stopped swinging and heard the sound of running grain. We had caused more damage than a million rats could have. All the sacks were slashed and the rice poured out all over the floor.

I thought a safer way of dealing with our unwanted visitors was to trap them. I laid out several powerful spring traps baited with cheese. I was trying to make them as sensitive as possible and as I set the bait bar I allowed the trap to lift up and trap my thumb. I still had a large dressing on my left thumb and now needed another on my right thumb. Nothing hurts worse than pain; both my thumbs throbbed for weeks. I was like the judge with no fingers, "Justice Thumbs".

Although we were training the scouts, we learnt so much from them. They were so aware of their surroundings and understood nature. They struggled with the military training, especially tactics. They were issued with Sten guns which were notorious with our own troops as being dangerous to handle. These were obsolete and had been out of service for years. The safety catch could be overcome if the weapon was dropped or knocked. We always kept one up the spout on our weapons that meant you just had to slip off the safety and pull the trigger to fire. You had no time in a contact to cock the weapon. The Sten was a sub-machine gun firing from an open bolt with a fixed firing pin, and any hard knock could activate it. So, to train the scouts to safely handle this was especially challenging. After four months of training we never had (as far as we know) any accidental discharges. We taught them ambushing, contact drills, patrolling and how to secure an area. They slowly came round to our way of thinking and we compromised on several issues like stand-to, sentry duty and the like. They were so used to being alert and couldn't see any need for the extra effort. They were always listening for anything different and could read tracks like a newspaper. They had a natural instinct that warned them of danger; they knew when they were threatened or in danger. We had to adjust to them as well, as they were excellent jungle warriors.

Our camp was secure and no visitors were allowed, but we did visit local kampongs. We used to buy fresh eggs, chickens and vegetables from them. The girls from an early age used to have their ears pierced and brass rings inserted. As they grew, more rings were added, stretching their earlobes, so by the time they were in their early teens their earlobes could be nine inches long. This practice was slowly dying out and some of the girls wanted them cut off. The ear bleeds a lot and care must be taken to avoid too much blood loss. I worked out a way of doing this and became a cosmetic surgeon. By injecting the ear with local anaesthetic containing a high percentage of adrenalin, it deadened the pain and helped to stop the bleeding. Only one side of the lobe was cut and clamped, before suturing the ear first, then the lobe. The patient was told to take it easy and come back in five days and have the dangly bit removed in the same manner.

It was a long process and we were always in demand. We used the schoolhouse for our surgery, and Frank used to come with me and watch me perform. He was our admin guy and did the cooking. One day I was out with the scouts and Frank went to collect the food. A young girl approached him wanting her ears operating on. Frankie said certainly, took her in the schoolhouse, sat her down, and produced a pair of scissors. Without any cleaning or explanation he tried to cut through her lobe. She squealed in agony and blood spurted everywhere. She ran away before he had time to dress it. I don't know what he was thinking of or what inspired him to do it. Her ear got infected and she had to go to Kuching for treatment. She never returned to her village, remaining in town where she went on the game and finished up doing the Dhobi for the Gurkhas.

The Sten guns were to be replaced by Armalites, a good, modern weapon. It was a real credit to the scouts that no accidents happened with the Sten. It was my job to go into town and pick up the new rifles. I had been working solid for three months and this was my first break: watch out, Kuching.

I went in with the boss dressed in OG with a border scout flash on my left shoulder and three months' worth of growth on my face. We had dinner together in the Aurora hotel, and split up around ten o'clock. His last words to me were, "Behave yourself, don't get into any trouble, and I'll see you in the morning." I went to the market for a few beers, sitting at a table minding my own business, when two military policemen turned up and said I was breaking the curfew. All servicemen had to be back in barracks by midnight. I told them I was a border scout and this didn't apply to me. I was talking in a mixture of Malay Pidgin English and drunken gibberish. They warned me that if I was still there when they returned in ten minutes, they would arrest me. Instead of being sensible for a change, I stayed in the market trying to prove a point: after all, this was my first break for ages. They returned on time carrying out their threat of arrest. I told them that if they dropped me off at my hotel I would forget this ugly incident. They were unsure of my identity as it was rare for anyone wearing a beard with Border Scout flashes talking Malay. I told them my mother was an Iban princess and my father was a Roman Catholic missionary: that's why I was so tall and European-looking. They bought this and offered me a lift, but I couldn't think of the name of my hotel. By now we had attracted quite an audience and the Chinese traders started putting in their two-penneth. The MPs were getting pushed around and their patience finally ran out and they took me to an army camp and left me in the guardroom. While I was in the Land Rover I hid cigarettes and matches all over my body, preparing myself for the inevitable. I retold my story to the guard commander, demanding to see the orderly officer. He eventually turned up still lacing his jungle boots. I started to rift him, telling him he was a disgrace to the British Army, sleeping while on duty and improperly dressed. He didn't take too kindly to this, his peace being shattered, and now having a raving lunatic shouting at him. He actually phoned a couple of hotels but got no joy, so he said I was there for the night. I disagreed with that decision and said I was going. There were three others beside the Rupert, and they stood up and blocked the doorway. I charged through them, skittling them over, and legged it to the wire. The camp was fenced in by a seven-foot fence with barbed wire on the top. I jumped on a sandbagged gun emplacement and leapt over this fence and kept on going. When I stopped there was no sign of pursuit, so I lit a fag and had a smoke. I carried on through the trees till I hit a road, and decided to thumb a lift. Inside a minute, a Land Rover appeared and stopped when I flagged it down. I gratefully went up to the door and said, "Cheers, mate," before realising it was the same Rover with the two MPs in who had arrested me. Some you win, some you lose, so in the back I go, only this time handcuffed. They gave me a provisional search and took my cigs and matches. In the back of the vehicle I pulled a ciggy out of my sock and a match from behind my ear and lit it. They couldn't believe it and I got a few drags in before it was confiscated. I drew another from my watchband and lit this up, getting the same response. I did this a couple more times and it was like a Tommy Cooper sketch. They tried to keep a straight face but struggled, and in the end let me finish one. I had Swan Vestas matches in my hair, beard and socks. If I combed my hair with enthusiasm I would incinerate like a Buddhist monk.

I was taken to the Marines' jail located on the airfield. Here I made another break for it, but only got a few yards before I was tackled. For my troubles they put leg shackles on me and gave me another search. I still managed to produce a couple more cigs after this, which didn't go down too well with the booties. There's nothing more annoying than a smart alec who, after a search, produces a cigarette and lights it. Well, there is. It's the smart alec who does it again after a further search. I was put in a cell with about ten others and all I wanted now was a sleep. Just before I dozed off I noticed a lot of boxes stacked high in the cell next door. I went to sleep wondering what was in the boxes.

At first light the cell was emptied of everyone but me. They still didn't know who I was and were taking no chances. I was thinking up different excuses and thought about playing the old malaria ply, making out I had a high fever that left me with amnesia. If the matches I still had in my hair and beard ignited I wouldn't have to fake the temperature. As I lay there perfecting my alibi, a man entered the cell next door and started climbing up the boxes. It was my boss. I said, "Good morning," and he answered before my voice registered with him. His next ten minutes of conversation are unprintable.

I was released and helped load the boxes, keeping a low profile. I still hadn't revealed my identity and returned to the safety of the jungle.

Things were very tense for a few days, but I was kept busy instructing on the new weapon. I was interrogated by the boss and told him I was framed. He listened to my story and said the colonel was coming in a few weeks and he would deal with it. The boss had to go back to town for a briefing so I could relax, but the future didn't look bright.

The training went well and the scouts loved the Armalite; it was an accurate weapon and easy to handle. The sights were easily adjustable, making zeroing easy. The normal practice for this is to fire five rounds from fifty yards and check the target and adjust as necessary. I was horrified one day to see them zeroing. They had a man at the side of the target pointing out each shot as it was fired. They couldn't see any harm in this. With some of the shots I've seen in the army I wouldn't stand in the same county.

When the boss came back his attitude to me changed. He told me of a group of soldiers who came up to him in the marketplace and bought him a drink. They retold my exploits and invited all of us to their mess anytime we wanted. They reckoned it was the best night they'd ever had. Things get exaggerated like the fence was twenty foot high, the guard was twelve strong, and I escaped ten times, but now I was a celebrity. Poor little Lofty locked up in the slammer: they didn't realise what psychological stress this caused or what mental damage I suffered.

When the colonel visited us I was dreading the worst. He had a touch of malaria and I hovered over him, giving him pills and copious amounts of tea. At the end of the day he told me to accompany him up to the LZ where a chopper was coming to pick him up. He didn't say anything about me bringing my kit so I kept my fingers crossed. He started telling me what a good job we were doing and how sensitive it was. The scouts were ready for their first operation and they had personally asked for me to be with them. He didn't mention a word of my Houdini exploits until the chopper landed. His departing words were, "Give my regards to your Iban mother." What a relief: I felt like going into town and celebrating.

When we were on operations we practised 'Hard Routine'. This meant no cooking, no dry kit, fully dressed all the time, including boots, no use of soap, toothpaste or anything smelly. It entailed getting up just before first light and standing to. All kit was packed and we moved when the light was good enough. March for an hour then stop, check for any follow-up and send the first signal of the day. We never used tracks and stopped every hour for ten minutes and sat and listened. At midday we stopped for an hour and sent the second signal of the day. At four o'clock we would check our back trail and sit on our kit, again listening. The final signal would be sent and we would move off and basha up for the night. This would be on the ground under a poncho, which was not put up till it was dark. It was hard work but we got used to it. On selection what really impressed me was Jick who was always the first up. I respected him so much for this and copied him. I had to be the first up and the last to sleep. To gain respect you must earn it and the best bit of advice I can give anyone is to be a good timekeeper and always get to your appointment at least five minutes early. We had so many top-class guys but they let themselves down with being late or couldn't get up in the morning.

Although we all came from different backgrounds, this style of life was completely alien to anything we had ever experienced before, but all the lads accepted this routine as a way of life. This was something that was special: it put the Special in SAS. No other units in the forces could do this. The Ibans found this routine difficult; they couldn't see the point of not smoking, cooking or cutting shelters. They had lived there all of their lives and habits die hard. Their senses were more developed than ours, and it was difficult to get them to realise that to leave no sign or indication of their presence they had to follow certain rules. In many ways they regarded our teachings as a game and, unless in danger, there was no need to be so careful. We found it best to give them the problem and let them sort it out their way. We gave advice, but they did their own thing. We always felt safe with these people and they never let us down.

Later on, when we went with them on ops, we were in for a few surprises.

On one occasion we were heading for an ambush site when the lead scout stopped and signalled us to get down. He drew his parang and I thought he was going for a silent kill. He was, but it wasn't a man it was a pig that was curled up asleep. He couldn't resist the temptation of fresh meat. It proved how silent our approach had been and they took this as a good omen. No way were they going to waste this pig, and it was more beneficial to let them cook it. So that night deep in enemy territory we had a pig roast.

Another time we were less than a thousand yards from an Indonesian camp, and stayed in a padi shack where the local villagers stored their rice. The scouts were interrelated to the tribes across the border and went in the village and mingled. If they felt at home, so did we. Under the floor of the shack a cobra's nest was discovered. The snake was big and was sitting on ten eggs. That night we had another feast. It was like magic: they could produce food from anywhere. Here we were skulking around not cooking, living on meat blocks, and these lads were dining in style. Cobra steaks garnished with eggs on a bed of steamed rice.

As soon as we started operating, rumours soon spread of our achievements. We used helicopters for insertion and extraction, and word soon got around. After one op we returned to the border, and while waiting for the helis the lads went hunting. They shot six pigs and butchered them just before the first aircraft arrived. The LZ was like a slaughterhouse, causing the pilot to hover longer than normal; he nearly fell out his cab when he saw the bloody meat hanging up.

During training the scouts were doing some medical training and were learning the treatment for burns. I got a spare set of OG and cut them about and set fire to them. Just as the instructor asked the scouts what would they do if someone was on fire, I rushed in the room screaming and smoking. They just stood there and laughed. By now, I was really getting burnt: the cotton OG smoulders for ages. After much shouting by the instructor, they picked me up and rushed me down to the river and threw me in. So much for bush medicine. I climbed out of the river just as a heli appeared. I went to the DZ streaming water and still steaming and smoking, and the crewman in the door nearly fell out when he saw me. I don't know what stories he told in the mess that night but that's how rumours get started.

It's quite normal that people don't like snakes, especially in the wild, but snakes get bad press and their reputations are greatly embellished. In all my time serving in jungles from Malaya, Borneo, Belize and the Amazon to Africa, I have only been involved with three cases of snake bite. Normally a snake, when hunting, is very alert and gets out of your way long before you get close. But when a snake has just fed it gets sluggish just like us after a Sunday dinner, and instead of retiring to somewhere safe, falls asleep. This is when we are most likely to come into contact. Venomous snakes use their venom to kill their prey, so if it has just killed, the amount of poison left is limited. This is very reassuring when briefing people about the danger of snakes. The army manual on snake bites states that the first thing you do if a soldier is bitten is to catch the snake for identification purposes. In fact, the first thing you do is to catch the victim and calm them down. People when bitten want to climb trees, jump in rivers and run away. The aim is to slow down the absorption of the venom as much as possible, achieved by laying the patient down, and keeping the bite low and cool. The use of a placebo is beneficial. The worst thing to happen is someone telling the victim that the snake is deadly. The locals grade their snakes' toxicity by comparing them to how long it takes to smoke a cigarette. If they gesture one fag, you're in big trouble.

We had a case where a lad was bitten on the leg by a snake of unknown origin. The snake was bashed on the head, and the patient dosed with a cocktail of drugs. If the patient plays up it's best to do this the other way around: bash him on the head and sedate the snake. We never carried the serum because, unless the species was correctly identified, giving the wrong serum could kill, acting like another bite. The drugs given were an antibiotic, antihistamine and cortisone. This was given as the placebo, but had positive effects as well.

A scout helicopter came in to evacuate the victim who was strapped into a stretcher. The snake was placed on his chest under his jacket for identification purposes back at the hospital. The pilot was flying tactically, following stream beds and keeping low. The medic in the back, being a good lad, decided to check on the patient's vital signs and unzipped his jacket to monitor his heart. Snakes are very susceptible to vibrations – that's how they hunt – and the helicopter is just a mass of vibrating rivets and aluminium flying in formation. This snake was only concussed and came alive at the disturbance. He was already in a bad mood, being hit on the head, and hated flying. The pilot hated snakes and when this thrashing reptile whipped around his feet he took them off the pedals and crashed the chopper, bouncing it down a boulder-strewn riverbed.

The patient was fine, being lashed down in a stretcher, unlike the pilot and medic who suffered abrasions and multiple fractures. The patient looked after the two casualties till another chopper came in. The moral of this story is you never know when you are well off, and if you are going to collect a snake, make sure it's dead.

Your body is under constant attack, and leeches become part of everyday life. We soaked our hose tops in mosquito repellent and this kept most off, but the odd one or two always got through. Hornets were very unpleasant and they helped to remind us of keeping the eyes moving and searching the bush. One night we bash'd up and were visited by night hornets. They are exactly the same as day hornets but with a more painful sting which we were about to find out. We used to read by candlelight and this kept the insects away. They would fly into the flame and drop to the ground. If you used a torch, everything with wings would be attracted and land on your chest. On the first night, Fred was stung and immediately blew out his candle. He said it was the worst pain he had ever experienced. Me and Jick laughed at him, calling him a big girl's blouse. The next night he refused to read and lay there in darkness. A hornet landed on Jick's book and he batted it away; unfortunately, it landed on Fred and stung him. Fred was up ranting and raging and moved his basha, saying, "You wait till you get stung and you'll see what it's like." We told him, "Get to bed, you big tart. Let the men read." The next night I was stung on the wrist. The only way I can describe this pain is by saying it was like a white-hot rivet being hammered through my skin. The pain lasted for days and I still have the scar to remind me. Needless to say, we upped sticks and moved our campsite.

On another occasion I was bitten by a scorpion as I stepped over a log. It stung me on the calf and was quite painful. I felt lousy for twenty-four hours, having a mild fever, but completely recovered. Compared to the night hornet it was nothing, but the after-effects were more severe.

Frankie, the guy who cut the girl's ear, wanted to get a set of false teeth. A Chinaman in Kuching was cheap and there was no waiting; unlike Blighty, where your gums would decompose before you got your new set of gnashers. He watched me pulling the locals' teeth and asked if I would pull his. The locals' teeth, because of their diet, came out easily compared to a European's. Most had gum disease which made the teeth loose, and their diet of rice and fish did nothing to strengthen them. Frankie had thirteen teeth left and I started extracting them, pulling two a day. Pulling is the wrong action for removing teeth: it is a side-to-side movement, gradually loosening the tooth. All was well till I got to the last two. I gave him extra lignocaine but he still complained of pain every time I started performing. I told him he had to be brave and stand a little bit of discomfort. I got one out and had one to go. He was a great talker, Frankie, and even when I had the forceps in his mouth he would still be chimpfing. I finished up with my arm around his neck with his head firmly locked under my armpit. I started pulling and lifted him out of the chair, and we finished up waltzing around the room. He tried to keep up with me to ease the pain, and I was moving away from him, trying to develop some leverage. Something had to give, and after dragging him around the room several times, there was a loud crack. I looked at the forceps and there was his tooth but on the roots was an inch and a half of white cartilage from his jawbone. I tried to hide this from him, ignoring his comments which were now unintelligible, then realised I had dislocated his jaw. I felt a bit sorry for him, but considered this justice after what he had done to the girl's ear. He had to go to Kuching for treatment and the dentist showed him no compassion; in fact, he was a bit harsh on him. A week earlier he had been drinking in the marketplace with his assistant and upset one of the squadron lads who was playing a guitar. He was warned several times to keep quiet while the lad was playing but kept on interrupting. He got a black eye for his trouble and his assistant a fat lip. Word soon got around to keep away from the dentist as he had taken a jihad out on the Regiment. Frankie's big mistake was to tell the quack he was Regiment. The lads would rather fly up to Labuan, a journey of two hours, than face the guy in Kuching. Words of wisdom. Never upset the dentist, keep in with the cook and pay bloke, and always blame your mate when things go wrong.

We had many good nights in the market, often seeing the sun come up. The Kiwis and Aussie used to join us and we would sing all night. The market was a mass of stalls selling beer and food. We used to haggle over the price of the beer and would drink at the stall that was cheapest. This might only be two cents, which was less than a farthing, but it's a squaddie thing: you had to haggle. You could get king prawns that were massive, they were more like crayfish. Three or four of these were all you could manage.

'He who laughs last' is certainly true on what happened to me at the hands of a proper dentist. While I was with the Kelabits a dentist came in to treat the scouts and families. I watched with interest and also weighed up how good he was. I had a wisdom tooth playing up and was about to go on a fourteen-day op. Just as Frankie watched me perform, I was now watching this dentist. I finally plucked up the courage to let him at it, and realised straight away that I had made a big mistake. The tooth crumbled and he couldn't get all of it out. The next day, I was deployed with a sack full of painkillers and an appointment with the dentist in sixteen days' time. You can imagine how I felt for the next fortnight. I couldn't eat, couldn't sleep, and wasn't the best of company. The op was uneventful and I missed my chance of a Victoria Cross. The way I felt, dying was preferable to living, and if there was any action I would have kept on going till I reached Jakarta.

When I got to Brunei for my dental appointment the cook made me a jelly: it was the only thing I could eat. This was made in a baking tray 18x12x3. I left half of it till after the treatment. The dentist had to cut out the root and took another tooth out at the same time. What a relief when it was all over: justice had been done.

Looking back, the most dangerous times were when we were on R and R (rest and recuperation). This was up to a week's break between operations. We would try and spend all the money we had saved up when in the jungle; no one wanted to go back in knowing they were in credit. We would climb up the outside of the hotel where we stayed. This was a three-storey affair with limited handholds. Sometimes we climbed into the wrong room, and one night I disturbed a matelot and his lady. He wasn't very pleased and tried to knock me off the parapet three storeys up with a broom. Another regimental ploy was jumping out of taxis while they were moving. It's very hard to judge the speed of a cab when judgement is impaired by ten pints of Anchor beer.

The Kiwis were magnificent, but the Aussies hard to bear. We nearly always finished up fighting. We trained both and the Kiwis listened, whereas the Aussies tended to do their own thing. The navy were always very entertaining when they came ashore. They were very similar to us in their outlook on life, and crammed as much into their run ashore as possible.

We had a remarkable pay bloke who we nicknamed 'The Bat'. We never saw him during the day; he only appeared at night. We could be drinking in the market at anytime and ask him for twenty bucks. He would pay you and always remembered who had what and when. He also had all the duty-free under his bed and you could help yourself. With all the drunken transactions taking place night and day, there were very few discrepancies: it was a unique system.

It was good to get back in the jungle; I felt safe there. People are the most dangerous species on earth and the least predictable. I never felt frightened in the sticks and had complete faith in the locals. Probably the most dangerous and nerve-racking activity was lifting an explosive ambush. These were areas of track laced with explosive devices designed to explode when disturbed. Laying them was difficult enough and a map was made showing the location and type of each device. We used these ambushes to deny tracks to the enemy, and they did exactly the same on their side of the border.

Lifting an ambush that you had laid was bad enough, but lifting someone else's was extreme. The initiation device had to be in the middle of all the devices, so that it was effective from both ways; so, regardless of approach, you were always in the midst of lethal devices. Animals or diverse weather could trigger these, so no one fancied this task. The best bet was to find the ring main and attach a charge to detonate the whole ambush, but this was easier said than done. Reading someone else's sketch map is misleading. What is six inches to some people is twelve to others: ask any woman. By the time the recce report has been folded several times and endured the rigours of being carried in a pocket through the jungle, it is hardly in pristine condition. Being used to swat the occasional fly and cover a mess tin of food does nothing to bolster the confidence of the reader. When I think about it, I can't remember an officer ever doing this.

Another scare I got was when I practised bullfighting. I was reading a book about the only English bullfighter to make it in Spain; he was called El Inglés. I thought El Lofty sounded good, and how hard could it be to be a bullfighter? We were in a village that had seladangs grazing on the padang: these were water buffalo, a large animal with big horns. I chose a calf to make my debut with, and tempted it with my poncho, shouting, "Olé!" and stamping my heels vigorously. Between me and the herd was a barrier of barbed wire coils, two at the bottom with one on top. Out of the corner of my eye I detected movement. The mother of the calf came through the wire as if it didn't exist and was in front of me snorting and stamping, festooned in tangled wire. My 'Olé' turned rapidly into 'Oh dear', and I was away as fast as my non-matador legs would carry me. Anything that could move that fast was dangerous. The next book I was going to read was on flower arranging.

I was now a corporal and was given my first patrol. Because of the shortage of men, we only made up a three-man patrol. We were used to plug a gap where a revenge incursion was threatening. I stated previously how important it is for everyone to get on, and with only three of us this was especially important. We were waiting for a heli and I was passing the time grappling with some Malay vocabulary, while Stan and Bob were grappling with each other. I couldn't believe it: they were rolling in the dust knocking bits off each other. As I pulled them apart, I thought, 'This is a great start to a long patrol', and wanted to know what started it. Apparently it was all over a rifle-cleaning kit. I sat in the middle of them keeping them apart, and I didn't want to take sides or add fuel to the flames. It was a long journey and I wasn't looking forward to the coming weeks with these two.

We were based in a village called Saliliran, not far from the border.

Across the border, about eighteen kilometres away, was a town called Labis. This had been attacked by the Gurkhas with devastating results. There was a chance that the Indonesians would launch an attack in retaliation. The headman's name was Nikinan who led the Gurkhas on this raid. He was a good man and we got on famously. There were three valleys which were all possible crossing places, and we had to check these out as soon as possible for any signs of enemy activity. So I decided to send two groups of scouts, one group taking the valley to the left, and the other group the valley to the right, with my patrol checking the main route in the middle with Nikinan. The scouts didn't have ponchos, so I lent them two of ours. This meant sleeping on the deck under one poncho. The first night, Bob was on the outside when it started raining. He complained that he was getting wet. So I changed places with him. Minutes later he complained he was lying on a root, so I got him to change with Stan. By this time my patience was running out and when he complained that the ants were biting him, I blew my stack. Bob was very lucky not to succumb to a lethal jungle ailment. Stan was all for it, and Nikinan wasn't bothered one way or the other, but I kept my cool. We did find lots of tracks, but couldn't discern who had made them, so to be on the safe side, a platoon of Gurkhas was posted in and defended Saliliran.

We were installing a cache in the area and prepared a small hole in the trees to receive the stores. It was my twenty-fifth birthday and the Gurkhas made a special curry for the occasion that we were having that evening. I was at the site waiting for the chopper and could hear him, but he was way off to the east. All I could do was go to the village and wait for the chopper and direct him from there. I told the lads I would be back as soon as possible and left them digging. We used to put caches in containing food, batteries, medical kit and ammunition, so in the event of the country getting overrun we could still operate without resupply. We tried to hide the locations of these from the locals, otherwise they would use it like Tesco's. The chopper landed in the village and I replaced the crewman who wanted a look around the village. I flew to our cache site, directing the pilot, and hovered over the small hole in the trees. Stan and Bob were below, ready to receive the stores. There were two loads, each weighing three hundred pounds rigged with a tape that ran through a set of rollers that allowed me to lower them to about one-fifty feet from the ground. The first load went as planned, but instead of cutting off the used tape, I tried to wind it back through the rollers. This caused a big knot and jammed the rollers. So I lashed the free end of the tape to the load and wrapped it around my shoulders and let in down using the old mountaineers' method of rappelling. As the load swung free of the aircraft it picked up speed, so that I was finding it very difficult to control its descent. It went faster and faster, building up a lot of friction on my shoulder and bare hands. I hung on as best as I could, but smoking flesh got the better of me and I let go. I had jammed myself in the doorway and braced myself with a leg either side of the threshold. I was wearing my belt kit, and as the tape was snaking out with the falling load, it took a turn around my water bottle and dragged me to the door. I was half out of the door looking at Stan looking up at me. I thought I would be with him sooner than expected. The load landed just as I was reaching a point of no return.

I was dropped off at the village and avoided shaking hands with the crewman who rejoined his crew. My hands were throbbing and my shoulder was burning. I sat with the Gurkha captain sharing a brew, when he noticed my hands. I ran through what happened and he summoned his medic. I was sitting with hands extended, palms upwards, trying to decipher what the captain was saying to the medic, and failed to notice the liquid he poured on my hands. I went skywards, leaping higher than the chopper that had just left. He had poured neat iodine into my raw palms and the pain was indescribable. I was running on the spot for minutes before they settled down sufficiently to let me stop, and then he spotted the burns on my shoulder. I was still wringing my hands, seeking relief, when the medic sneaked up behind me and soaked the friction burn on my shoulder with a drop of the same. Oh what a happy birthday. That night a fair amount of G10 rum was consumed: it was the only way I was going to get any sleep.

My hands took a long time to heal but at least I had the satisfaction that no infection took place. I wouldn't recommend the treatment to anyone: it could kill a human.

As I got to know Nikinan better he took me more in his confidence. In his longhouse he kept fruit bats, and on special occasions would serve them up for dinner. One day he invited me to go with him to his padi shack, a small shed in the middle of a paddy field. He was very enthusiastic and I wondered what treat he had in store for me. As we got nearer the smell of putrefaction attacked my nostrils. He opened the door and motioned me to follow. In the shack a swarm of disturbed bluebottles filled all the available space and I retreated, choosing to wait outside. Nikinan was dressed in a loincloth and T-shirt when he went in, and after a few minutes when the door opened I got the shock of my life. Emerging from the gloom was a TNKU soldier dressed in camouflaged clothing carrying a Garand rifle in one hand and a soggy head in the other. It took me a few moments before I realised it was Nikinan dressed in an Indonesian's uniform taken from a soldier whom he had killed weeks earlier. The head was his pride and joy, and he brandished it under my nose several times.

What an op this was: smoking palms, soggy heads and eating bats. What a life!

The Australians had a bad experience with an elephant. They were patrolling when they were confronted by a gadger who was blocking the track. They made the fatal mistake of firing at it. High-velocity rounds go straight through flesh, and unless they hit a vital organ or a bone, have little stopping power. The shots just annoyed the jumbo who charged the four-man patrol. Unfortunately, it was the signaller who was caught and died from the injuries he received. He was trampled and it was the radio he was carrying being wrecked that further complicated the situation.

It's always best to back away if confronted by a wild animal and only fire as a last resort. We use the buddy system and wherever possible use your mate. So if I get attacked by a dog, I tell my mate to run for it and I stand still: guess who gets bitten?

I had a unique experience while flying into Bario. I was in a single Pioneer, a small aircraft where I sat behind the pilot. One minute we were flying slow and level, getting ready to land, when we suddenly dived to the right and skimmed the trees, flying down a riverbed. The pilot had spotted a Mitchell bomber and two Mustangs flying low over the airstrip and had taken evasive action. My bowels had taken evasive action as well, and fear is definitely the best laxative known to man. These aircraft used to buzz the strip as a show of force, and would immediately head back to the border.

Another achievement that I will never forget was meeting the Punan. These were the last nomadic people of Borneo. They still lived only on what the jungle provided and kept themselves very much to themselves. Because they lived in the thickest bush, their skin was light-coloured, more white than brown, and they were extremely shy. The only reason they made themselves known to us was we were with some scouts whom they recognised. Sometimes they would approach a kampong if they had something to trade. They would build temporary shelters and move on again when the game or fish ran out. If they didn't want to be found, you would never see them. They recognised no borders and wandered wherever they could find food, always staying far from civilisation.

Our HQ was based on Labuan, an island not far from Brunei. I was on R and R and got drinking with a couple of Aussies. They wanted to go diving the next morning and borrow the assault boat. This was a twin-engined aluminium assault boat that we used for recreation. They wanted me to run them through operating the boat, which I promised faithfully to do. I carried on the movement, and before I knew it they were back in the bar ready to launch. I was still in the same place as they had left me hours earlier. They staggered under the weight of their scuba kit, while I staggered under the weight of a barrel of Guinness. They couldn't give me a hand with this, as I had drunk it.

We launched the boat on a beautiful tropical morning at sixish. The twin 40s were working well and I showed them all the controls and how to trim the boat while heading out to their dive site. There were numerous islands scattered around, all with palm trees growing on sandy beaches. After twenty minutes of me showing them the ropes, they were satisfied with the controls and offered to drop me back at the jetty. Like a fool I said no, and dropped back over the stern and waved them goodbye. I lay in the water for a long while looking at the odd cloud high in a beautiful blue sky. My head was still throbbing but the sound of engines had long gone. The water felt great and the gentle wave movement was very relaxing. When I looked around I didn't recognise anything; I was completely disorientated. I couldn't see the wake of the boat, all the islands looked the same, and I didn't know which one to head for. No one would know I was out here, only the two Aussies who wouldn't be back in camp till the evening. It's funny how the mind works. One minute I was in complete harmony with my surroundings, the next on the verge of panic. You start imagining things touching your legs, fish biting your feet, and sharks stalking you. What wasn't imagination was the power of the sun, which got hotter as it got higher. The glare off the water was painful and the salt water stung my eyes. I was already dehydrated from the booze and had plenty of time to reflect.

I lay on my back with my shirt over my head regretting the error of my ways. I've got to keep on going, otherwise I won't be able to finish this book.

What would Alan do in this predicament? It's one that you can't talk your way out of. You quickly realise your limitations and fears, and the biggest fear you are likely to face in life is fear of your own weaknesses. You can impress other people with bullshit, but when alone with no one to rely on but yourself, you have got to deliver.

After eight hours of bobbing up and down I finally crawled up a beach: let's get back in the jungle, it is safer.

No one had missed me at base, only Fred had phoned around to try and find me. It just goes to show:

WHO CARES RINGS

CHAPTER ELEVEN

HOME AGAIN

I returned from the jungle a conquering hero riding my white stallion down the High Street and sweeping my future wife off her feet. Well, it wasn't quite like that. I returned covered in sores and Rosalind, my mate's wife, arranged for her sister Marilyn to meet me. We met outside the entrance of a large store by the revolving doors and we started going around together. It was love at first sight and we were married a few months later.

I am a big believer in coincidences. My mate Rob went on a diving course to Portsmouth and met June who was to become his future wife. June was best friends with Rosalind and lived opposite each other in Southsea, Portsmouth. Rosalind joined the army (not the SAS, although she could have done), and met a guy called Hughie, who later passed selection and came to Two Troop. They married and invited Mabby, my future wife, to stay with them: that's how we met. June and Rosalind were notorious matchmakers, and like a lamb to the slaughter the returning warrior Lofty is snared and settles down. Fifty-odd years and seven children later, we are still going strong.

The wedding was brilliant, costing eighteen pounds, one and six in old money. My mother gave me twenty pounds which we squandered on the reception and I borrowed ten quid off a mate to buy a ring. We got married in the old Coal Office next door to the Fleece and celebrated there till closing time. Then we retired to the married quarters where Rosalind and Hughie laid on a party. Everyone took some booze and it worked out a treat. It tickles me when I read about weddings now costing thousands. We were lucky enough to move straight into a married quarters and we wanted for nothing.

In between trips to the Middle and Far East we went on training exercises at home and abroad keeping busy. We used Lossiemouth for free fall training. Although it is far to the north, the climate there is affected by the Gulf Stream, producing its own microclimate which is good for jumping. We stayed with the navy and shared their rum ration. The senior ranks tended to hoard their ration and once a week would hold a party. After one such session my mate ate a heather plant that a matelot had been nurturing for months. It was all woody and spiky, but he was like a camel and just devoured it.

The highlight of the trip was when we did a jump on their open day. Four of us jumped onto the airfield which had the tallest windsock in the world. We had to circle around this to land in front of the crowd. I was first down and looked around for the other three, but could only spot two. I heard a ripple of laughter from the crowd and followed to where they were pointing at. On the end of the windsock was Jimmy. The periphery of his chute just caught the end of the pole and Jimmy was still pulling down on his lift webs, wondering why he hadn't hit the floor yet. We had to use the helicopter to lift him off.

If you had tried to do this, you never would be able to. We passed it off as a stunt that had taken years to develop.

We had to go in a pressure chamber for high-altitude training. The RAF run this and they allowed a young WAAF officer to join us. She was a petite, shy girl called Annie, who was in charge of safety equipment. In the chamber you are taken to altitude wearing oxygen, and to see what effect the lack of oxygen has on the body, you take it in turns to take off your mask. You are asked to perform various tasks like touching your toes, doing some simple sums, and writing your name in a notebook. Everyone performs pretty well the same, but Annie was a star. As you go higher the gases in the body expand and you pass wind like exploding bagpipes. Annie took her mask off and from a shy, demur girl turned into a lager lout. She gyrated around the chamber, ripping off the loudest farts imaginable and dancing seductively. She started shouting, "Let 'em go, Annie," and tried to blow the gusset from her pants. The beauty of all this is that they video everything, and at the debrief play it back. She couldn't believe it when she saw herself acting like a drunken teenager at a pop concert.

We went parachuting to Culdrose, another naval air station in Devon. The navy pilots had fewer restrictions than the RAF and took us higher. As a favour to the commandant we agreed to test their security and see if we could break into their armoury. This was manned twenty-four hours a day and a sailor actually lived inside the building. We knew a conventional attack would fail as everything was reinforced and covered by alarms. The commandant and his master-at-arms, who was responsible for security, were quite smug and confident that we would fail.

We had a good look at the building, looking for weak spots, but none were found. The roof, which often offers the best means of entry, had been covered. All windows had metal grills and bars fitted, and the door would have done justice to Fort Knox. No sewer or air-conditioning ducts were found, and the building was really tight. It was going to be difficult, but no way were them two smug b'tards going to defeat us.

What we did was on the lines of the Trojan Horse. We informed them that our quick move box was coming from Hereford which contained weapons and had to be kept in the armoury. In fact we got a crate from the MT and fixed the lid so it could be opened from the inside. Taff was the smallest member of the troop and we volunteered him to get inside, where he lay down on a sleeping bag and took a bag of goodies with him.

We delivered the box and placed it between the racks of weapons. In the night, Taff opened the lid and removed a rifle, sub-machine gun and grenade launcher from the racks and deposited them inside his new habitat. In the morning we recovered our box and went to breakfast. I was summoned with our boss to see the commandant and his sidekick, noticing they were in a jovial mood. The commandant had his fingers steepled in a superior manner held in front of him like a bank manager does when you are asking for a loan, and he said, "I didn't hear much activity last night: how did you get on?"

The master-at-arms was swaying on the balls of his feet with his arms behind his back with a smile on his face from ear to ear. I produced the weapons and said, "Not too bad: we can always get more." Their looks were a sight to behold and they both exploded into action, trying to do too many things at once and failing in all of them. They leapt up: one grabbed the phone, the other tried to run out of the door and got entangled with the mat. He returned and put on his hat and the other ran out of the door taking the mat with him, dropping the phone in the process. Someone shouted at the clerk who ran in and picked up the dangling phone, tripping on the upturned mat. We stood back well satisfied and straightened the mat as we left. We were not invited to Culdrose again: shame really.

Manchester was graced with our presence where we took on an old colliery workhead as a demolition target. Dolly was in charge; he was the madman who fired at the hornets' nest in Borneo. His first test charge was quite modest for him, and a few bricks flew, but he hadn't warned the Coal Board who had men working underground at the time of the explosion. We were soon surrounded by angry wives and policemen demanding to know who had given us permission to let off charges. They thought it had been an underground explosion and were not very happy. One of the wives said she had never heard such a bang, and one of the lads said we were just blowing the lock off the gate before we could lay some proper charges.

Next door to the mine head was a steel fabricator's, and I was told to go and warn them of the next explosion. They had a lot of men working in the yard and I told them when they heard three blasts of the whistle to take cover. When the charges were ready I went and blew the whistle and watched all the workers take cover. The explosion was not very large and no debris came over the boundary. I did exactly the same when the next set of charges was ready, but the workforce just laughed and carried on working. It was a fine day and the sun was shining, so I got my head down and waited for the bang. I felt the shock wave first, then a shower of granite blocks filled the sky, blocking out the sun. I could hear rock bouncing on metal for ages before the dust cleared sufficiently for me to see into the yard. The whole area was strewn with rubble and the workers emerged one by one from under piles of rock and dust, rubbing their eyes. How no one was killed is beyond me. What Dolly had done was to load a gallery up with explosives under a chimney, and this acted like a giant mortar barrel showering the masonry over the steelworkers' yard. I didn't have to warn them the third time: they had all gone home refusing to work while we were there.

On the first blast a granite set had gone through the secretary's car roof, finishing up on the driving seat. The next blast sent a granite block through the roof of her office, through her desk, and finished up in the waste paper basket underneath. How's that for neatness? It proves demolitions need not be untidy. I tried to live up to this when I ran the demo cadre.

Health and Safety were unheard of back in the sixties, and looking back, I must admit it was dangerous. But I'd rather have it that way than pamper to all the umbrellas and bullshit that industry has to suffer to do their job nowadays. It's just an excuse in many cases to screw money out of firms that cannot afford it or benefit from it. Don't get me started on politically correctness, either, as I think with this and Health and Safety we have really shot ourselves in the foot. Here endeth my political broadcast on behalf of the 'old-fashioned way of doing things' society.

We had a demolition range on the Eastnor Castle Estate near Ledbury, and when we used it, we had to place out signs to warn the public away. I will tell you more stories of this later. We carried railway line up to the range which was a good mile from the road, so we got fit if nothing else. Rails weigh eighty pounds a yard and we carted a few yards up the hill. We used to fire 3.5 rockets, expediently firing them from the tube that they came in, rather than carry a six-foot bazooka-type weapon. The rocket is an anti-tank missile and will penetrate about nine inches of armour. The practice was to strip out the electrics from the base of the rocket that was used to conventionally fire the missile and replace it with a bunch of matches wrapped round a piece of safety fuse and insert this in its place. I stood with a guy called Dave who was wearing a plastic mac which we all envied. He was waiting his turn to sight the rocket and fire it, making sure that he had rammed up the fuse as far as possible when the matches ignited and from his hands the rocket took off in a shower of flames with a scorching back blast, incinerating anything in its path. Amazingly, no one was hurt. The rocket landed in a field where spud pickers had been hours before and Dave's mac was perforated like a Tetley's tea bag. After this the rules were changed to use only safety matches, not Swan Vestas.

Dolly ran another demolition course on the tank range at Sennybridge. There was a three-pound limit for charges, but little things like this never affected Dolly. The first thing he did when we unloaded the trucks was to fire a 3.5 rocket vertically. This shot in the air, trailing smoke, and as it got higher, disappeared. Dolly stood there puffing on his pipe and said, "I've always wanted to do that." We were all huddled in a group looking skywards concerned that 'what goes up must come down'. It's either still going up or landed over the ridge miles away: we never saw it again.

His pièce de résistance was with a five-hundred gallon aircraft drop tank full of avgas. This was to test our own home-made soap dish incendiary device. A normal plastic soap dish filled with thermite at the bottom, with two ounces of plastic on top, which was sufficient to pierce a metal container and ignite anything inside. The theory is that the plastic blows a hole in the vessel, allowing the liquid inside to run out and mix with air, while the thermite, which burns fiercely, ignites anything volatile. Avgas was a very pure form of petrol, high in octane and specially refined for aircraft. One gallon was equal to a pound of explosive used as a concussion charge. Five hundred gallons would have kept all of our cars running for months, but

Dolly wanted to do a full test. To initiate this device, a detonator was inserted with a length of safety fuse crimped on, which was ignited by the guy laying the device. It was near the end of the day and only nine inches of safety fuse were left, which was good for a 30-45-second delay. One of the golden rules of demolitions is 'never run from a burning charge'. Wally was nominated as the mug to go and initiate the device. He wasn't the quickest in the group; in fact he was the slowest to hide when Dolly was looking for a volunteer. We were five hundred yards away on top of a hill when Wally went down to the drop tank muttering about lunatics and pyromaniacs. He lit the fuse on the second attempt and sprinted up the slope dropping the matches, as weight was going to be critical. Dolly shouted at him, "Never run from a......" A wall of heat hit us, followed by an intensely hot blast wave. One minute we were watching Wally's progress up the hill, shouting encouragement at him, when he disappeared engulfed in a fireball. The noise followed the blast and the air was alive with hot fragments, dust and flying debris. Wally emerged scorched, smoked, seared and shaken. He was partially stripped of clothing and skin, burnt between medium and medium rare.

Africa was a magical continent. We had worked in North Africa in places like Tripoli and Libya, which were deserts, but Kenya was something special. Out of all the countries I have visited I think East Africa was the best. The wildlife, climate and landscape were stunning; the only drawback was the locals. Teaching Africans was challenging and I like to illustrate this with a story. There was an African, a Scotsman and an Englishman locked up in a jail. They were each given two six-inch-diameter, spherical steel ball bearings. After one hour the jailer checked up on his prisoners, looking through the peephole in the door. The Scotsman was doing exercises with his, lifting them above his head. He moved on to the Englishman, who was playing bowls with his. He checked the African, discovering he had lost one of the balls and broken the other. This was what it was like training them:

never a dull moment and very frustrating.

We had a great job training Jomo Kenyatta's bodyguard. This was a first and involved lots of new skills. We took recruits from the police and trained them in close protection. They were very fit men but lacked all military skills and common sense. We had to tell them everything and show them many times before they could grasp what we were talking about. I spoke Swahili, albeit with a cockney accent, and this further confused them: I could have been talking Japanese for all they cared. This reminds me of a story that happened when I left the Army and got involved with a world conservation scheme. It involved saving the rhino in Africa, building wells in Asia, breeding pandas in China, and all that kind of thing. Off the coast of Kenya a sinking Japanese fishing boat was rescued. It was upside down with all the crew clinging to the hull which had a large, gaping hole through it right where the bridge used to be. The captain was the only person missing and all the crew were in a state of shock. When asked what had happened, all they got was "gombe, gombe," and the crew made a mooing sound and pointed skywards with gestures of something falling. Eventually an interpreter was found and couldn't believe the story he heard. Apparently the captain was on the bridge drinking tea when a cow fell from the sky and went straight through the wheelhouse and out through the bottom, taking the skipper with it. They all thought that the crew were mad or the interpreter was speaking the wrong language. What didn't help to make this story plausible was that the skipper was asking for a drop of milk at the time.

What had happened was a Russian aircraft was moving cattle as part of a hearts and minds campaign, and the animals were not sufficiently anaesthetised. One started kicking up so they lowered the ramp and jettisoned it. Unfortunately for the Japanese who were underneath, the Russians scored a bull's-eye.

I am always telling people to keep their eyes open and look around them, especially up. Another tragic story about an airdrop happened in Somalia just north of Kenya. The locals were starving and a resupply of food was dropped to them. One minute a man on the ground was praying for food, when a one-ton pallet of rice fell on him and killed him: where's the justice in that? The moral of this story is when you pray don't ask for too much, or be careful what you pray for.

All the students on the course had to be loyal to Kenyatta so they were mainly Kikuyu. They had names like Wellington, Winston and Nelson. A guy called Livingstone was put in charge of them and he never ceased to amaze us. On demolition training we showed them how to make a time delay using an alarm clock. Just by taping the contacts on the back, which closed when the alarm lever started turning, couldn't have been simpler. Livingstone came back in five minutes with the clock completely stripped down; he even took the hands off. He had a handful of cogs and springs and in an Oxford accent said, "Sorry, old chap: had a spot of bother with the jolly old timepiece."

He was late for a briefing one night and we all sat about waiting for him, wondering what excuse he would come up with this time. After another thirty minutes he appeared, crossing the lawn bathed in moonlight, in leather slippers wearing a brocade silk dressing gown with a cigarette holder dangling from the corner of his mouth. "Sorry about the short delay, chaps: couldn't get the hairdryer going." It was like a scene from a Noël Coward play. He was a blood relative of the president, so no way could we get rid of him.

The other lads worked well but it was hard-going. They had a short memory span and, unless you repeated everything regularly, it was like teaching a new subject every time. Nanyuki was a great place to train: it had loads of space with spectacular scenery. On one horizon was Mount Kenya and on the other Kilimanjaro. I was teamed up with Dave, the world's worst driver, the one who drove me on the survival course. He was running vehicle ambushes and had a car that he wanted to tow over to the demolition range.

It was badly shot up, but would make a good target for car bombs. I stupidly agreed to be towed in this wreck while Dave towed me in a Land Rover. He tied the tow rope, leaving a lot of slack between vehicles. I sat in the car surrounded by jagged metal. When a bullet hits the car, it leaves a little hole on the outside but a big, jagged exit hole on the inside. This car had been hit hundreds of times: it was like sitting in a cheese grater. I told Dave to take it easy and take up the slack. He did neither. He dropped the clutch and the slack was taken up that violently that my seat broke off its runners and I finished up in the back bouncing around on the floor covered with broken glass, impaled by jagged metal. I fought my way forward again just as Dave descended into a lugger (a dried-up watercourse). Halfway down the slope I overtook Dave, having no brakes and very little skin left. When I finally got out of the car I was like a pound of raw mince. I did salvage the air horns from the car and took them home with me. The boss got his wires crossed when he heard I had some horns. He tried to get permission from the Game and Fisheries Department giving me authorisation to take them out of the country. He thought they were animal horns, not automobile ones.

We needed a safe up country to keep all the classified documents in. They sent one up from Nairobi but without the key. When we informed them of this situation they said, "No worries, there is a spare key." We asked them where it was and the answer was "in the safe". Typical African efficiency: we finished using the safe as a demolition target and carried on keeping the documents under a bed.

Tony, the guy in overall charge of the group, had been a policeman for years. He had a servant with him who washed and ironed his kit. He always looked immaculate and changed several times a day. We changed once a week if we were lucky. His boy's name was Goi and he had found him when raiding a brothel in Nairobi. Goi was ironing a bra and was about six years old at the time. He had been with Tony for years, and waited on him hand

and foot. One night, Goi went to his bed about seventy yards downwind from our tent where four of us shared. Tony had a pressure lamp by his bed and called for Goi who had been in bed for hours. Goi came running and Tony told him to turn the light out. We couldn't believe it and called him all the laziest, selfish names we could think of. Tony said, "That's how we do it in Africa." No wonder there's trouble in the world.

Just as my wounds were healing from the car incident, Sandy was chased by a buffalo. This was an old male who had wandered onto the range. Sandy was alone and pasting up targets when the animal charged him. To escape he jumped down into a lugger, landing right in the middle of a thorn bush. He arrived in camp looking worse than if the animal had caught him. He had laughed at me; now it was my turn. Two bottles of iodine later, I had him at my mercy. "What must I not do when Lofty gets hurt?" I asked him. I also gave him an injection of antibiotic. You can mix this so it's thin, which is less painful when you inject. I left this jab pretty thick and enjoyed every moment.

Most people are under the misapprehension that fire keeps wild animals away. One night, four of us were sitting around a campfire telling lies to each other when a rhinoceros came into camp and did a cha cha cha on the fire. Whether it had cold feet or not, we didn't stay around to find out. This is a rarity, but there is always an exception to the rule.

I met some interesting characters in Kenya and had the honour of going for a drink with Kipchoge Keino. He was an Olympic gold medallist from the Tokyo Games, and I met him at Kiganjo police college where he was a police inspector. I thought it would be a quiet night with a few drinks and an early night: how wrong I was. We started in the market where we ate two-inch squares of fat. I love fat but others in the party were a little put off. We soon attracted a crowd as he was a national hero. We washed the fat down with gallons of beer and moved on to different pubs and clubs where he was eagerly received. If this was his training schedule, I was definitely in with a chance at the next Olympics.

Tony was also an Olympian: he shot rifle and rapid pistol at the same games. Every day when we were up country we would go out and shoot for the pot. He was the best marksman I had ever seen and I learnt a lot from him. We would drive all day and watch all the different animals. He knew everything about the wildlife and was a pleasure to be with. One day we stopped by a river and I couldn't wait to dive in. The water was refreshing and as I lay there floating on my back I asked Tony what was the name of the place. He said, "Crocodile Jaws." I was out of the water up the bank and dressed in seconds. He couldn't stop laughing, reckoning the place got its name from the shape of the pool, not the presence of reptiles. Better to be safe than sorry.

Later on I was to meet a world champion shot who won several gold medals for Great Britain. He was a pure target shooter, whereas Tony had all the skills of fieldcraft and stalking.

You never know who is watching you. We organised an exercise where we had the lads following certain dignitaries who were not aware of our presence. This was to teach the recruits surveillance, and we did this in Nairobi. One target was a bank manager and we discovered he had a mistress. So always look over your shoulder, you never know who's watching.

We also trained a unit called GSU, General Service Unit. They were policemen and the unit was raised to offset the power of the army. A lot of training was conducted in the Northern Frontier Division, which is a barren expanse of land up on the Somalia border. We thought that the recruits would have an instinct for water discipline, but assumption is the mother of all ….ups. We dropped the recruits off on a navigation exercise where they had to make RV points where we checked their condition before sending them on. It was blisteringly hot, no wind and no cover. They carried all the kit they needed, but we had a jerrycan of water so we could top them up if they ran out. At the first RV, that only took two hours to reach, every one of the thirty recruits had run out of water. We stressed the importance of rationing but it fell on deaf ears. At the second RV, while I was dressing blisters, a recruit picked up a jerrycan of water and attempted to drink the lot. What he didn't spill he vomited, and this seriously depleted our water ration. The trucks wouldn't be back for three days and we had a critical situation developing.

We signalled base, alerting them of our situation, and changed the exercise. We had two men missing and had to wait for them. We sent all the students with two DS to a village about forty miles away with the last of the water. Two of us waited behind for the missing men. Hunger is one thing, but thirst is ten times worse. Between the two of us, we had less than a pint of water, which had to last us at least two days. Things were not looking good and we feared for the missing men. We had decided to stay put till rescued, and settled in whiling the time away. Pictures of icebergs and waterfalls kept on creeping into the subconscious, and a strong desire for salt was never far away.

Africa is so full of surprises. On the second day the two stragglers turned up carrying a full goatskin of water that they had bought off a nomad. Cyril and Stanley became my best mates. They looked as if they were out on a Sunday stroll unaware of all the drama that had happened.

Our two lads who went with the main group had a hard time. They made a bad decision to drink their urine. They had a small bottle of orange juice which they used to dilute their waste. They finished up taking longer to recover than us. We waited for transport and were none the worse for wear when we were picked up.

The lessons learnt from this are: always protect your water source, guard it at all times, and never drink urine. In the army it's ok to take the p..s, but not to drink it.

Another thing about Africa is it's no good for parachuting. Air currents cause a stormy ride in the aircraft, and the thin air makes the descent under the canopy faster, so you hit the ground harder, which is very unforgiving. So to keep safe, carry plenty of water, don't let Dave drive you, and forget about parachuting.

We went to Jamaica and had a good time achieving a lot of firsts. We crossed the island from the south to the north, a feat which the locals couldn't believe. The central spine is very rugged but we did it.

We were also credited with the first free-fall display on the island. I don't know how true this is, but that was what we were told. All the newspapers, radio and TV stations carried the news of the four displays that we were doing, so they were reluctant to cancel for any reasons. We were delighted to find out that the Jamaica Defence Force had a Twin Otter aircraft which was one of the best aircraft for parachuting. It could climb fast, fly slow, and had a sliding door. The only snag was the pilot had dengue fever and was got off his sickbed to come and fly us. I went to the airstrip to arrange everything and admired the aircraft. There were only four of us jumping so we had room to play football inside the Otter. When I was introduced to the pilot I nearly fell over. He was a Jamaican but had a pale yellow patina to his skin, that was bathed in sweat. He continually wrung out the towel that he wore around his neck and the whites of his eyes were more like egg yolks. It was midday and our first jump was scheduled for three o'clock. I didn't think the pilot was going to last that long; it was a pity that he was the only pilot qualified to fly the aircraft. I was the only one to talk to him: the others kept well clear. I only hoped that whatever he had was not contagious.

The plan was to fly over the DZ which was a school, drop a streamer, then climb to altitude for the display. After we jumped, the aircraft would land and pick us up for another display later at Montego Bay. We were to give a packing demonstration at the school and sign autographs and give a brief interview to a local radio station. Looking at the pilot I would have bet money that this wouldn't happen.

When we took off the four of us linked arms and legs at the rear of the aircraft, as this is the safest place to be in a crash. Taking off from a proper runway helped the aircraft to soar into the sky and in no time at all we were at two thousand feet. The pilot was swigging orange juice faster than the plane was burning fuel, and I was glad we were wearing parachutes.

Mick was a novice so we dropped him out first using him as our drift indicator. He used to land in some interesting places, never once landing on the intended, the DZ. This time he landed by a swimming pool of a big house up on a hillside where he was treated like royalty by the houseowners.

The three of us landed in front of the crowd and were immediately swamped by a mass of schoolkids. We had landed on a football pitch that was surrounded by scrub with the odd cow grazing in the long grass. Eventually we had a space provided for us to pack in front of a dilapidated grandstand. We encouraged the kids to help us fold and tension our canopies as we packed them for the next show. I gave a short interview with Jimmy to the local radio and I knew they couldn't understand our accents. Jimmy was talking about the donkey leg in the wind, not a dog leg, which even confused me. I heard the aircraft making low passes but was absorbed in what I was doing. Mick reluctantly rejoined us, being quite willing to have stayed with his newfound friends with the mansion on the hill.

I looked around and saw the aircraft at the far end of the football pitch parked amidst the long grass and bushes. They had taken down the goalposts and the teachers were ushering the kids to the sidelines. I thought there must be an airstrip there, but couldn't recollect seeing one on my descent.

I had a chat to the pilot who was still wringing out his towel, and asked him where he had taxied from. He looked at me with glazed eyes and pointed to the penalty spot. Apparently, he had landed on the pitch and had backed up in the bushes to give him more space for take-off. I knew this aircraft had a good, short take-off and landing capability, but I didn't think it was this good, especially with the pilot running a 103° temperature. We reluctantly climbed back into the aircraft and braced for take-off. Again sitting well back with interlaced limbs, we took off. We hurtled into the air, leaving behind a cloud of dust, stampeding cows and cheering schoolkids. As we climbed, I looked back, noticing that they didn't even take down the other set of goalposts.

The jump at Montego Bay went well for us, but not so well for Mick. We used him again as a drifter, and he landed in a pigpen miles from anywhere. I didn't want him to land in the sea, as the canopy would not be dry for the next day's displays; so I dropped him a little too deep. We landed on the beach amidst a large crowd and were treated to a barbeque. By the time Mick was recovered, the last sausage had gone.

Our OC thought it a good idea if we completed a fifty-mile speed march to get us prepared for an exercise that was coming off in Germany in a few weeks' time. My troop was deployed in a place called the Cockpit Country which was a wonder of nature. Imagine an egg box turned upside-down, and, instead of being made from cardboard, was made of limestone with each peak being a hundred feet high. It was infested with mosquitoes, and the peaks acted like storage heaters, trapping the sun and making the floor like a furnace. It was hard to navigate as everything was the same. Just these pyramid hills erupting skywards with no breeze, and when the sun was high, no cover. We got a signal telling us to go to a place that on the map was called 'you no look me no see', a small village on the edge of this freak of nature. The OC did it on us again. The colonel was coming from the UK and he had volunteered us to look after him.

The colonel was in his early forties and had stepped straight off a plane from the UK and driven to the RV. It was boiling hot and when he asked us what we were going to do in the next couple of days, he aged considerably when we told him of the speed march.

We set off at a good pace and covered about ten miles when we spotted an ice cream van. The CO insisted he treat us, so all twelve of us sat in the gutter licking ice creams like big kids. If the CO hadn't have joined us I would have headed for the main road and caught a bus. I could see the colonel was suffering and was struggling to keep up, so I diplomatically hinted that we were being held back and it was unfair that the CO wasn't acclimatised. He took the bait and inquired about a taxi. We had Taffy with us who was long in the tooth and when the CO, told him that he was going to order a taxi and take him with him, he at first resisted. I was winking furiously at Taff, telling him to go, which he eventually agreed to do. As soon as the colonel departed in the taxi I changed course for the main road. There were three other troops making the same journey and were spread out along this route. We jumped on a bus and settled down to what turned out to be an eventful journey. We had a lookout at the front of the bus who told us to get down as we passed the other troops. A local got on at one stop and sat next to Mick. The conductor went to collect his fare and the new passenger said he wasn't go to pay, and drew a knife. The conductor removed his ticket machine and he pulled a knife. I thought, 'Here we go: witness to a murder and caught cheating as well'. Their knives were sharpened hacksaw blades set in a wooden handle. On my pack I had a real knife, a fourteen-inch parang which I drew. Mick was in the middle of this dispute so I ordered the passenger off the bus, waving my parang menacingly. In the middle of all this the lookout shouts, "Get down!" so we called for a short amnesty till we passed a couple of Three Troop striding down the road. My imagination is running riot thinking, 'How am I going to explain being involved in a knife fight on a bus, when I should have been tabbing?' Faced by the conductor and myself, the fare dodger thought it prudent to get off the bus, but not before we had another alert and had to get down once again. The conductor told us that this was normal and happened every day. I suppose it helps break up the journey.

We got off the bus on the outskirts of Montego Bay and headed down the beach. We had hours to kill before we dared make the final RV, and had a swim and a brew. We met a man from Leeds who was on holiday and he went to his hotel and fetched some beers, so it all worked out nicely.

The colonel got to the final RV literally five minutes before One Troop arrived. He asked them how they had covered the ground so quickly, and Spud said they used a shortcut. They had got on a bus before us, not many of the squadron walked the full distance, if any.

Just before we came home we had a night out in a local club. It was poorly lit and in the corner was a bundle of rags, and all the tables were in the centre of eighteen-inch raised platforms. You would be talking to somebody one minute and they would vanish the next, falling off the platform as they leant back. As the drinks flowed people forgot about the step and would disappear into the gloom, evaporating like magic. At ten o'clock the bundle of rags came alive and got on the microphone and started singing. He had one of the best blues voices I have ever heard. An hour later he went back to his corner and collapsed again.

I was at the bar when a Yank who had been playing up all night started becoming a nuisance and drew a pistol. I gave him a slap and disarmed him. His mate took him home which set me thinking that I had better be on my toes here: he might come back seeking revenge. I was surprised when his wife turned up and thanked me for doing what I did, saying that he deserved everything he got. It's nice to be praised for a change.

Another great island for training was Cyprus. Here the Squadron could carry out free fall, mountain, diving and mobility training all within easy reach of each other, making administration a lot easier. Cyprus was of strategic importance and we were always asked to test the security of its airbase, Akrotiri. We would infiltrate by day, passing off as transit passengers, and lay low till darkness when we would sneak around laying charges and attacking vital points like the control tower and fuel installations.

After a free fall session we all posed for an end-of-course photograph. This was on a small airfield where the C-130 could land, but because of limited resources had to keep the engines running. The pilot left the engines idling so he could be in the photograph. The entire course was sitting facing a hangar with the aircraft behind, trying to look intelligent as Joe tried focusing the camera. It wasn't staying in focus and it took a few minutes for Joe to realise why: the aircraft was inching forward. It gradually picked up speed, forcing all to scatter. The pilot and his crew jumped aboard, desperately trying to stop the moving aircraft. They found out later that there was a hydraulic failure, making the brakes inoperative, and the propellers gave it sufficient momentum to cause it to run down the slope. Unfortunately, the nose hit the hangar so there was a court of inquiry. There was not a lot of damage done to the aircraft, but the pilot was found guilty of leaving the aircraft and fined a nominal sum, something like a day's pay.

A year later a story hit the papers where a pilot was reported as doing a tandem jump with one of the lads. They inferred he left the aircraft to the co-pilot and jumped out with the course; that's what you call leaving an aircraft. In fact, he was a pilot, but was on leave at the time of this incident.

At home we used to take it in turns to be the standby Squadron. This meant that we had to fill in a weekend book stating where we would be, and if we went anywhere had to leave a contact address or telephone number. Not many people had telephones and a telegram was sent if we were needed. We had a code word that would be sent and on receipt of this had to get back to camp ASAP. We were limited to how far we could go and usually stayed close to camp. The pay in the army was not that good, so most of us went moonlighting. We worked for builders, bakers, the chicken factory, or anywhere there was work. On one particular leave when we were the standby Squadron, the code word for a quick move was 'free beer'. Most of the married lads had casual jobs working at Bulmers where they made cider, Mother's Pride the bakery, and the chicken factory, Sun Valley, which was the biggest chicken processing plant in Europe.

Football pools were very popular in the sixties, giving you a chance to win £75,000. We had a troop syndicate and hoped to win a fortune. It was a ritual checking the evening paper on Saturday seeing how many draws you had. My wife said, "You are wasting your time checking them," and I strongly resisted saying, "Nothing ventured, nothing gained" sort of thing, and "If you don't speculate you don't accumulate." She said, "Never mind all that rubbish, I forgot to post them." Imagine my horror when Mabby, my wife, told me this. I started ranting and raging, saying that if I forget anything it could be the difference between life and death, and men would perish. Just then the doorbell went and I answered the door to find Bob my sergeant major on the doorstep. He said, "Free beer." I answered, "Great, Bob, I could do with a drink." He said again, "Free beer." I looked a bit puzzled and said, "What, your place?" He had been working at Bulmers so I thought he had a few flagons of cider for me. I was at the chicko and got him chickens. His van door was open and I offered to help him unload. He repeated the code word for the third time before Mabby stepped in and said, "It's a quick move, you dickhead," and showered me with words that meant I was forgetful. So much for catlike reactions and laser-like applications.

On a Friday night the Regiment made up the night shift of Mother's Pride, the bakery. The adjutant was the shift leader and we took it in turns to man the ovens, clean the baking trays, and make cakes. If we were ever called out on a Friday night there would be a famine on the Saturday.

The chicken factory was a good job for getting you acclimatised for the Arctic. An eight-hour shift in the cold store stacking chickens was enough to make you give up the will to live. Loading fishmeal at the chicken feed factory was another hard job, but beggars can't be choosers and we worked where we could.

The best jobs were on the building sites: plenty of fresh air and good fun. Me and Jimmy worked for a Greek Cypriot called Hegatron. We plastered out his factory where he was making electronic components. Although neither of us had any qualifications, we did a good job saving him a lot of money. We kept asking him for a rise but he always had an excuse. One morning we turned up and I said good morning to which he responded, but he ignored Jimmy. Jimmy told him if he didn't cheer up he was going home. Hegatron said, "Mr Jimmy, I have piles." Jimmy said, "So what? Half the world's got piles." Hegatron responded and said, "Mr Jimmy, the Turks have invaded Cyprus and my mother and father have disappeared. They may be tortured or murdered." This didn't faze Jimmy at all, who said, "I couldn't give two f…s. If you don't cheer up I'm going home."

It was because of the casual work we did that I met Tony who was to become a good mate. He ran a contract at Madley where they built a satellite station. I earned more money working for Tony than I got from the army. There was a pair of carpenters who were ex-national servicemen and we had a good laugh together. I would bring in a mess tin and brew tea over a Tommy cooker for them. They had to make a vandal-proof shed that would house some calibrating instruments for testing the new satellite dish. It had to be placed on the Black Mountains to do this, so it had to be strong and sturdy. The only way to get it on the mountain was by underslinging it on a chopper. The post office had contacted the Regiment to do this and they had agreed. I kidded the chippies that I was a pilot and would be flying the load. I also told the lads that they had to be in the shed when we moved it. They really milked it building the shed. It took them all week and they used the finest of materials. They were unconvinced that I was a pilot, but I got Tony to back me up and got them thinking. When I went back to work I told Pete, the pilot, of my scam and asked him to tell me when he had to go to Madley to confirm details, so I could go with him. Sure enough, a few days later we flew to the site with me sitting in the left-hand seat. I was wearing a helmet and looked exactly like the pilot. When we landed I saw the chippies and gave them a wave. They couldn't believe it, they said they wouldn't trust me driving a four-tonner, let alone a heli. While Peter got the technical details of weight and dimensions, I kidded the lads where they had to sit in the shed for take-off and landing. They said no way were they going to fly and would be sacked first. Peter agreed a date of the lift and we returned to camp.

I was out of the country when Pete lifted the shed. He was flying towards the Black Mountains when the shed started oscillating. It got so bad that Peter had no option but to cut it away. It fell out of the sky and demolished another shed and greenhouse below it, and to this day the chippies swear blind that I had jettisoned it on purpose.

We also worked as bouncers at weekends in the local dance hall. The only trouble was usually started by a bouncer. The locals were great, and once you got to know them they would always help you out. There is always a local nutter who likes to be thrown out by a bouncer, but usually it was a quiet night. For this we were paid a fiver.

We used to take it in turns to cross-train and half the troop went climbing and skiing, while the other half went boat training. I think some blokes took it in turns to cross-dress, but that's another story. We finished up in a trendy German ski resort dressed to thrill. We had battledress trousers that were cut off at the knee and elasticated, which we wore with long, submariner's socks. Over these we wore a parka with a fur-trimmed hood, making us look like pantomime bears. On our heads we wore cap comforters with yellow-lensed welder's goggles to protect the eyes. The Germans are so meticulous about how they look, and when we turned up looking like the Legion of the Damned they must have thought every lunatic asylum in the country had been emptied and sent to them. Our skiing was not much better, and we tended to run into people and knock them over. The only way to stop sometimes was to grab someone, so we left a trail of devastation down the ski slopes.

Scouse was a short guy who had as much coordination as a sack of spuds. He was waiting for the ski lift to come and whisk him up the ski run, and stood with his backside stuck out, hoping that the T bar would hook him up. His mate Billy was the other side, and he reached the T bar first and twisted it just as Scouse leant back. The bar went inside his parka, pitching him head down and making him run to keep his balance. As the ground fell away, Scouse was left suspended head down with the bar inside his parka from waist to neck. He decided to remain still in case something gave way and that's how he arrived at the top station. As soon as he had ground under him again he started struggling. With arm and legs thrashing he jammed a ski into the giant cog that ran the lift, and everything ground to a standstill. The lift was full of Germans suspended from the cable all the way up the mountainside. Scouse was kicking and pulling, trying to extricate his ski. All you could hear from the tourists was 'crazy Englanders'. All you could hear from Scouse was unprintable.

There was a group of Finnish students on the slopes and every morning they would start with a series of vigorous stretching exercises. They made skiing look easy and took it seriously. They were doing their stuff one morning when Blue hurtled down the slope out of control, screaming like a banshee. He tore through the stretching group and finished head down in a snowdrift.

It goes to show:

BLUE SCARES FINNS

CHAPTER TWELVE

RETURN TO DESERT

When the army was closing its bases in Sharjah, trouble was expected in the area to disrupt this process. The squadron was recalled from leave and given a briefing about the coming dangers. Trouble was expected from the Musandam Peninsula, which is a finger of land at the head of the Strait of Hormuz. We were told of a warlike tribe called the Shuhu, who were going to revolt and march on Sharjah. The ops officer who was giving the presentation was new to the Regiment and really hyped up this briefing. One of his lines was: "Look at the man sat next to you, he may not be coming back." That's all the encouragement you need at the beginning of an op; it's not surprising that no one wanted to go. The Shuhu were an ancient tribe who still wielded stone axes and lived in houses built of rocks. The door was small and low, forcing anyone entering to duck low so the head was vulnerable and could be chopped off if the occupants didn't like the visitor. The peninsula was hard to get to, being surrounded by mountains, and few people had contacted this tribe. Khasab was the capital of the region and an important trading port; it was very isolated and had been unaffected by Western influence. We sat at the briefing picturing these wild men wielding axes and trying to behead us. It was with this in mind that we departed for the desert once again.

As soon as we landed in Sharjah we were whisked away into the desert. There was no camp and we sorted ourselves out in troops using thorn bushes to hang our kit on.

I was called forward to see the boss and introduced to a political officer who was responsible for the Musandam. My job was to go with him, taking a signaller with us to Khasab, and send out as much intelligence and geographical information as possible. My job was to look after this guy and provide a secure radio link with base. With Geordie, my signaller, and Simon, the PO, we flew in a Skyvan with a Land Rover in the back, to the north. From the air the landing strip was barely discernible; it hadn't been used for years. What with the briefing and now this, emotions were running high. We bounced to a stop and unloaded the vehicle and all of our kit. It was about twenty miles from Khasab where we were going to set up base. I could see potential ambush sites around every bend, but we had an uneventful journey to the port. The PO had acquired a house for us right next to a mosque. It was the time of Ramadan where everyone fasts, and prays at least four times a day. The house was a simple two-up two-down construction with a small courtyard surrounded by a low wall. It was recently built and still had piles of sand and bags of cement in the yard. As soon as we arrived, the mullah called the faithful to prayer. Loudspeakers were used and the noise was shattering. When he started up, every dog in the neighbourhood started howling, and every now and then a loud, high-pitched screech would come from the mass of speakers.

I quickly assessed the house and felt very vulnerable. The walls were of mudbrick construction and wouldn't stop a fly penetrating them. The roof was flat and overlooked by all the other houses in the area. There was no water, electricity or toilet – just like Downham really.

I wanted some form of early warning system in case we were attacked. Dogs were out of the question: they only barked at pilgrims. At home we had geese on one training establishment and these were excellent sentries. I asked Simon if he could get a couple of geese when he went to the souk for supplies. He came back with three ducks, saying these were tastier and had more meat on. I was trying to beef up security, not run a gourmet restaurant. Simon was very laid back and felt at home in these strange surroundings. He spoke excellent Arabic and dressed as a local. This worried me slightly, as there was a condition known as 'Lawrence Complex' where people fall in love with the desert and go native.

We all had a room each. Geordie slept by the radio upstairs, with Simon next door to him. I slept downstairs with my feet braced against the front door: anyone entering would have to get by me. I didn't sleep well on the first night. When I dozed off I was chased by mad axemen and was woken by the mad mullah crying into his mike. I wished I was back with the troop.

We met the Wali of Khasab: he was the equivalent to a mayor. He ruled the district with a rod of iron and all the locals paid him the greatest of respect. I witnessed a fisherman who was hauled up in front of him for fighting. He came from another village and had a dispute with a local and started fighting with him using pebbles from the beach as weapons. He prostrated himself in front of the Wali and kissed his feet continuously, as though begging for his life. It was like a scene from the Middle Ages. He was fined and crawled backwards away from the Wali, reciting praises as he went, a very relieved man.

We scouted inland, visiting isolated communities. With the briefing fresh in my mind I was taking no chances. I kept my distance as Simon approached the huts and was surprised to see him greeted by the whole family. It was rare for Arab women to welcome strangers, but everyone turned out and they were the warmest and most hospitable Arabs I have ever met anywhere. We were given tea and dates with unleavened bread; they really made us welcome. So much for all the crap we were told in Hereford.

We made maps of the area, putting on all the villages, recorded the inhabitants, and filled in topographical features; our next task was to recce the coastal villages. For this an Arab dhow was put at our disposal called the Muntissa. This was the flagship of the Sultan's navy, a good strong, traditional dhow with twin .30 cal machine guns mounted on the bridge. These were taken from the old piston-engined Provost aircraft that were replaced by jets.

Of a morning we would walk to a jetty where a rubber inflatable would pick us up to take us to the dhow. Once on-board we would head out to sea and have breakfast with the crew on the open deck. The cook looked like Oddjob. He was as wide as he was tall with a polished head, and was busy either cooking or preparing food all day long. The crew were burnt black and looked a right bunch of cut-throats. I felt like Sinbad the Sailor, son of Popeye.

There were five minesweepers running a blockade along the coast. They stayed just over the horizon so no one could see them from the shore. We took it in turns to visit these boats, and the matelots couldn't believe their eyes when we came alongside. We had a shower and a meal on-board and scrounged whatever we could. We were soon named by the flotilla as the 'scourge of the Seven Seas'.

We stopped a lot of dhows and fishing boats to make sure they were not gunrunning. One dhow we stopped was en route to India. The crew were all big-built, which was unusual, and as the lads searched the boat you could detect a certain tension. It wasn't till they were well underway that Simon asked me what I thought they were carrying. I didn't have a clue. Apparently, they were gold smugglers. They would buy gold in Dubai and take it to India. If the customs stopped them they would give them a gold bar worth twenty grand. If the Indian Navy stopped them they would dump the gold over the side and retrieve it later. This dhow had four hundred thousand pounds' worth of illegal gold on-board: no wonder he never told me till it was just a speck in the distance.

We checked out the coastal villages, making a note of all personalities, and made sketch maps of the area. All the locals seemed so friendly, and a mother actually breastfed her baby in front of us. We never found any signs of dissent, let alone terrorist activity.

The days were long and I even looked forward to going back to our hovel. The madman had quietened down a lot as it was now Eid where everyone celebrated. The locals liked throwing swords in the air and catching them, which kept me busy suturing their wounds. A cut of the web between thumb and first finger was the most common one and quite tricky to suture.

I felt sorry for the ducks that Simon had bought, so I dug a pond and lined it with cement. I put a duck in the pond and he sank. He had never seen so much water before and his feathers were not waterproof... Oops.

We passed all the intelligence back to base and they started planning the next phase of this op. I rejoined my troop who were busy practising night jumps. Trouble was brewing in Southern Oman, and we heard that B Squadron was deployed there.

Two Troop was elected to jump into the mountains and observe some villages while the rest of the Squadron carried out a sea assault against a town called Bukhara.

While we practised for this insertion we found out that the pilot who was flying us was Julie Andrews's stepbrother. We would get ready to exit the aircraft and start singing "Just a spoonful of sugar" before leaping out of the door. Night jumps are always difficult, and trying to land in the mountains was especially hazardous. Our intended LZ was surrounded by peaks as high as 6000 feet. Although we had jumped onto the road in Aden, we considered this to be the first operational free fall that the regiment had ever done. It was a mixed troop made up of half A Sqn and half G Sqn.

The RAF were very strict about the carriage of arms and explosives, but on this occasion that went out of the window. We didn't know what to expect on the ground so we all chambered a round in the aircraft. Fred was jumping with a 40mm grenade launcher, and he cocked this as well.

I was first out and acted as low man, with the remaining following. The exit point was calculated on time and distance from a known spot on the coast which was about fifteen kilometres away. There was a three-quarter moon giving plenty of light, and jump conditions were ideal. At ten thousand feet you could make out all the features of the jebel, but as you got lower, and entered the shadow of the earth, things got darker. Just before I deployed my chute I glimpsed someone spinning to my right, falling below me. The idea of me going low was to allow the others to follow me in, as I was the most experienced. We were smack on target and directly over two large holes dug in the ground the size of tennis courts that acted as water reservoirs when it rained.

We landed in a tight group but one man was missing. We split into two patrols to search for him: one took the high ground to the south and the other patrol to the north. After thirty minutes the other patrol reported they had found Rip, the missing man. He was the man I had seen spinning, forcing him to delay his opening till he regained stability. If he had been over the wadi he would have got away with it; unfortunately, he was over high ground, and just as his main was deploying he hit the mountainside.

There are no words that could relay our grief, and in respect for Rip we carried on as though he was still with us. He loved a laugh and would have seen the funny side of us all sat huddled looking at Fred sorting his kit out. Fred had a bad landing and had pitched forward onto his knees, tearing both legs of his trousers. One boot had a toecap missing, and he had a large graze on his nose. Fred's bergan had broken away when he lowered it and everything inside was smashed and flattened. One water bottle was squashed flat but didn't leak, and he said he couldn't get the top off. We said, "You will when you get thirsty." All the 40mm grenades he carried were flattened, and it's a tribute to British standards of safety that no rounds exploded. The only good grenade he had was the one in the weapon that he carried. Willie had a large tin of green beans with him which he shared out. I have no idea why he packed these but they went down well.

Rip carried the Bren Gun which I think was the cause of his instability. We all carried heavy loads which is fine if you are stable, but hard to control if you get in a spin. Whether a strap came undone or a poor exit was to blame, no one will ever know.

Small consolation is that Rip is not alone. A year later, Geordie, who thought he was the astronaut, had a tragic accident on the same DZ. I'm sure these two have plenty of brews together wondering why Willie carried a large tin of green beans in brine.

There was also a small hitch with the sea assault. The lads went in, silently surrounding the town at first light. When the light improved they arrested the Wali. He was asked if he was the wali of Bukra, which he denied vehemently. After much confusion they determined he was the Wali but the Wali of Batar, not Bukra. Someone had got the villages mixed up. A small geographical embarrassment of fifteen kilometres.

This was probably the only time in history that the British Government acted before anything happened; however, it was brewing up nicely down south.

Communist-inspired terrorists rebelled against the Sultan and engaged in an armed uprising in Dhofar, a mountainous region in Southern Oman. The lads were used to train loyal tribesmen (Firqats) to fight the enemy (Adoo). I was flown into an airstrip called White City, which was the first stronghold we had on the jebel. From here other positions were inserted and they were all supplied from White City. I was like the airport manager who administered the position.

Skyvans would land at first light full of jerrycans of water, which I distributed amongst the position. We had a Firqat, Gesh, Baluchis, and two squadrons of SAS. There was a village built of stone huts that was centuries old where the Firqat families lived. In all there were over a thousand people there.

The Gesh were the Sultan's own troops of regimental strength, and the Baluchis manned two twenty-five-pounder guns. This position was attacked every night by mortars, rockets and machine guns, so everyone had to be dug in. We lived in holes in the ground which resembled the First World War. Rats infested the position and I woke up several times with rats chewing on my beard, after the last remnants of curry that I had eaten that night. The locals slaughtered cattle just to the side of my trench and in the night wolves would come in and eat all the leftovers. To hear them howling and crunching thigh bones was dramatic and not the lullaby I needed to sleep.

One minute there were over a thousand troops on the position, but overnight all that were left was thirty Baluchis and five Gesh; the rest had been deployed to other parts of the jebel. I felt a little bit exposed. I had two lads with me and that was all. No way was I going to live in that hole any longer. I thought, if I'm going to die it will be with dignity above the ground. So I built a café made out of ammo boxes filled with sand and covered by a tent. This is where we slept, fed and entertained visitors.

From here we unloaded the Skyvans and positioned water for the choppers to come in and ferry it forward to the newly installed positions. From first light to midday it was hectic organising all the loads of water, ammunition and food. In the afternoon it was generally quiet. We made tea for everyone passing through White City, which was quite a few. I would take a wheelbarrow to the Gesh storeman and borrow a sack of sugar from him. A hundredweight sack only lasted a few days.

Since the big evacuation the nightly attacks fizzled out. The Adoo attacked the new positions which suited us. Two lads had a cup of tea while waiting for a chopper to take them forward to join their troop. They had been on a course and looked forward to some real soldiering. They got on the first available aircraft and I was still drinking the same brew when it returned with one of the lads stretchered out in the back. They had landed during a contact, and one of them was shot in the thigh before he could get to cover. The aircraft returned after the contact and picked him up; that's how quickly things happened.

I was missing a pair of boots. They were modified with a sewn-on extension and, being size elevens, would be easy to spot. The only way off the hill was through me and I observed everyone closely. One day I spotted a Baluchi stumbling down the strip like Charlie Chaplin. On closer inspection I saw that he was wearing my boots. I told him to contact his superior and come and see me. I heard nothing so I got on the radio and started threatening the Baluchi gun crew. After a minute the OC of D Sqn came up and said, "Do you mind keeping your problems till later? I'm trying to organise some gun support." I didn't realise the guns were being used and the lads were in the middle of a contact.

A little bit of luxury for me was that the Baluchis used to send me half a dozen chapattis first thing in the morning. They were very tasty and one or two were sufficient to eat with breakfast, depending on how hungry you were. The real luxury was using what was left as toilet paper. It gets a bit sore around these regions and a soft, warm chapatti was like Heaven with the gates shut.

I used a spray to keep the flies down and it was a heavy, oil-based solution that stung on contact. We had the brigadier, colonel and 2 I/C come for a visit, and when they were due to return to Salalah I lined them up and told them I had to spray them for health reasons. They had a signaller with them, but I left him out. I had the Tuans strip to the waist and drop their trousers. I sprayed them from head to toe and between their legs. The colonel asked me why the signaller was exempt from this and I told him it was for commissioned ranks only. I was a staff sergeant at the time and I could see my field marshal's baton slipping away. They walked very gingerly towards the chopper trying to walk and keep their thighs apart.

A cat took a liking to me so I started feeding her. She was always with kittens and I called her Spartacus. The locals lived in baits (stone houses) that were rat-infested, so I started trapping these and would feed them to the cat. I built a rat pit six feet long, three feet wide and four feet high, out of ammo boxes. All the rats I caught I put in here. When the cat was hungry she would help herself.

Jack was a small arms instructor who was attached to us, and came to White City to see how we operated. He had on a brand new vest and sat with me drinking a brew. There was always a breeze blowing which caused you to underestimate the strength of the sun. I told Jack this and he started on about being at Suez, was an old soldier, and had 'seen it all before' sort of attitude, and didn't like being told the obvious. Anyway, he asked me where the enemy was and I dramatically explained to him how we were surrounded and probably under surveillance all the time. I pointed to a rock and said, "From there to the bushy top tree lots of Adoo. From the bushy top tree to the rocky outcrop many Adoo," and went through 360 degrees pointing out features and enemy strengths.

Jack flew to a forward base the next morning still sporting his new, immaculate white vest that was still gleaming. I was always busy and soon forgot all about him. Two weeks later, I got a message from Amatol (a forward position): 'casevac to you'. When the chopper landed I saw a prone figure wearing a dirty, saggy vest with lips like Mick Jagger burnt crimson: it was Jack. He was badly sunburnt and couldn't move without agonising consequences. So much for the old Suez veteran. I treated his burns and fed him plenty of liquids, and started thinking of the best place to put him so he could be in the shade, get some rest and recover. It was always hectic in the tent where people would be tripping over him all the time; he needed isolation. I had a flash of inspiration: the rat pit. I could fit a camp bed in easily and Jack could sleep to his heart's content. I led him to his new accommodation and he looked at me with eyes full of gratitude. His new vest was now black and the armpits had stretched to his waist. He couldn't speak because of his swollen lips, but his eyes said it all. It was cool in the pit and I helped lower him gently onto the camp bed.

All the rats had hiding places in the bottom ammo boxes and must have wondered who their new neighbour was. Jack lay there with arms folded across his chest, a picture of tranquillity. What I hadn't taken into consideration was Spartacus. She would come regularly and grab a rat to feed her kittens. When she did this the rats would go in a frenzy trying to avoid this furry feline. Just as Jack was slipping into a much-needed sleep, Spartacus arrived and surveyed the scene from the top rim of ammo boxes. Sure enough, the rats went potty, swarming all over Jack, seeking out parts of his body for new hiding places. He lay there paralysed mumbling like old Blakey from *On the Buses*, "I hate you, Lofty."

After a few weeks on the hill two figures emerged asking for food. They were from D Sqn and somehow were left behind and forgotten. They had dug a trench that was so deep that they didn't come out of it much and were surprised to find that their squadron had all been redeployed. They had been working with the Gesh and that's where their squadron thought they still were. I was curious and went and looked at the trench they had constructed: it was more like a mine, it went on forever. They had a large communal area with a separate bed space at each end. It was all hewn out of solid rock. They were two Paddies and must have loved digging and dynamite. Danny had size thirteen feet and said to me as he was rejoining his squadron: "Lofty, if I get shot, push me over."

The 2 I/C was a regular visitor and would always stop for a brew. He still hadn't forgiven me for when he was giving a briefing before all the troops pulled out. I was friendly with all the pilots and I asked Low Level Grevell to make a low pass over Henry where he was briefing the lads. He was just over a small hump at the end of the strip, where he had all of his maps propped up on a Land Rover, and was in full swing when the sound of engines got louder and louder. Everyone looked towards the noise and a Skyvan emerged just feet above the Land Rover, scattering Henry one way and his maps the other. He leapt up, shaking a fist at the fleeing aircraft and shouting, "That's how you write aircraft off." Henry was a cracking bloke and I don't know of anyone who didn't like him.

He was wary of me because of all the stunts I pulled, and was still smarting from the spray I made him undergo. I was cleaning my weapon and had a large aluminium can of oil on the table. G10 rum started coming in the same containers and it was only a matter of opening the lid and sniffing to tell the difference. You couldn't mistake the smell of rum: it attacked the nostrils. Henry picked up the oil and asked if it was G10 rum as he was responsible for getting this issued. Before I could answer he took a swig. All the clues where there. I was cleaning a weapon, it was ten o'clock in the morning, and the can smelt of oil. Henry spit out what he could and through clenched teeth said, "You b.....ds: is this all the gratitude I get for getting you rum?" I hadn't done a thing and carried on pulling my weapon through.

It was a funny war, as people from the same village had joined different sides. A lot of these surrendered and were immediately signed on with the Firqat. One minute they were trying to kill you, the next minute they were on your side.

Jerrycans were the bane of my life. I had to send them all down the hill daily, otherwise the next day we would be short of water. One day I saw a camel loaded with full jerrycans of water heading out to the south. This was unusual because we had no troops in that direction. I got on to a Firqat enquiring where they were going with my cans, but the language barrier was put up. When they wanted something it was so easy to be understood, but when they didn't want to answer, questions fell on deaf ears. It was only when the camel was long gone that they told me it was for the Adoo. They had run out of water, so had come to their cousins for a resup. What a war!

Besides running the Firqat we ran a hearts and minds programme. This included tips on farming, looking after cattle, and drilling for water. We got a rig into White City and it started drilling, hoping to find water at about four hundred feet. This impressed the locals: it really would change their lives for the better.

Cattle were very important to the locals, and in many ways dictated how the war was run. The Firqats would only agree to do something if there was a chance of getting cattle. The Jebali were renowned for being argumentative, and when operations were being planned there were always lots of arguments and compromises to be made.

The Adoo actually outgunned us. Their 75mm recoilless gun outranged our 81mm mortars. To try and make up this difference, the lads poured petrol down the barrel and used more augmenting cartridges than was advised. This gave the extra range but put a dangerous load on the mortar. These had to be checked regularly, so they sent a guy out from the UK to test our mortars. On White City I had some large cardboard cylinders that aircraft rockets came in. What we did was substitute these with the actual mortar barrels. They stood ten feet high and fitted into the bipod nicely. The inspector couldn't believe his eyes and was too proud to inquire as to what they were. He used a jackknife to scrape the surface, gingerly looking around to see if anyone was watching. It took him some time before he realised he had been tangoed.

On my next trip to Storm (operational name for the Dhofar War) I was the SQMS, which was responsible for resupplying all of the jebel. This tied me up in base but I still managed to get out now and again. We lived in a tented camp at UAG (Ul A Gwarath) which was south of Salalah, and the first thing I did was to make four small, concrete bases into one large one. This was so we could have a place to play volleyball. Every night we played and I invited the lads on the jebel to make up a team and come and play when they could. We lost more men injured at volleyball than all the Adoo activity put together.

I slept in the stores, which had an electric supply. The luxury of a fan and a bedside lamp was priceless. I shared with the RQMS who was a great character and a good long-distance runner. Last thing at night we would have a brew and a slice of bread loaded with cheese and pickle. Me and Drag had been arguing over something stupid, and I made the brew and sarnie to make it up with him. He stood by the fan and opened his mouth to take a bite when I hit the fan with a tent peg. There were centuries of filth, crud, and dust on the fan cage and it came off in one big lump and completely enveloped Drag's head. He looked like something out of Quatermass. It filled his mouth, coated his sandwich and brew with a two-inch layer of dust, and profiled his head to look like an idol from Easter Island. He couldn't talk for ages and was getting crud out of his eyes for ages. I was not a big fan of his after this. He had only been with us a week and was getting over a nasty case of sunburn, which was partially my fault. When he arrived from the UK I went to the airport to pick him up. He had been here before so I thought he knew his way around. On the way back to UAG I stopped the open-topped Land Rover at the fort to book some ranges. It was lunchtime and I told Drag I would see him in the cookhouse, which was the other side of the fort. Drag was as bald as a badger and deaf as a plank. I booked the range and went through to the cookhouse and had lunch. There was no sign of Drag, so I thought he must have gone straight to the stores and had fallen asleep after his long journey. I was busy in the armoury when Drag came staggering around the corner two hours later. He had waited for me in the Land Rover and fallen asleep, exposing his head to the mercy of the sun which took no prisoners.

I was responsible for the cleanliness of the camp and every morning would go round the camp and pick up all the rubbish. There was a tip a few miles out in the desert where I took the rubbish. I took Sean my storeman with me, and to make a mundane task more exciting would soak the rubbish with petrol before driving slowly away with Sean on the tailgate pouring out petrol till the can was empty. We would then strike a match and watch the flames race over the ground and ignite the rubbish. 'Never play with fire and you won't get burnt' is a very sensible statement, one that I should have listened to. Like many times before, we tipped the rubbish, soaked it in petrol and drove slowly away, trailing petrol. The idea was to get as far as possible from the tip and watch the flames. This day we were only just clear of the tip when the flame started chasing us instead of the other way around. Unbeknown to us, the tip was smouldering from the day before, igniting the petrol prematurely. Sean shouted a warning and tried to throw the jerrycan away, but it hit the canopy and bounced back in. I knew something was wrong when Sean leapt over the front seat to join me in the front, then dived out of the passenger door before I could say anything. I felt the heat and was aware of the inferno behind me. All I could think of was accelerate which, luckily for me, worked. The can fell out of the back when I hit a bump at speed, but not before it left its mark blistering all the paintwork and breaking the glass on the lights. I have recalled several incidents concerning petrol, and you would think that I should have learnt my lesson by know, but there is more.

To deny certain areas to the Adoo, it was decided to burn all the grass that gave them cover. To do this we devised a plan to drop barrels of avtur into the wadis that would ignite on impact, from Skyvans. The only snag with this was getting the safety fuse to burn at a consistent rate so you could get maximum coverage on impact. The other major concern was to make sure the barrel would leave the aircraft when the fuse was lit. Manhandling fifty-gallon burmoils in the back of an aircraft being thrown around by turbulence is a tall order, but 'he who dares' and airborne initiative solved the problem. If the aircraft flew too low it would be vulnerable to small arms fire, and if too high, needed a long fuse. Because this fuse comes coiled up in a tin its natural tendency is to coil up, and the danger of it doing this is that it can take a shortcut across the coils and ignite the barrel too soon.

We had a couple of near disasters and I was glad when it was scrubbed. I knew the pilots were. We never used to tell them the whole story, we just told them to fly at a certain height and direction. I would have been more confident wearing a flameproof overall and a parachute, but had to make do with shorts and flip-flops. On RAF flights you cannot smoke or carry anything that's combustible in hand luggage; matches and lighters are confiscated. So there I am in the back of a Skyvan igniting barrels of avtur and heaving them out of the door.

Petrol not only is dangerous when ignited, but also can seriously damage your health if drunk. We had a couple of cases where the petrol jerrycan was mistaken for the water can. All water cans are black, and petrol cans green. This cannot be seen at night so it's important to keep them well separated. One lad took a swig and finished up in bed for two weeks on morphine; lucky he wasn't a smoker. We threatened to send him home strapped to the wing like a drop tank.

The cooks used No. 1 burners that ran on petrol. While they were cooking these would be red-hot. If the cook didn't fill them up regularly, they would run out halfway through cooking the meal. The cook would panic and try to fill the burner while it was still hot, because if the meal was late he would face the wrath of the lads. Just a little spillage would ignite the lot, and the poor old cook would become blistered, burnt and blackened. Those lads should have received danger pay.

Every evening we had a briefing that brought everyone up to date on what was happening on the jebel. It would be given by the ops officer and would start 'across the board in the last twenty-four hours'. A large map was displayed with all the locations marked. He would then go on to say that the Adoo were running short of sugar. This always tickled me as it implied that once they ran out of sugar, they would surrender. Five years later we were still told they were running out of sugar. But as we gradually retook the jebel, the amount of stores we recovered including sugar could have fed the world.

The drill at White City was always mentioned and it took eighteen months for them to hit water at eleven hundred feet. The odd cook got a mention on the state of his burns, and the winners of the volleyball competition were announced.

Up at the airfield there was a swimming pool where we spent a lot of our free time. We practised swimming underwater and had competitions to see who could do the most lengths. The morning after a farewell party I was record breaking in the pool and came up gasping for air just short of three lengths. I broke the surface inhaling deeply, surfacing in the corner where some reveller had been sick. It's not nice having a greasy ring of tomato skins around your neck and bacon rind up your nose. The taste of regurgitated food does nothing for the appetite and can seriously affect training.

We held all sorts of challenges. One was to drive a nail through a beer can underwater with a wooden mallet. We would throw all of these items in the deep end and the idea was to dive in, collect them, and holding the empty beer can on the bottom, drive a nail through it. It's the first time I have ever seen anyone scream under water. Jakey was doing this and hit his thumb with the mallet, forgetting where he was.

There was a Field Surgical Team on the airfield who worked miracles on the injured. To one side of this was a temporary morgue, and on the other side the back of the cookhouse. After a contact, the FST was busy and asked for volunteers to give blood and help out. A volunteer was told to put a body in the morgue. He asked directions and was told, "Outside to the right you will find the cold room." He followed directions but went to the back of the cookhouse and put the body bag in the kitchen's cold room amongst the spuds and onions. Story has it that a young chef opened it up thinking that they were delivering the vegetables in different packaging. This could cause anyone to become a vegetarian.

Back in the stores, Drag got a new chair that you can pivot around on and change the height of at the press of a lever. He forbade everyone to use it and would show off spinning around. Someone stole his chair and threw it in the static water tank. He searched high and low for it and finally saw it still afloat in the tank. It just goes to show:

NEW CHAIR SWIMS

CHAPTER THIRTEEN

TRAINING WING

Time waits for no man, and from being one of the youngest members of the regiment I was fast becoming one of the oldest. After many years in a Sabre Squadron it was time to move on to a training post. Training Wing was responsible for selection and training all members of the Regiment in the skills that they require.

My first stint was running the demolition cadre. This was a great job and entailed destroying everything from bridges to power stations. Most lads have a destructive streak in them and this was an opiate for the junky. I can't help breaking things: handles and knobs come off in my hands, chairs break underneath me, and handles come off teacups. Imagine how devastating I could be if I put my mind to it. Freezer handles and wardrobe doors are my speciality. All over the world these items are waiting for me to come along and touch them so they can fall off.

Two of us went to Heathrow to gain experience of a Jumbo Jet's (747) flight deck for anti-terrorist training. We were introduced to an instructor who took us into a flight simulator. He told us what a great bit of kit this was, and at thirty-four million pounds each, very expensive. My mate asked him if it was soldier-proof or had any weaknesses. The instructor said that thousands of pilots had used this simulator and to date nothing had broken. I sat down in the seat and lowered the armrest which came off in my hands. He couldn't believe it: his jaw hit the floor before the armrest.

So demolitions were right up my street and I had acquired a lot of experience from different courses and from different countries.

It's funny how people like watching explosions and want to take photographs. This is fine if you have a camera with a telephoto lens so you can stand well back and film in safety. Johnny only had a cheap camera and wanted to record the destruction of a concrete silo. We all took cover behind a wall while Johnny poked his camera around the corner, resting it on his right knee. I told him to snap on six and counted down, two, four six. I pressed the firing button, keeping well tucked in behind Johnny and saw the building distort as the charges went off. A mushroom cloud of dust and smoke formed in front of us, with a granite block emerging in what was like slow motion, heading towards us. The silo was still making its mind up either to drop or not, but the block hit Johnny on the knee, causing him to pirouette several times before he dropped gracefully to the floor. I had my arms on his shoulders and I felt the impact going through his body. It was just as well that he was a stocky lad with big legs, otherwise this could have been nasty. The swelling and bruising were enough to earn him the front seat of the vehicle for the return to camp.

When blowing stumps it's best to stay about a hundred metres away and look up. You have enough time to dodge all the debris thrown in the air which goes straight up and lands between 200 and 300 metres away. On one occasion the boss brought his wife and left her in my care to watch proceedings. I told her what to do but she panicked. When the stump was blown, a shower of mud, stones and wood was thrown into the air. She grabbed me and I had to take my eyes off the debris, and a big clod of mud hit me on the right shoulder. I thought I had been punched by Cassius Clay. I still get twinges in the shoulder to this day.... Stupid woman. She thought I was being heroic and protecting her, whereas I was being heroic and protecting her.

We used to mix our own chemicals and make explosive and incendiary devices. This was all done in an old air-raid shelter that was damp and had one unprotected light bulb dangling from the roof. Some of the stuff we mixed was sensitive and, looking back, I now realise how dangerous this was.

You had to keep an eye on the students as they all wanted to experiment to try and make the most devastating device. We would let them fire their devices on the range, giving them marks for performance. One lad made his mixture, which was a mild incendiary which burnt for a long time. When he fired it there was a big explosion and a blinding flash. This caught us all out: we were expecting a low, constant flame. Instead of being behind cover we stood and watched it burn. I accused him of not following the formula, but he insisted he had. Back at camp I watched him mixing an identical device. He had all the chemicals he needed which came in jars. One jar was in a cardboard carton packed in a coarse powder for protection. He thought this powder was the chemical and used this and not the ingredients of the jar that was at the bottom of the carton. I don't know what was in the powder, but it was good for removing eyebrows and moustaches when mixed with aluminium.

On one course we made an incendiary device that had to be baked in an oven for twenty-four hours. So we made it in the shape of a fish so we could use the oven in the cookhouse. We told the duff sergeant it was harmless, but in reality it could have destroyed the kitchen. We took it to the range and used it for our opening demonstration while waiting for the keys to the barrier that gave access to the range. The four-tonner was full of explosives and was parked on the road outside the demolition range; the driver had gone to the camp for a brew.

In theory you just had to scrape a small area on the surface of the fish and ignite it. This was a first for us and we didn't know what to expect. After half a box of matches were used there was still no sign of life; we even tried using sugar-chlorate, which will burn anything. One of the lads kicked it away in disgust where it finished up under the four-tonner and was forgotten.

We were all busy unloading the truck when an intense light similar to a welding torch lit up the underside of the truck. The dormant fish had come to life in a cascade of light and smoke. It started burning downwards, eating through the road surface. I jumped in the cab to move the truck but there were no keys. I got the lads to give us a push and got the truck rolling. Without the engine on there is no air pressure in the breaking system, so now I'm now gathering speed going down a hill in a runaway truck with no brakes full of explosives, unable to steer because the steering is locked. It was just another day in the life of a demo man.

The fish burnt for twenty minutes, burning a hole in the road three feet deep, the size of a manhole. Kitchen-sink explosives were good fun but not without their dangers. After a range day I asked Jimmy to sweep out the back of the truck. There were a lot of chemicals spilt with pieces of det cord and the remains of the haversack lunch that we hadn't eaten strewn all over the floor. Jimmy swept all of this rubbish into a pile and it exploded and burst into flames. It wasn't an explosion but rapid combustion, but enough to put Jimmy off. He threw down the broom and said, "You can sweep your own f…ing truck out."

There are different formulas for cutting steel, concrete and wood, which can be quite a mathematical challenge to work out. The lads are not renowned for their academic talents, so the general rule of thumb was P for plenty. I asked one student, "How many degrees in a circle?" and he answered, "It all depends how big the circle is." Trying to explain Pythagoras' Theorem to calculate diameters was like talking Greek. The only Pi most knew was meat pie from the NAAFI.

We had an old cement works with many buildings scattered over a large area that we could use as targets. Here we could experiment with different charges on a variety of walls made from different materials. The best way to destroy concrete is to drill it first and tamp the explosive in the holes. These have to be spaced at precise intervals to penetrate at least halfway through the intended target. By drilling down at 45 degrees it's easier drilling and easier to load up these holes. I left the lads preparing a large wall which had been drilled. We had plenty of explosives and a pile of sand for tamping. When I came back all the holes were filled, but the pile of sand had hardly decreased. It was a Friday and we all wanted to finish early, so we didn't hang around. I blew this wall and it vaporised. They had used the entire stock of explosive, filling the holes to the top, leaving little room for tamping. The resulting shock wave threatened a listed church two miles away, which the vicar claimed had dropped the stained-glass window an inch. It's a good job he wasn't praying at the time as he might have seen this as a sign. We called Fridays 'poets day': piss off early, tomorrow's Saturday.

You had to keep an eye on the lads and try to get through to them that the skill is to use the least amount of explosive as possible.

Another incident happened in Wales. A motorway was under construction outside Neath, and in its path was a weir across a small river. I met the engineer in charge and he took me across fields to reach the weir. This was a solid, reinforced concrete structure impregnated with pebbles. The best way of attacking this was to drill it, placing multiple charges all over it. The motorway was a good five miles away and the engineer said that we could use any size charges we wished, as we were miles from anywhere.

Three weeks had elapsed before I could go and blow the weir. I contacted the engineer to set up a time and date. He explained that he was on holiday and his second in command would look after us. All I needed onsite was a drill and compressor. Olly and I set off early and met this guy as planned and started drilling. It was hard-going because of the pebbles and we were making no impression on the weir. So we decided to scrub the drilling and lay large charges using riverbed stones for tamping.

We laid six large charges, covering them in stone, and hooked them up to the firing wire. I had forgotten to put the large reel on the truck and only had a 100-metre firing wire to use. As long as you are not directly in line of the blast and have some sort of cover, it is alright to be fairly close. I surveyed the tranquil scene of gurgling water tumbling over the weir, with birds singing in the trees and bushes that hugged the river banks, which cut through lush pastures where cows were grazing contentedly: all very

Constable. My biggest worry was the cows, but we herded them to safety in another field. Up the river was a steel bridge, but it was a good eight hundred metres away. I sent Olly and the young engineer up towards the bridge while I lay under a bank with the firing device. I was a bit too close for comfort so I curled up in a ball. I shouted, "Fire in the hole," and blew the charges. Day turned to night as tons of stone went flying in all directions, blocking out the daylight, and a mass of water emptied the stream bed as it erupted up into the stratosphere before returning to earth minutes later. This deluge helped settle the dust, but it took ages before I could see anything. I heard stones bouncing off the steelwork of the bridge and my head felt like a bell tower with all the bells ringing at once. When the dust cleared, the landscape looked like Iwo Jima. The trees had branches missing and the bushes were stripped of foliage. There was no sign of any living creatures, and the stream had altered its course. The air was full of very fine dust, and I was trying unsuccessfully to clear my ears. Olly and the engineer turned up covered in dust and looking very pale. I heard the sound of powerful engines, and minutes later a possession of earth-movers and -scrapers came from the direction of the bridge, crossing the stream at speed, before disappearing in the distance. I was just going to inspect the weir when a Land Rover pulled up and a guy with a yellow safety helmet on leapt out of the truck, demanding to know who was in charge. I pointed towards the young engineer and told Olly to wind up the firing cable. The new arrival was a big man and I was glad that we only had the short cable. He grabbed our friend by the throat, nearly lifting him off his feet. "Who gave you permission to use explosive on this contract?!" he shouted. "See you down the café, George," I interrupted before the pair of us legged it to the café. Apparently, in the three-week interval between seeing the weir at first and blowing it, the motorway construction had reached the bridge. They were laying the road when, without warning, the sky was full of debris, showering them with fragments of stone, forcing all the plant and heavy machinery to a standstill.

As we were leaving I spotted an old crow that had got injured in the blast. He was hobbling around the ground and the old saying of 'stone the crows' came to mind.

I promised to tell the story of the hunt: here goes. There was a guy called Blaster Bates who made a living giving after-dinner speeches about his demolition exploits. He tells a story about a hunt, and whether he got this from me, I don't know, but this actually happened to me. On our range at Eastnor Castle we prepared some railway line for demolition. The course had laid their charges and retired to the safety area. I stayed behind to do a final check and was about to join them when I heard 'toot a toot' and the local hunt appeared. There were about twenty horses with men and women resplendent in their hunting livery in the saddle. I couldn't believe it. We had signs out warning people to stay clear and this lot had chosen to ignore them. I said, "Didn't you see the signs?" and an older moustached gentleman replied, "Tell him it's a public footpath." He didn't speak directly at me, but went through a minion who rode beside him. This got my back up even more. "Tell him that if you had come a minute later you would all be in the abattoir," I said. This caused a few giggles from the women and I felt like detonating the charges but felt sorry for the horses.

The pack leader said to his flunkey, "Ask him if he's seen any hounds." This cracked me up. Evidently they had became separated from the dogs who probably had more sense and made a detour. They rode off looking down on this wild man who was now sweating profusely. An older woman, bringing up the rear, stopped and inquired what all the fuss was about. I explained it all to her, remarking how much her horse was sweating. She said, "Sonny, if you had spent the last two hours between my thighs you would be sweating also." I was already lathered and not about to take up her offer.

A suitcase was left unattended on the side of the road in camp and I was summoned by the ops officer. He asked me how much damage it would cause if it was filled with explosives. I told him that the whole camp would be at risk, and without more ado, he told me to evacuate the camp and call the bomb squad. With that, he disappeared, leaving me in quite a predicament. Trying to evacuate the camp would be a nightmare; no one would take it seriously. Secondly, the bomb squad would want more details. Remember this is in the early days before terrorism became all the fashion and a regular occurrence. I went back to the suitcase and, using my knife, cut a hole in the side. I was just pulling out a well-worn pair of underpants when a voice said, "What are you doing with my case?" He was a lad from the MT going on leave and was unaware of all the fuss his case had generated. I slung his pants at him and reported back to the ops officer, telling him that everything was fine. He threatened to sack me. I stood there amazed, thinking maybe I was on *Candid Camera*. He ranted on about me disobeying his instructions of not clearing the camp or calling the bomb squad, and to make matters worse, my mate was standing behind him pulling faces and grinning. This set me off, especially when he threatened to sack me; I couldn't control myself any longer. It reminded me of before I joined the army and being sacked was routine, but now this twat who didn't have the balls to close the camp was blaming me. This bloke had a funny-shaped ear, and if you focused on this and kept on staring at it, he completely went to pieces. In the end I just turned my back on him and walked away, ignoring all his hysterical threats that followed. We never did see eye-to-eye or in his case eye-to-ear. I had obviously made the right call, otherwise I wouldn't be around to finish the book.

Ireland was becoming a problem, so security had to be stepped up. Our camp was open with a public right of way straight through the centre. People from the council estate used the camp as a shortcut. There were many false alarms and, being the demo man, I was always summoned. I was called to the officers' mess where a briefcase was found in the foyer. I asked everyone present if it was theirs, but got no joy. So out came the trusty knife again, and I cut through the top. I managed to get a chequebook out and when I read the name I saw it belonged to the second in command. He had come in and left it in the foyer before going to the toilet. The mess caterer had assured me that he had asked everyone present, so I left to him to explain to the 2 I/C why his beloved briefcase had an extra vent. He was of a nervous disposition and constantly found suspicious articles that he reported regularly. I would think twice now before doing anything to a suspicious object. But in those days we didn't have the facilities we have now to deal with them.

The mail clerk used to screen all the incoming mail, and parcels or anything suspicious would be placed in the centre of the parade ground. One day he had a parcel that wasn't expected with the wrong amount of stamps on, so it was placed on the square and the bomb squad alerted. Everyone was looking through windows observing it from afar, but no one physically guarded it or prevented access to it. My mate Fred, unaware of all the drama, cut across the square and saw the parcel. He thought it was Christmas and picked it up and threw it in the back of his car. He went home and was just about to tear off the wrapper when the bomb squad and half the ops room descended on him.

In the classroom I was demonstrating potassium permanganate and glycerine. By mixing pott. perm. with sugar, and putting a small drop of glycerine on it, it eventually bursts into flames. The course all had their mixtures in front of them eagerly awaiting ignition. We had a new padre posted in and he was making a visit to everyone, and happened to come in the classroom as we were doing this. As I offered my hand to shake his, a mixture went off just by his hand, and as I pointed out different students the chemicals in front of them, completely by luck, flared up. He thought I was some sort of witch doctor. He had heard all about the Regiment and said we didn't need a padre as much as a missionary. He was really impressed by our fire making and never did know how we had done it. It was a dangerous practice to light fires in the classroom but we thought nothing of it, even though a basha had been burnt down previously. This happened when an instructor was giving a lecture on arson. He had the fire triangle drawn on the blackboard stating that heat, fuel and air are required for combustion, when the classroom door started blistering and smoke filtered in through the door surrounds. The students thought this was an excellent training aid and all part of the lesson.

In the passage the lads were making improvised shaped charges. Wine bottles are used for this because they have a built-in cone at the base. The bottle has to be cut in half, and this is done by wrapping string around the bottle and soaking it in petrol. When this is lit by holding it upright, the top of the bottle is heated. When hot enough, by plunging the neck in cold water the bottle cuts cleanly where the string is wrapped.

Someone knocked over the jerrycan of petrol which was ignited by a piece of burning string. Someone else emptied the fire bucket over the flames which only spread them further. The end result was that the whole building was destroyed. When the fire brigade came they initially attacked the flames with gusto, but when they found out that the demolition display was mainly live stuff they retreated. Next door to the demo display was a survival display, and out through the windows came burning mannequins and blazing stuffed animals.

My next stint on training wing was as the survival instructor. Survival training was about as popular as a fart in a spacesuit. Survival was all about going hungry and living off the land while evading a hunter force who, if they captured you, gave you a hard time.

My first task was to redo the interest room. This entailed making models and display boards. I took my son to work with me as my wife was pregnant with our fourth child, driving her blood pressure through the roof. So to give her a rest, I took Dave to work with me. Imagine a big, hairy-arsed paratrooper going to work armed with potty, nappies and titty bottles.

To keep him quiet while I was working, I fed him some survival chocolate. This was a vitamin-enriched chocolate that was carried in lifeboats. It was old, wartime issue but it did the trick: Dave loved it. It did have one side effect, however. Dave didn't pass a motion for a fortnight. I was working away doing some intricate drawing and was overjoyed when an unmistakable smell attacked my nostrils. I looked in the potty and was disappointed to see it empty. I couldn't have been mistaken so I looked further. Dave sat on top of the desk gazing at me with a tear in his eye. Alongside him was a big, black, steaming object that looked like a piece of submarine cable. It was the biggest turd I have ever seen, no wonder he had a tear in his eye. For the uninitiated, submarine cable is five inches in diameter and covered with a black, tarry cloth. I was trying to think of a way of incorporating this specimen in my display.

We only ran two main courses a year, each of three weeks' duration. The first week was all instruction on survival techniques. Knowing what you can and can't eat, ways of finding water, navigation without map or compass, obstacle crossing like rivers, fences and walls, and lock picking. The second week was on evasion and resistance to interrogation. How to evade tracker dogs, navigate across country without leaving any sign, was also taught. The third week was a realistic exercise where everything that was taught was put into practice, ending with the dreaded interrogation phase.

A medic called Fred used to do the water lecture and his party piece was to urinate in a glass, treat it, then drink it in front of the class. What he did was use two identical glasses, one which was filled with weak orange juice, the other with his urine. He would put a sterilising tablet in the glass that he had topped up, and place it behind a screen. He would leave it for a few minutes while he went on about the dangers of drinking urine, then produce the glass with orange juice in and stir this before swigging it down. Well, I couldn't resist swapping glasses while he was distracted. He would swallow half the specimen before he realised the switch. The next time I just used to pretend to change the glasses, but leave them where he had placed them. He would outsmart himself and take the wrong one. His face was a picture when he realised his mistake. When he got used to this, I would mix both samples together and would catch him out nearly every time. Through clenched teeth he would utter, "You bar- glug glug -stard."

We had many first-class lecturers teaching in the first week. One of these was a mycologist named Jill. She had a great personality and really got the blokes' attention. When she started her lecture she was a little nervous and would always turn to me for support. Her voice would falter and she would say, "Lofty and I collected all these specimens in the woods yesterday, didn't we, Lofty?" I would say, "Yes, Jill." In front of her was a heap of fungi of all different shapes and sizes. She would carry on saying things like, "We got these boletus from one field, didn't we, Lofty?" I would answer, "Yes, Jill." Then she went on to say, "Last night, me and Lofty went foraging and Lofty came back with puffballs, didn't you, Lofty?" Well, the course erupted. She didn't realise what she had said, but the course did. I thought they don't need to know about that. There was a large fungi called phallus impudicus and it looked like the name implied, a big dick. When she picked this up and started waving it about it always got the same response: a hundred and twenty soldiers, sailors, airmen and Marines would start fantasising, slumping down in their seats, and when she said it had a funny smell, it brought the house down. The common name for this fungi is stinkhorn.

Lock picking was a very popular subject and was covered by a father-and-son team who came from London. They were hilarious, leaving us wondering what side of the law were they on. It was a good double act holding everyone's attention. After this lecture we had to be especially vigilant, since if things were not secured, they would disappear. Desk locks were easy pickings and storerooms, cupboards and lockers were opened with ease. All of a sudden there was a shortage of stationery as this store was always being broken into. We taught the course they had to be scroungers and never to return home without something that they didn't leave with. We paid the penalty for this and tried to leave nothing lying around.

Distinguished high-ranking officers would lecture on their wartime experiences, and it was my job to make sure they had everything they needed. The wives' club was next to the blue room where all of our lectures took place. A general was explaining how he escaped from Colditz and knocked the jug of drinking water over, so I shot out to get him a replacement. In the wives' club was the thrift shop where all the wives brought in things that they didn't need and were sold off cheap. The only thing I could get that would hold water was a baby's bottle. I filled this and took it back to blue room and the general paused in mid-sentence when he saw me. I offered him the bottle saying, "With or without teat, sir?"

The final exercise started on Sunday when the course was assembled and individually searched. We encouraged them to make escape kits and hide them on their person. They were stripped off and we searched them from head to toe, looking in every crease, crack and cranny. Appetite for Sunday dinner was severely curtailed after looking up a hundred-odd backsides. The Marines were always the most ambitious, secreting many items up their jacksies. I pulled a compass, map and watch from one sailor, and he said it was just as well his missus wasn't on the course as she could have got through with his motorbike. One Marine had a Rolex watch taped to his penis. I asked him, "Got the time on you, cock?" If they made a good attempt at procuring items we would let them keep them. Any money we found was confiscated. This went in a kitty that was used for the end-of-course party.

The students could keep their pants, vest, socks and boots, and were issued a BD jacket and trousers with overcoat. This old-style battledress was made of wool and was warm when wet. The reason it kept you warm was you never stopped scratching.

We used to have 'specials' for people we didn't like. If he was a tall man we would give him the smallest size. We would cut off all the fly buttons and the bottom of the trousers. We had an Aussie who knew it all, so he qualified for a special. We cut one arm off the jacket and one leg off the trousers. He complained but we told him to stop whingeing and get on the truck. "You're not Trooping the Colour, sport." Each man was issued an escape compass and sketch map.

They were transported to a holding cage where a stool-pigeon would tell them of an escape plan and the location of first RV. When it was dark we would drive them to the exercise area where we had a prearranged ambush planned which allowed the prisoners to escape. On one course I took a friend's Stafford Bull Terrier called Trampus with me in the lead truck that I was driving. He sat on the passenger's seat enjoying every mile. When we hit the ambush site, rockets and thunderflashes went off which scared Trampus. He jumped down through my legs so I couldn't reach the brake pedal. The road was blocked by a Land Rover which I ran straight into. It was a realistic start to the exercise.

We taught the lads well, as there were always complaints from inhabitants in the exercise area. Milk and papers disappeared off doorsteps, chickens went missing, and from one farm some piglets went AWOL. All of these complaints were followed up, and we tried to encourage the locals to report anything suspicious and report strangers. But they never did; they always helped the underdogs. They gave the students lifts and fed them; everything was fair game to the students, the cardinal rule was 'don't get caught'. Washing was taken from clothes lines, and coats from barns and outhouses.

At one address a woman complained that two German officers had knocked on the door at midnight demanding to be fed. I obviously thought that this would be two of our lads impersonating Germans. But when I questioned everyone it turned out to be the only two Germans on the course. They claimed this is what they did in Germany: not very subtle, no wonder they lost the war.

Every time we did the dog evasion lessons I would finish up taking a student to casualty. Either the police or a special army unit would come with their dogs and demonstrate their efficiency. We would pad up a student, putting a large padded arm on him, then he would attempt to outrun the dog. We would give them a short start before releasing the dog. The idea was to offer the padded arm when the dog got close and let him bite this and take down the student. This sounds easy enough and quite straightforward, but fear and pressure put demands on the body and all common sense goes out of the window. Students have turned the wrong way offering the unpadded arm, but it's all the same to the dog: they take what's offered. Sometimes the pad dropped off, and seeing the student trying to run with both arms high in the air is hilarious. Eventually the arms get tired and as soon as one is lowered the dog takes it. The dogs loved it and got more enthusiastic as the day wore on. Their bites always required two to three stitches, which led to me having my own bench in the casualty department for being such a frequent visitor.

One day a police van arrived with a dog in the back and the policeman said, "Whatever you do, keep away from this dog, it's deadly". As he said this while undoing the cage, his hand went near the dog which bit through the mesh, fastening its teeth between the copper's thumb and forefinger. The copper looked down, saw the blood, and fainted. What chance have I got when the handler is still feeding the dog and is flat out on the ground? The solution is, get your mate to do it. Whenever you find yourself in a tight situation, use a mate. If I'm walking down the road with my mate and get attacked by a dog, I tell my mate to run for it and I stand still. The animal will always chase the runner.

If I'm walking down the road with my mate and get confronted by a gang of yobs, I tell my mate to stand still and I run for it. He gets beaten up; it's definitely easier to survive with a mate. If you ever share a room with your mate and they snore, the best policy is, just before you go to sleep, kiss them full on the lips; they won't sleep a wink. If they kiss you back, you won't sleep a wink. Back to the police dog.

I shouted for my mate and between us we managed to close the cage door, forcing the dog to let go of his master. The copper came round, and before I took him to casualty he gave his dog a good thrashing. This reminded me: never bite the hand that feeds you.

A Marine fled from a pursuing dog and jumped in the river. The dog just bided its time, following the Marine as he drifted downstream, trotting along the river bank. The pad on his arm became waterlogged, getting heavier and heavier, eventually forcing him to come ashore. The dog nipped him on the buttocks for all the extra work, then fastened on his arm as usual. There was no escape from these cunning canines.

During the final week all the students were eventually captured and held in an interrogation centre. They would be isolated and kept in stress positions. I had to make sure this was not overdone, as soldiers become sadistic and cross the line between giving the prisoners a hard time and outright torture. After a long, softening-up period, each student would be interrogated. The interrogators were despicable bastards whom we despised. They would compare notes on how they abused, insulted and intimidated the prisoner. What makes a man want to be an interrogator? It's like who wants to be a politician? I suppose someone has to do it. I haven't mentioned that a year previously, I had to attend a Tactical Questioning Course and got an A grading.

They would infer that you were queer, your mother was a slut, and your girlfriend or wife was on the game. Just like a normal night's discussion in the Tavern really. I always remembered the first time I was caught on exercise and interrogated. It was in Denmark just before Christmas, and it was freezing. It was a relief to be taken for interrogation as this was conducted inside and it helped to pass the time. You could only give your number, rank and name and to any other questions, "I cannot answer that question, sir."

You couldn't say yes or no, because in training this was enough to fail the course if you did. Being held for thirty-six hours, of which twenty-four could be spent being interrogated, was a long time and you know how time drags when you're enjoying yourself. This was the first time in my life when I fell asleep standing up. I fell into barbed wire coils and lay there comfortably before the guards hauled me upright again. They eventually handcuffed me to a hot water pipe which was like Heaven with the gates shut.

My mate was caught and when he was strip-searched it revealed that he was wearingtights. This was a common practice as they kept the legs warm, but Buddha had frillypanties sewn into his. The interrogator had a field day exhibiting Buddha on the table wearing pantyhose.

Every time we held an interrogation exercise a psychiatrist had to be present. On the NATO course the army's chief psychiatrist would be in attendance. If that man was sane, I'm glad to say I'm nuts. He was peculiar and so unpredictable that he put everyone on edge. When he arrived for a briefing he would warmly introduce himself to everyone in the room, then, in the next breath, tell everyone to clear off and leave him alone. He was a sandwich short of a picnic, definitely a candidate for the funny farm. On occasion, other shrinks would come, and when they greeted each other, one would say to the other, "You're alright, how am I?"

Navy pilots hated this course and tried everything to avoid it. But it was part of their training and they couldn't go operational without passing. It cost millions to train these guys and they knew that they wouldn't be sacked if they got caught cheating. They used every ruse in the book. They would find out where the final exercise was taking place through their contacts who flew the hunter force. They would pre-book a hotel room in the area or get a girlfriend to pick them up from a prearranged RV. We were wise to this and thwarted them when possible. It got so bad that their headman came to see why so many of his pilots were failing the course. It was my duty to accompany him and introduce him to the course. My old mate Dolly was running the course and he asked me to fix up a special demonstration for the Chief. In the woods at Eastnor Castle I had one of the lads called George dressed in rabbit skins, sitting in front of his survival shelter, gnawing on a bone. Dolly asked me to find a plant with red berries on and transplant it near to the shelter so we could hide a bottle of red wine under it; so when I fed the chief on a variety of survival foods, he could have a swig of wine. Later he changed this for a white-berried plant so we could produce white wine. I was getting fed up with all these changes, and when he asked me did I know what juniper looked like, I had to tell him to leave it to me, I would make the visitor welcome my way. I got his drift: juniper is used in gin. On the actual demo the chief arrived with his entourage, following Dolly to the camp. We had a good fire blazing and when they arrived me and George stood to attention and blew a bosun's pipe. I then pulled on a piece of para cord and a bottle of rum descended from the branches of an overhanging tree, with a large note attached, that said, "Hello, sailor." Dolly nearly died but the admiral loved it. He sat down and tucked into hedgehog, frogs and fungi.

He wanted to take part in an interrogation to see what caused a lot of his men to fail this stage of the course. He was treated like everyone else but kept on calling for an umpire. He had lost all track of time and he started hallucinating. Every time he complained to an umpire it was about how long he was left and how ill-treated he was. All that he had actually done was to be left for less than two hours in the holding pen standing facing a wall with his arms up. He did only a short stint with an interrogator before he demanded to be released. At the debrief he came out with all sorts of things like "I don't know how you replaced my fingernails that you pulled out or the teeth you extracted." In his mind all these things had happened, but in reality he was less than three hours in the centre. This was why we had to have shrinks present to handle such cases: he was a classic case that they could easily diagnose and treat. Like the man wearing nothing but cling film pants, the psycho said, "I can clearly see you're nuts."

My final tour on Training Wing was a few years later as sergeant major responsible for selection, but before this there is a twist. Remember it's the early bird that catches the worm, but the second mouse gets the cheese.

Sometimes the lowest hand wins at poker so:

TWO PAIRS WINS

CHAPTER FOURTEEN

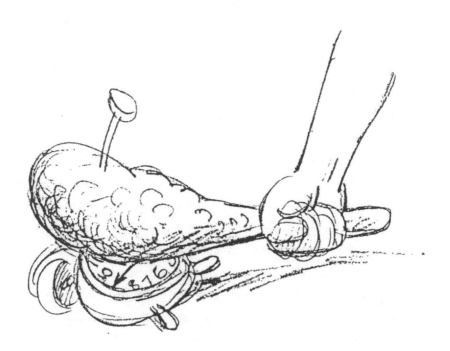

A SLIGHT SETBACK

At the age of thirty-three I was a substantive WO2. This meant I could only be demoted by a court martial. My field marshal's baton was about to be well and truly broken with the pieces inserted somewhere delicate.

I took over B Squadron and worked with the OC who was nicknamed 'The Duke', and who was a magnificent man. He was very popular with the men but not so popular with the hierarchy who, in honesty, were a little bit jealous of the relationship he had with his men. He was laid back and in between ops he would be in his office filling in his football pools, while I would be next door in the Squadron office with an engine on my desk grinding in valves. I bought a rally car and fancied my chances rallying. It was a Lotus Cortina and I was overhauling the engine. He would come in the office and ask for a file, and while I was searching for it, I would get him busy with the grinding paste.

B Squadron under The Duke had initiated the campaign in Dhofar, and The Duke recognised what a great effort the lads had put in and treated them like the men they really were. He didn't call for unnecessary parades allowing the lads to rest. I remember when I first met The Duke when B Sqn were finishing their tour on Storm and handing over to A Sqn. He had pulled all of his men off the hill and said, "My men have had enough and they are not going out again." I thought about this and realised that a lesser man would have deployed his men. It took a very brave man to make this decision, and the men really appreciated this. I admired The Duke and we got on famously: the morale of the squadron was tremendous.

On Operation Storm we were about to finish a four-month tour when an incident at Mirbat occurred. This has been well documented as one of the biggest battles that the SAS had been involved in. At five in the morning The Duke told me to get him down to the airport as quickly as possible. I used to do this route every day, practising my rally techniques. There was a checkpoint that acted like a chicane which I could take nearly flat out. On this particular morning I excelled myself and when we arrived at the airport The Duke said to me, "You will kill yourself in one of these one day." It was a Land Rover he was referring to. It's ironic that months later The Duke was killed in a Land Rover in France when he was 2 I/C of the Regiment.

He conducted the battle from the airfield, skilfully managing the relieving troops, coordinating the jets and all the airlifts.

We had many casualties on this trip and the key phrase amongst the men was 'beat the clock'. We had a clock tower in Hereford where every fatality was named. No one wanted their name on the clock, hence the phrase.

While The Duke was second in command he summoned me to his office where he instructed me to form a counter-hijack team. Half the squadron was involved in training, so I now had a job for the remainder of the squadron. It was a top job, one from which I derived a great deal of pleasure. This was the team that was to put the SAS firmly in the spotlight and overnight become world-famous. It was the hostage rescue incident at Princes Gate that I refer to. I have met people all over the world who have claimed to have been on this mission. The number of people who have told me they were on the balcony of the Embassy are so numerous that the balcony would have to have been as big as the stage in the Sydney Opera House.

All the harmony and great morale of the Sqn were about to be torn asunder. Along came a new guy who had two major flaws amongst a million minor ones. He was ignorant enough to believe he knew the system and arrogant enough to want to change it. I think he must have had a personality transplant, no one liked him. Lovely bloke! We fell out when I lost my temper and the chance of a field marshal's baton went with it.

I wasn't perfect and trod on thin ice. I was an easy target for criticism. But I told him with all of my faults I was SAS, as I knew nothing else; I was a result of the system. I told him he was not SAS and never would be. I think I upset him when I told him I could do his job but he couldn't do mine.

Anyway, to cut a long story short, I resigned from the Sqn and went to the TA (Territorial Army), the part-timers.

I have seven children, and when asked why I have so many I tell them that every time I got promoted I had a child. In theory this would have made me a field marshal but I did get busted.

Under The Duke we would parade in open order and when he appeared I would call the Sqn to attention. I would say, "Right, lads, look in tricky movement, atten….shun." The Duke would stand them at ease, say what he had to and leave me to dismiss the parade. Drill was never our strong point and was to be avoided at all costs. The new guy wanted a Trooping the Colour-like ceremony. He wanted a right-hand marker to march out so many paces and halt. Then the Sqn in individual troops would form up on the marker. Then, given an open order command from me, the OC and I could inspect the troops. I knew the pitfalls of this and how the lads would react: it was fraught with danger.

Arthur volunteered to be the right-hand marker and I should have known better to have allowed him to do this. He claimed he had done this in his parent Regiment where he was a drill pig. He looked the part and no one else was going to volunteer, so I was stuck with Arthur who was renowned for his antics. When the OC appeared I called, "Right-hand marker," and Arthur just stood there. I repeated the order and Arthur said, "Do you mean me, Lofty? I'm sorry, do it again." This got the lads chuckling, and when, after I repeated the command, Arthur kept on marching instead of halting after eighteen paces, the ranks started swaying uncontrollably. Arthur would have kept on going if I hadn't have called him back.

Witnessing all of this was the new OC who was getting more uptight by the minute. He was pacing up and down while this fiasco from *Dad's Army* was taking place. When the Sqn marched to form up on Arthur they tripped, pushed and pulled each other. The scene was more like a football crowd going to the game than Britain's finest forming up for inspection.

Finally the Sqn was ready for inspection. The front rank was easy enough to do, but it was a bit of a squeeze doing the second and third ranks as I had forgotten to give an 'open order'. I started between the ranks a smart man with a millboard and pen. I emerged the other end with my epaulettes pulled open, my shirt hanging out, my trousers pulled out of my puttees, and no pen. The lads had groped, pushed and poked me: I looked like a human cannon ball who had missed the safety net. Even the paper was missing off my millboard.

The new guy was fuming. He gave a pep talk on what he had seen and threatened everyone with extra drill. He finished up by remarking on the standard of saluting, saying, "If you're not sure, salute anyway." When I dismissed the parade several guys in tracksuits saluted immaculately, even giving a wiggle wiggle. He exploded, saying, "Never salute when not wearing a beret," and the lads ran away swearing under their breaths, muttering, "You can't please some people." He ordered me to stay behind and threatened to send me on a drill course. This was the one where everyone borrowed the one set of bulled-up boots. I told him that I would die first.

Talking about saluting, we had guys who came straight from the TA and had never done drill in their lives. One lad, while he was on his Para course, was pulled up by an officer whom he had ignored. "Don't you know how to salute?" demanded the officer, and Geoff answered, "No." He wasn't lying but could have made a gesture. I mean, saluting is not that hard. Because of this, anyone coming from the TA in future was sent to Para Depot to do basic training.

Geoff also got into trouble when he took his dog with him on a course. The dog attacked the adjutant's horse who was in foal at the time, and bit the horse's legs. It was reported that the dog did:

CHEW MARES LIMBS

CHAPTER FIFTEEN

TA

After my fallout with the man, I reverted to staff sergeant and was posted to the TA for my sins. This was arse about face as you got posted to the TA before getting promoted, not the other way round. Most lads were reluctant to do these postings, but once they were introduced to it and settled in, loved it. I was no exception. The TA lads were magnificent and I had a great time with them. It was all part of the promotional process. Senior NCOs became Permanent Staff Instructors (PSIs) and had to do a tour with the part-timers to get made up. They got experience in administration and training that you couldn't get in Hereford. I was posted to London where the lads were known as the Chelsea Chindits. They came from all walks of life. Lawyers, dockers, taxi drivers, accountants, salesmen and farmers: every profession was represented. There were some amazing characters amongst them. We had a Lord, a Harley Street specialist and an eminent surgeon, to name just a few. However, they all had one thing in common and that was the desire to be first-class soldiers. They were so keen and eager to learn, it was a pleasure to train them.

One of the biggest characters I met was Alphie. They say that first impressions are important and stay with you; in Alphie's case they were stencilled in my brain. He was ex-Long Range Desert Group and was the paymaster. Alphie knew everyone, and no matter where we went, he always bumped into someone he knew. He also bumped into many objects and was accident-prone. He took us out regularly and was great company; there was never a dull moment with Alphie around.

When Jimmy was posted to us from Hereford, I mentioned Alphie, telling him, "He probably knows you already." Jimmy was adamant, saying, "No way, I've never heard of him." True to form, Alphie comes across and introduces himself. "Where you from, Jimmy?" he inquired. "Teddington," was the answer. Alphie pondered this for several minutes before asking

Jimmy if he had a brother called Buddy. Jimmy was flabbergasted. Alfie had taken Buddy through his basic training when he was a national serviceman in the Queen's Regiment.

Alphie was accident-prone and always sported a limp or had a plaster or bandage somewhere on his body. In between meeting people he would hurt himself. We once went on an exercise to Denmark. Alphie started out fit and strong but by the end was a physical wreck. As he climbed into the minibus, a bloke in the back kicked the sliding door shut: this trapped Alphie's head in the door. The catch embedded itself in his cheek, leaving him with a big cut and a bruised ear to go with it. He never complained and would occasionally burst into song. He was fiddling with the seat mechanism and got his finger trapped. This removed a large area of skin that had to be bandaged. It didn't end there. When we arrived at the docks, Alphie, in his haste to make the toilets, tripped over the trailing seat belt and twisted his ankle. As he fell he also grazed his nose, adding to his list of ailments. He was a medical salesman's dream. He used more dressings and medication than any other man I know.

He got aboard the ship without further injuries but placed his hand where a seagull had deposited three days' worth of regurgitated fish. It was wiped on his jacket and soaked into his bandage.

In the lounge Alphie started mixing and got talking to the first mate who, it turns out, knew his uncle. From him he got the captain's name which Alphie kept repeating, saying, "I wonder if he's related to…" and his brain went into overdrive. He sent him a note and the captain joined us for a drink. They discovered they had a mutual friend whom Alphie had served with in the war, but the icing on the cake was that Alphie had met the King of Denmark who had launched this ship a few years previously. I told you he knew everyone.

His party piece was on the piano where he would sing "Lili Marleen".

He would start in German, change to Italian, and finish in English. All the ship joined in: Alphie was a star. I can hear him now. He always started any conversation, "My dear chap".

At the end of the exercise, Alphie organised a party, which he was good at, having a lifetime of experience. He invited everyone, including the local mayor. He had a top table where all the dignitaries were seated, that was covered with freshly laundered bedsheets. He had made a rum punch that was in a bucket that was decorated with tinfoil. This was placed in front of Alfie so he could top up everyone's glass. He stood up to make a speech and staggered slightly because of his injured ankle. One of the lads helped him up and pulled the chair out of the way to give Alfie some room. Alfie was in full swing, praising everyone for their support. He got everyone to raise their glasses for a toast before sitting down amidst a raucous round of applause. The only trouble was the chair was missing and the raconteur disappeared under the table, taking the tablecloth and rum punch with him.

Another stalwart character was Rocky. He had served many monarchs – the first one was probably Canute. He was part of the furniture in Chelsea and looked after the vehicles. His claims to fame are many, but one was his curries. After every drill night when the militia paraded, Rocky would produce a curry. To call it hot was an understatement. After one of his gastronomical delights no one dared pass wind for days just in case, and everyone had a backside that looked like a Japanese sunset. Someone claimed that after one of his curries, he went to the toilet, and his piles went down for a drink. To prepare for one of Rockie's curries you put the toilet roll in the fridge.

After one boozy night, Rocky staggers down to the Tube station which is deserted apart from a big black fella. Rocky had to obey the call of nature when the Guinness and curry started fermenting. The only place he could find open was a cleaner's cupboard. He did what he had to and used the cleaner's overalls to wipe himself.

All was well until a large Irish charlady arrived and headed for the cupboard to start her daily chores. Rocky quick as a flash stopped her and said he had just seen the black fella coming out of her cupboard. She seemed a little confused till she opened the door. When she saw and smelt Rockie's deposit, she grabbed a broom and brandished it under the unfortunate bystander's nose, threatening him with his life. "Don't come over here with your filthy habits," she shouted, as Rocky slipped deeper into the shadows.

I took over B Sqn which was stationed in Dulwich not more than five miles from Downham. It was like a homecoming, and initially I stayed with my parents. This was ideal, but it did have certain drawbacks. My mother was deaf and every time I said something she would give me something to eat. I would say, "Nice day, Ma," and she would reply, "What's that, son? A bacon sandwich, it won't take me long," and I would be fed. My dad hadn't lost the art of arguing so we continued where we left off.

One of the perks of being with the militia was we received lodging money. We had to provide our own accommodation and feed ourselves. Being typical soldiers we would sleep anywhere to save a few bob. The CO warned everyone about sleeping in the drill hall, but this was often convenient on a drill night. I had a cosy room in the drill hall and after a hard night's training, five-a-side football and a few pints, the room was most welcoming.

We had an annual inspection and the CO came early to ensure everything was shipshape. He had heard about my room, threatening me with torture if I didn't clear it out. It was on the second floor of the drill hall with the door locked, so he decided to get a ladder to check. He climbed up, entering through a window; he need not have bothered as it was like Mother Hubbard's cupboard. One of the lads who was picking up litter spotted the ladder and removed it. The top brass were arriving and we were getting ready for the parade, but there was no sign of the CO. Loud banging was heard, and cries of "Let me out of here!" I had to go and unlock the door to release him. He was only just in time to welcome the top sheds of London district, but still found time to accuse me of skullduggery. Can you believe that I would do anything like that?

Charlie was the caretaker, and his wife Margaret used to make a fuss of us. She was always making tea and sandwiches. The drill hall was on a very busy road that linked Catford with Brixton. Margaret had a fear of crossing the road, so if I saw her I would go and help her across. One day I spotted her carrying two bags of shopping, so I went to give her a hand. No one ever stopped: you had to cross one lane at a time and keep your eyes open. I took the shopping and Margaret took my arm, and I led her across the road. We negotiated the first lane without difficulty, getting to the centre unscathed. This was the easy bit, as the road was on a steep hill, but now we had to cross where the cars were really motoring downhill. The traffic was unrelenting and I waited a long time for a break. I spotted a slight lull and went for it. I dragged Margaret with me, but she hesitated and let go of my arm. I finished up on the pavement, and Margaret was stranded in the middle of the road. She was not far off becoming hysterical and I shouted to her to keep calm. I couldn't get back to her and she was frozen with fear. It seemed ages before I could get to her, and we finished crossing back to where we started. She lit a fag and calmed down before we made a second attempt. Exactly the same thing happened. We could have died of starvation for the length of time we spent there. If it wasn't for a funeral cortège coming along, we would probably still be there.

All the TA lads had to pass selection to become Sqn members. This was slightly modified from the regular selection but just as challenging. These lads would put a weekend in where they tabbed all over the mountains, and on Monday had to report to work. Not only that, but many had families to support as well. If I worked the weekend I didn't surface till Tuesday and would spend most of the week doing nothing, sometimes without a break.

Eric was a postman, and was so keen to pass selection he carried bricks in his mailbag. All the people on his round in Brixton had mail with brick dust on it. He used to run up and down the stairs of the buildings and run back to the depot when he finished. Eric was the fastest postman south of the river.

Eric was a one-off. He was five foot six and played the bagpipes. Here was a cockney kid playing Irish tunes on Scottish bagpipes. He practised in the drill hall and drove everyone mad, but when he learnt to play he was in constant demand. Although Margaret and Charlie were due for retirement, it was Eric's practising that helped make their minds up. When they retired, Eric became the caretaker.

I was best man at the wedding. His wife was shorter than Eric and all of their friends and relatives were less than five foot six; even the vicar was a short arse. At the reception it was like being amongst a tribe of pygmies. I towered above them all and felt like Gulliver.

I have already stated that it's only the Brits that admit to not liking parachuting. The TA lads were no exception. On one occasion to give them that extra incentive to leap out of the door, Eric was strapped on the tailgate of a C-130, playing his pipes. After a few bars of "Danny Boy", even the pilot wanted to jump. This was a special jump marking the anniversary of a wartime operation.

It was a homecoming for me and I found myself surrounded by the same kind of mates I had as a kid. They were a great bunch and I was invited to weddings, parties and even funerals.

Apart from drill night, that was once a week and the odd weekend, I had a lot of time on my hands. The biggest chore of the week was the pay sheets. Each sheet held twenty-five names and I had fifty-one blokes to pay. To open a pay sheet, reams of information had to be entered with regimental codes, type of training, duration etc. One night, I got hold of a guy called Wilson and told him I had to sack him. He was a good lad and was very upset. "Why?" he demanded to know. "I haven't missed a drill night or a working weekend all year." I told him that I had to open up a new pay sheet just for him. It was only a wind-up and I told him I'd sack someone else. He was relieved when we got a guy called Yates on the books. If they attended so many drill nights and working weekends, they would qualify for an annual bounty. This was a large sum of money, and when it was paid out the celebrations lasted a week or longer.

A typical drill night would start with calling the roll. Then the lads would attend any training that was organised. They did a lot of this themselves depending on the subject, or I would get someone in; occasionally I would lecture. I would interview new recruits and see that everything was running smoothly. After training we would play football. It became very competitive and we had lots of injuries. After an hour or so we would all retire to the bar and discuss next week's training. It was all very sociable and good fun. I held the keys to the bar so could open it at any time.

There were a lot of tradesmen in the Sqn so we gave them permission to rebuild the bar. They built a base out of natural stone with a hardwood top. They got the timber cheap because it was split in several places, but after they glued it together you couldn't see the joins. The stonework was set off with fancy pointing, and after a fresh coat of paint on the walls, the bar looked stunning.

I didn't have a lot to do and was always looking for work. Imagine my surprise when they gave me an assistant. Archie had fallen foul of someone in Hereford, so they posted him to the TA. Now there are two of us without a lot to do.

Jimmy was up in Chelsea and I visited him daily. One day I was waiting for him in his office when the phone rang, so I answered it. The caller asked for Jimmy who was down the pub. I said, "Hello, who's calling?" and a posh voice said, "Who's that?" I said, "I asked first: who's that?" After much spluttering the voice said, "Major ….who's that?" I replied, "Jimmy B," and hung up. I forgot all about this and was making a brew when Jimmy turned up. As I was pouring the tea, the training major burst through the doorway, out of breath after running from his office across the road, and up the stairs. He confronted Jimmy with sweat steaming off his head. "You diminutive little bastard," he shouts at Jimmy. "How dare you hang up on me." Jimmy was taken aback, completely unaware of the situation, replying spontaneously, "You f…… queer c…" The major, already on the point of collapse, couldn't believe his ears and looked around for moral support. I exited stage right and left the two at it.

To say things like this do not affect your career is a lie. These people write our annual confidential reports. There is a hidden code in these reports that is not obvious to the reader. If it says "not recommended for the TA", it means you have a drink problem. If "not recommended for a boys' unit", it infers you are gay. Often you get described as "life and soul of the troop". This means you're loud and a troublemaker.

It was easy to be led astray in London: we had time on our hands and watering holes everywhere. One day I needed a lift back to Dulwich when my vehicle was in for a service. Jimmy volunteered but only after we had a few beers in Chelsea. After a few beers and a few more beers, we arrived in Dulwich, just in time for a few more beers before they closed. It was late-afternoon by now and I had the keys to our bar in my pocket. So we retired to the bar and got down to some serious drinking. A few other lads joined us and we finished up on the Guinness. It was a drill night and the lads started assembling. Jimmy wanted an arm wrestle and challenged me. I was behind the bar and he was on the other side. I gripped the bar and took Jimmy's arm and heaved. There was an almighty crack and Jimmy came through the bar in a shower of rocks and splintering wood. The whole bar collapsed and the wooden top was shattered. Jimmy lay on top of me and we were both buried under a heap of rocks…. Oops, bloody cowboy builders.

It was Jimmy's birthday so Alfie took a group of us to a nightclub where he was a celebrity and naturally he knew the owner. He was a Greek whom Alfie had met in the war when he was liberating Greece. At two o'clock in the morning he ordered a birthday cake and, lo and behold, one appears resplendent with candles. Jimmy is all choked up and when we started singing "Happy Birthday", tears formed in his eyes. To defuse the situation I picked the cake up and balanced it in the palm of my hand. I said to all present, "This is an old SAS custom," and thrust the cake in Jimmy's face. I was expecting the cake to crumble and disintegrate but it remained unchanged. The candleholders bent and the flames extinguished on his skin, but the cake was still intact. This thrust had knocked Jim off-balance, causing him to fall into the arms of the waiter who was a bit light on his feet. Jim's nose had spread and his face was branded by the candles and scratched by the holders. I was examining the cake for cracks while Jim regained his balance, fighting off the advances of the waiter. He was just about to erupt when I attempted for the second time to spread the cake in his face. This time, I gave it a few turns as well, but the cake never distorted. You can't have your cake and eat it.

Jim's face looked the worse for wear: he had little blisters and scratches where the candles had branded him. His nose took the brunt of the attack and looked like a blind cobbler's thumb. The cake was probably left over from Christmas and we were now in August. Alfie calmed everyone down by singing "Lili Marleen". He had a change of headgear that matched the language he was singing in. One verse a German helmet, the next an Alpine feathered hat; he brought the house down. When he finished he called the waiter over. "My dear chap, give the lads a drink."

Jimmy disappeared but I tracked him down to a broom cupboard where he was sitting fast asleep on a mop bucket. He was easy to track as he left a trail of body fluids behind him.

We would walk back to Chelsea early morning, cutting across Berkeley Square, where Alfie, without fail, would sing, "A Nightingale Sang in Berkeley Square". There was a dog stall on the embankment where we had breakfast. It was always swimming in grease, but went down a treat. Sometimes it came up a treat, but someone had to feed the pigeons.

My drill night was Wednesday and I would spend all of the next day recovering, doing all the paperwork and admin. Depending on what was happening at the weekend I would get away if possible. The RSM grabbed me one day and accused me of going home early on Friday. His wife worked in the office as a secretary and we always shared a laugh. Pete, the RSM, had a squeaky voice, and had phoned around on Friday afternoon, but got no answer. He was laying into me and I caught his wife's eye: she was trying to remain serious but couldn't suppress a big smile that filled her face. "You went home early on Friday morning," he insisted. Well, I can't lie, so after denying this several times, I made out to cry, and grabbed his missus sobbing on her shoulder, complaining that he was shouting at me. It brought the office to a standstill. Pete was dumbfounded as his missus gives me a cuddle and starts consoling me, patting me on the back and saying, "There, there." I told him that I got away early on Thursday morning and promised him I wouldn't do it again. Well, not this week.

Just before one Christmas leave all the PSIs were invited around to the CO's house for drinks. We officially didn't break up till the next day and was warned that we would all return to work till lunchtime. The party was at Putney and we all got stuck into the booze. Alfie demonstrated how to open wine bottles without a corkscrew. He would bang the base of the bottle on the wall hoping that the generated gas would blow off the cork. All he succeeded in doing was to smash the bottle. He tried three times before admitting defeat. We can all open bottles like that, but the carpet suffers. The house was full of bottles of duty-free liquor that had been collected over the years. There were unusual and rare spirits that we had to sample. Some of the whiskeys and brandies were limited editions. After a hectic session we all went our merry ways. I woke up in Hereford in my car by the racecourse. Archie had driven back and couldn't wake me, so he just left me. No wonder he was posted to the TA. The only bloke who tried to get back to work was a REME lad. He fell asleep on the Circle line and woke up with a pocket full of tickets that he bought off the ticket inspectors every time he completed a circuit. After leave, the CO fined Ernie but said nothing to the rest of us: at least he tried to get back.

Champagne Terry was the OC of the Sqn and he volunteered me for a Round London Marathon. His name describes his lifestyle and he was one of life's best. The marathon involved driving an inflatable boat down the Thames and transferring to the Regent's Canal, overnighting in Little Venice, then back the next day to the Thames and on to the finish. I had a TA lad as a partner with a backup crew to transport us. Because it involved an overnight stay, I had to fix up some accommodation. I wanted this in Central London and asked around the lads. We had a Harley Street specialist on the books and he allowed us to use his pad at the back of his practice. I went to have a look at this in the week, and was shown around and given a key to the back door. This was at the end of a long passage and up a short flight of stairs. I went out the back and counted the lamp-posts from the corner to the flat as a reference, and had a good look around so I could recognise everything on the Saturday.

On race day we got away to a good start and arrived at the first obstacle without any problems. The tide was slack so we had a good climb up to the canal. We had worked out a routine where one man would climb up and fix a rope. Then we would pull up the engine, boat and fuel separately, reassembling when we got onto the canal. It was a good twenty-foot climb and a mass of bodies were clambering up the lock gates at the same time. We avoided these, making up a lot of time.

We were in and out of the boat on the canal negotiating the locks: guess who fell in? Joe Soap was getting aboard when my mate gave the engine a big handful and I missed the boat and disappeared over the stern. It was about two hours from the finish so we carried on; I pretended not to be cold. We got picked up by our crew and I was keen to get some dry clothes on. We drove round the back of Harley Street and I counted the lamp-posts to find our flat, then tried the key in the lock. It went in easily enough but wouldn't turn. I was getting fed up now and needed warmth. I gave the door a little nudge which sprung the Yale lock, so we carried all the gear inside. We climbed a few stairs and everything seemed different. I couldn't remember seeing this large ornament full of dried flowers or the portrait of the naked woman on the wall. Surely I would have remembered her. I went back outside and tried the flat next door and, sure enough, the key opened the door. I went back, telling the lads about the slight mishap, shouting at the same time, "Is there anybody there?" but got no answer. So I locked the door and beat a hasty retreat.

I was thrilled when I found out that my bag with my dry kit in was soaked in petrol. Numbnuts the driver had put a jerrycan on top of my bag and hadn't secured the top properly. We had a look around the flat and found under every cushion a pair of knickers: this place had seen a lot of action. We wanted to go out and have a meal but the driver didn't have any civvies with him. The quack who owned the place was well over six feet tall, and the driver was just over five. There was a pinstriped suit hanging up and we got the driver to wear it. He had to roll up the sleeves and legs, which made him look like Herman Munster. Although the nearest pub was miles away, we never stopped laughing. I smelt like a petrol pump, and Herman kept threatening to set light to me if I didn't stop laughing at him. We got some strange looks when we entered the pub.

I had a driver called Ron attached to the Sqn, who looked a bit like Quasimodo. He was out of work so I used him as my personal chauffeur. He would sit hunched behind the wheel looking like a gargoyle, and was the only bloke I knew who frightened taxi drivers, not by his looks but by his driving. He was fast and aggressive, just the qualities needed to drive in London.

We had a demonstration coming up at Motspur Park and Ron wanted to get involved, pleading to be allowed to carry the GPMG (general-purpose machine gun). I told him that he didn't have enough experience, and his pixie-like jaw dropped. He had a girlfriend named Jane who was twice his size and whom he wanted to impress, so he badgered me all week to carry the GPMG. Finally I relented and warned him if he messed up I would spoil his looks. He quivered with delight, looking like a little puppy looking at his master with adoring eyes.

The demonstration was for the BBC who held an open day every year for all its employees. The plan was for a Pink Panther to come roaring into the arena with all guns blazing, attacking the bad guys who were defending a fort. This was erected by the props department made out of wood and canvas supported on scaffolding on the inside. It looked very authentic and was strong enough so the lads could scale the walls. There was a sandbag emplacement in front of the door, and this is where I intended placing Ron with his Jimpy.

We had a static display where the kids could climb over all the kit and ask the lads any questions. Ron, with Jane by his side, was proudly exhibiting his Jimpy to an audience of excited kids while she was preparing his kit for the demo.

I retired to the beer tent where the OC promised to buy me a pint of real ale. He told me it was strong stuff and had to be treated with respect. I barely got the froth off the top of the glass when a loud explosion took place. At first I thought, 'This is really strong beer,' but then realised it was a thunderflash. The demo didn't start for another twenty minutes, so I was a little concerned. I went to investigate, looking towards the source of the explosion. I saw Jane with a GPMG under one arm and poor little Ron under the other.

He had been preparing his thunderflashes, stripping off the outer cover to expose the striker. In his haste he accidentally ignited the pyrotechnic and didn't know what to do with it, so he just hung onto it. They are quite powerful and he was lucky that only his thumb was dislocated.

Jane carried the Jimpy better than her partner, so I let her hang onto it while I supported Ron. We went to the first aid tent where they recommended I take him to hospital. Now Ron had told me weeks earlier that he had a wish to be in hospital. This is so unusual and probably a cry for help. He just wanted to lie in bed and be waited on. I found this very strange and something to be avoided. I told Ron that I could reduce his thumb, having done it a few times on the rugby field. He reluctantly gave me his hand and fainted. So Ron got his wish and finished up in the Woolwich where they kept him in.

While this was going on, the attack started and just as the lads got halfway up the fort, the whole structure burst into flames. The canvas was set alight by a stray spark and quickly spread. The lads, being good soldiers, went for cover and found the beer tent where they waited for fresh instructions. The OC was busy taking Ron to the hospital and I was trying to wrestle the Jimpy out of Jane's hands; they had a long wait.

One of the lads had a toy factory in North London and let us use it as a target for a demolition exercise. We had two patrols who were to attack the target at separate times. The first patrol made enough noise to awaken the dead, and triggered off the perimeter lights. I was inside monitoring their progress. They laid their charges and left. A neighbour was alerted and phoned the police, who arrived just as the next patrol was entering. This patrol did everything right but became a victim of circumstances. There's little justice in the world: the noisy patrol got away and the good guys got arrested. It was difficult explaining to the police why we wanted to blow up a toy factory, and they never saw the funny side of it.

A guy called Tootsie fell in a river on his way to the final RV. He went to a launderette and stripped off, covering himself in a blanket. He put all of his kit in a tumble dryer and started cleaning his weapon. This was in West Ham and no one took a blind bit of notice. Through the glass door his boots were seen going round and round followed by his maps, clothes and belt gear. It was probably a daily occurrence in West Ham: it didn't raise an eyebrow.

Keeping an eye on the kit was a full-time job. Recruits would get issued with a full scale of clothing and equipment, which some used for work or camping holidays and you would never see them again. Tracing them and recovering kit was a headache, so we exploited any means to make up deficiencies.

One lad had a tragic accident while on holiday abroad. I said to the OC, "No wonder the lad drowned, he was wearing two parkas, had a pair of binos around his neck, with three blank-firing attachments in his pockets." The OC didn't get it at first and asked what he was doing with blank firing attachments on holiday.

We were always desperately looking for recruits as we were never up to full strength. Various recruiting drives were tried and the latest one was to put on a demonstration stand at the Royal Tournament at Earls Court. Alphie was put in charge of this project and told to behave himself and get plenty of recruits.

This coincided with Jimmy going to the Palace to receive an award for gallantry. I had planned a party over at Dulwich, inviting all of our families and friends to celebrate Jimmy's achievement.

I went on a recce with Alfie and the first person we met whom Alfie knew was a barman. This was a private bar for the performers, not the public. The barman vowed to stay open as long as Alfie requested – obviously he didn't know Alfie too well. There were six of us in total to look where we were performing, and where to site our stand, leaving Alfie at the bar to cement relationships.

We stayed and watched the afternoon performance which was based on the First World War. Alfie knew all the songs and conducted the choir that was made up of the six of us with a few mates we had made on the day.

After the show, the lads carried on the movement and Alfie spirited them away to one of his clubs. I went home to my parents' place where Jimmy and his family were staying. The plan was for my parents to look after Jimmy's kids while he went to the palace with his missus. I had to go to Earls Court, and we would all meet up in the drill hall at Dulwich for a party that evening.

We were up at sparrows in the morning, arriving at Chelsea at sevenish. Jimmy and Eileen went to collect his mother, leaving us to have a cup of tea and allowing for me to show my dad around the barracks. Being an ex-military man, he took great interest in all the paraphernalia that hung on the walls.

His concentration was interrupted by a figure crawling on all fours trying to get up the marble staircase. My dad offered the prostrate figure a hand. "You alright, mate?" he inquired. "My dear chap, I'm tickety-boo," replied Alfie.

He had just returned from one of his evening escapades. "Be with you soon, Pop," he added, straightened himself up with exaggerated motions, and marched off with a list to starboard.

Four more figures came lurching in supporting each other, singing four different songs. They found difficulty in negotiating the different floor surfaces. They slid and slipped on the tiles, just about managing to stay upright. As they got the hang of this, they came to the carpet. This caused them to stumble and pitch forward. Eventually they mastered it, but then had the parquet flooring to contend with. One pace forward two back was the norm. This was our recruiting team: we were in for a good day.

Alfie reappears in his captain's uniform sporting three rows of decorations. His powers of recovery are amazing, and he greeted my parents like long-lost friends. My dad, not renowned for his diplomacy, said, "You better get that jacket off, son, before anyone sees you." He couldn't believe that Alfie really was a captain and thought he was skylarking.

Another two figures came staggering in, walking in zombie-like fashion to the showers. They were unaware of anyone present.

My mother, who was busy looking after Jimmy's two kids, was bewildered by these goings-on. She just stood there in amazement.

Alfie soon got everything organised. He looked as fresh as a daisy compared to the other lads, who looked as if they had been shipwrecked. We parted company, with us going to Earls Court, and my parents to the palace.

Our stand was shabby in comparison to the others around us. We tried to jazz it up by borrowing stuff off the other exhibitors. They were not aware of their generosity and we certainly were not going to tell them.

The Royal Signals had the best display, their stand was decorated to look like a jungle scene. They had camouflaged nets hanging everywhere with vegetation intertwined. To crown it off, they had a stuffed crocodile lying by a fountain of running water. The only running water on our stand was the lads going to the toilet.

Alfie went to his mate, the barman, to ensure the beer hadn't gone off, and based himself at a table in the corner. The barman didn't like drinking alone and loved his long-lost friend. So at nine in the morning we could get a drink, which was just as well, as it is very thirsty work recruiting.

On our stand we had a selection of weapons, medical kit, parachutes and climbing gear. To the side was a Pink Panther, and on the opposite side, a Gemini inflatable boat. Each one of us were dressed differently, representing different theatres and skills. We had a free-faller, climber and frogman, a jungle warrior, desert rat and Arctic warfare specialist. All dressed up and nowhere to go, we had an hour to kill before the doors were open to the public, so we retired to the bar for a liquid breakfast and to brief Alfie.

Our stall became the most popular one, with hundreds of kids and parents climbing over the vehicles, stripping down the weapons, and being entertained by six lunatics in fancy dress. We offered free holidays packed with adventure and worldwide travel with all expenses paid by the Queen. It was hard work protecting the kit, and we caught one youngster nearly at the door wearing a gas mask and carrying an Armalite. We were thankful when the matinee started so we could relax.

Alfie was in top form and conducted the choir involving everyone present. We attracted many followers which created a carnival atmosphere. Alfie pointed out that the only thing our stand was missing was a crocodile. I knew where this conversation was heading and I said, "I wonder where we could get one of those from." He gave me a knowing look that I understood only too well.

It was an informal request but, like a good soldier, I obeyed orders without question, and also without common sense. I marched to the Signals' display stand, brushed away the exotic foliage, picked up the croc and marched away with it under my arm.

I didn't think I was too conspicuous, but it's difficult not to draw attention to yourself when you are six feet four, carrying a twelve-foot reptile under one arm, and dressed for Arctic warfare. This was the start to a string of events that led to twenty charges being raised against us by London District.

I put the croc on Alfie's table and the next song sung was "See you later, alligator". Everyone was in high spirits except one warrant officer from the Signals who had come to recover his reptile. He got off on the wrong foot, demanding to know who had stolen his crocodile. Everyone said, "What crocodile?" He said if it wasn't replaced within two minutes heads would roll. "My dear chap, have a beer," offered Alfie, but this was declined and misery guts marched away.

Five minutes later a young bespectacled lieutenant appears with a nervous stutter. "Can wwwee have our crcr croc back please?" "What's your name, son?" Alfie asks. "Lt Lewis," was the answer. "No, what's your first name?" He answered, "Simon." "Well, Simon, what would you like to drink?" Simon relaxed and had a beer and we all got introduced. He told us that they had hired the amphibian, which cost a lot of money. Alfie, for the crack, had summoned the duff sgt to come to the table with his carving knives and bread. He sharpened a knife on a steel with professional ease and sized up the croc, pretending to carve it up. "What do you want, breast or tail?" he inquired. Simon went pear-shaped. "You can't eat it, it's stuffed." He leapt up with arms spread to protect his pet. We all sat there with pieces of bread in outstretched arms. "'Course you can eat it, we are survival-trained," someone said. "Make it snappy," said another.

The croc was on loan from the Natural History Museum, and a large deposit had to be made to ensure it arrived back in good condition. By now, Simon couldn't care less and said, "Cut the b'rd up. I'll have a sarnie as well."

Simon stayed with us for the rest of the day, and was the only recruit we managed to acquire. He got that drunk that I had to hide him in our support van which was parked behind our stand.

We had to get ready for the next performance which we aimed to eclipse, pushing the exciting levels to extreme, forcing me to answer the call of nature. I was on my way to the toilet just as the finale was about to begin to end the matinee show. A bugler stood opposite the big double doors to the arena, doing his lip exercises. He was to go in and play the last post when the doors opened. I couldn't resist it: I took the bugle off him. He pleaded with me to give it back and every time he came towards me, I moved back further from the doors. He was torn between staying by the doors so he wouldn't miss his cue, and retrieving his instrument, but without the bugle was snookered. I gave it back to him just as the doors opened. I remembered how touching this scene was yesterday: it was the highlight of the show. His first couple of notes were shaky, but he soon settled down.

By now we were all in top form. The diver was dancing with a girl wearing his flippers, and another girl was wearing parachutes doing the hokey-cokey. I was asked about the climbing rope, so I obliged the young lady by tying her up. I wound the rope around her from head to toe so she finished up looking like an Egyptian mummy. She couldn't move a muscle, so I propped her up against the pinkie and forgot about her. The medic was offering cosmetic surgery and free abortions. Springs and working parts were flying out of weapons as they were demonstrated to a keen audience. Jungle Jim was flashing his parang asking anyone if they needed circumcising. Taff was announcing, "Come and see the drunken officer," and leading people to see Simon flat out in the van.

It was pandemonium from the moment we started to the time we finished. Alfie was invited by the organisers of the tournament for afternoon tea. Each of the services was represented by a senior officer. I was unaware of this and sent Nobby to find him, telling him to bring him back regardless. Nobby did exactly this: he found out where Alfie was and barged into the room unannounced. Just as the squadron leader was pouring tea from a bone china teapot, Nobby said, "Get your arse back to the stand, Alfie, Lofty wants a break." With diplomacy like this it is no wonder we lost an empire.

The military police happened to checkout some toilets and became suspicious of a locked cubicle with snoring noises coming from it. They investigated further by looking over the top, discovering our frogman fast asleep on the khazi. They banged on the door which annoyed Bill, who threatened to punch their heads.

The Honourable Artillery Company had a 25-pounder gun on show, and every time I looked in their direction, someone was cleaning the gun. It gleamed under the overhead lighting. During a break, two of us went over to the gun and started talking to the gunners. They were very stand-offish and didn't like us touching their gun. It was the same type that had saved the day at Mirbat, so we had more than a passing interest in it. When they refused to let my mate sit on the seat and operate the elevating wheel, I made my mind up: we would hijack this piece at closing time.

The evening session got underway, so now it was time for us to pack up. The girl I had tied up was released and she was still very excited. I found out her name was Sue Blair from Gravesend. Someone from London District gave Alfie a key, so he could lock up the display cubicle, threatening him with dire consequences if he forgot or lost the key. Alfie did both: another black mark against us.

I hitched up the 25-pounder behind the pinky and they set off for Chelsea. They were stopped at the gate where they tried to convince the orderly officer that they were going to Hyde Park to fire a twenty-one-gun salute in honour of Jim's decoration. Their cunning ploy was exposed, forcing them to unhitch the gun. It was pouring with rain and the gun was left outside, the security only too pleased to see the back of them. I drove the minibus which still had Simon flat out in the back. Alfie sat in the front, still in good voice, giving it, "Goodbye-ee, goodbye-ee, wipe the little tear from your eye-ee," an old wartime favourite. I was just going past the big double arena doors as the Royal Naval gun crew came running out. It's a good job that they are tough lads, as we collided, scattering matelots everywhere.

The evening in Dulwich was a big success, finishing off an exciting day nicely. There were many thick heads in the morning, but mine quickly cleared when Alfie phoned telling me the CO wanted to see us urgently.

The CO was not very pleased with our recruiting efforts. All we had managed was to poach Simon from the Signals. On his desk he had a list of twenty complaints against us. Alfie and I were standing to attention, listening to the complaints that the colonel was reading out. When he got to the London District guy complaining about leaving his cubicle open, Alfie could stand it no longer. "That bloke hated us from the start, he despises the regiment," blurted Alfie. This won the CO's sympathy and Alfie knew exactly what buttons to push, saying how we were victimised from the start.

The colonel, being the great bloke he was, said he would look into this further; we never heard another word about it.

The woman, whom we had tied up with the climbing rope, wrote a letter to the colonel, saying how much she had enjoyed herself. She sang our praises and said she had never enjoyed herself so much. There is no accounting for taste; it's just as well we are all different.

I was tied up with the administration of our annual exercise in Germany. The lads were deployed where they dug hides and lived underground for two weeks. This was a job that few men could do: it was worse than living in a submarine.

If you could imagine the smell created by six sweaty bodies, fourteen days of stored-up faeces and urine, and stale air impregnated by curry and cigarettes, you get some idea of the conditions they endured. A sewerman would think twice before working in these conditions. When I went round to open these hides I was knocked back by the odours escaping. The lads loved it and blinked like pit ponies coming up to the surface, gulping in lungfuls of fresh air.

There was always a fearsome party at the end of such exercises, and on a scale of one to ten, the one we had after this exercise was rated fifteen. It started normally enough with everyone catching up on the local gossip and comparing notes on how they had done. Every patrol had a story to tell: some were hilarious. The venue was a German canteen which was about to become Madison Square Garden.

Champagne Terry started the ball rolling when he started comparing the TA lads with the regulars. A lively discussion took place, but us PSIs didn't bite. It was all good-natured stuff, but the demon drink does funny things and changes people's characters.

We started playing touch rugby and the touches got heavier and heavier. The scrums were well contested and the odd punch was thrown. I finished up underneath a pile of bodies and was caught on the nose by a full-thrown punch. I grabbed the offending arm and traced the limb to Len. Right, I thought, two can play at that game and the punches started flying. I was on my back, and the floor did nothing to help my head absorb the punches. Mysteriously all the bodies disappeared, leaving Len sat on my chest with a victorious look in his eyes.

There is good and bad everywhere and B Sqn was no exception. There was a group we called the Mafia, who were a law unto themselves. The leader was a typical East Ender with a big mouth: he flossed with a skipping rope. As they all poured out of the door leaving Len on top, I heard big mouth say, "Another PSI bites the dust." Early on in the night, I heard him boasting about how they had got rid of three previous permanent staff.

He said, "We've already got rid of a cripple, nigger and a Rupert." I must apologise for writing these words. I hate them, but they are genuine quotes, and hopefully justify my actions. The cripple he referred to was a lad who was never posted to the TA. He was wounded on Storm and was recuperating in Dulwich, which was handy for the Woolwich hospital where he was an outpatient. The nigger he mentioned was a Fijian who is one of the nicest men I have ever met. He was posted to the Sqn but wouldn't play their stupid games, and went back to Hereford. The Rupert was a training major who dismissed an ex-B Sqn OC from the ranges for being incompetent. On the Monday morning this turd complained and the training major was sacked. This guy had a lot of influence in the City and that's how powerful the Mafia was. A lot of senior officers had investments with him.

So when they thought they were winning, they left the scene, but I don't like biting the dust. No way was I going to come second-best, and I proceeded to knock seven bells out of Len. When big mouth looked in, he was surprised to see me on top and tried to rescue his mate, but I wasn't having any of this. I flew at him: he was the one I wanted. The fight went up and down a flight of stairs and went from room to room. Anyone who came within reach got a clout. Finally Terry, who was instrumental in starting the scrap, became the peacemaker, but not before justice was done. Henry Cooper couldn't have lived with me that night.

Eight of us needed stitches and our eminent surgeon performed the honour. Poor old Len was suffering from concussion amongst other things, and lashed out at the doc, giving him a black eye. The doc gave him the benefit of the doubt and didn't complain, and because of Len's condition had a medic by his bedside all through the night.

When the doc woke Len in the morning to monitor his progress, Len lashed out again and caught the doc a fair one on the other eye. This time he did complain and a court martial was mentioned. Funnily enough, Len was my mate; he wasn't a bad bloke, but was easily influenced. Our incident to me was nothing but a punch-up settling some old scores, but the powers that be made it political, and tried to use me as a pawn in their power game. One side wanted to hang me out to dry, but the CO, whom I respected, looked after me.

When I was marched in front of him, he threatened me with everything, but when he dismissed everyone else in the room, he rubbed his hands in glee and said he was going to put me in for my long service and good conduct medal. Needless to say I didn't get this, but I was posted back to Hereford. The doc who was summoned to give evidence still looked like a panda.

I have a golfing mate who was at Suez, and forty years later they agreed to issue a medal to all those national servicemen who took part. Cedric was delighted when the postman turned up with his medal Special Delivery. While he was signing for it, he said to the postman, "I've been waiting forty years for this." The postman said, "Don't get onto me, mate, I have only just started in the post office."

I often think about Sue Blair whom we tied up at Earls Court. I wonder what she did for kicks. It was nice of her to sing our praises, and I am glad that:

SUE BLAIR SINGS

CHAPTER SIXTEEN

BACK ON TRACK

I got my rank back while in the TA and was requested by popular demand to be sergeant major of Training Wing. I would miss the TA: they were a great bunch and we had a lot of fun. I was best man four times in my eighteen-month stint there, but all good things must come to end and now I faced a new challenge.

No court martial resulted from the fracas in Germany, as all the evidence was mishandled. There was a top barrister in B Sqn who advised Len and got him off the hook. I have the greatest admiration for the T.A. lads: they do an excellent job. Many turned up on selection and joined the Regiment.

We would start the selection course with about one hundred and twenty men from all branches of the army, and later all the armed forces. At the end of five months we would be lucky to have twelve left.

It was a mammoth job calling the roll on each parade, so I would say, "Excuse rank, answer your name. Smith, Brown, Jones." There was always someone who would say, "Do you mean Captain Brown?" I would answer, "If your name's Brown, then answer up, you stupid boy." This was enough to crack the less resilient ones up: they quickly learnt or left.

I couldn't help the odd crack when I called the roll, and it got the day off to a good start. Things like: "Bakewell, you big tart", "Jacobs, you must be crackers", "Baker, use your loaf."

There is so much nonsense recorded regarding selection, and it's started by the ones who fail. They have to justify why they didn't pass, and exaggerate the distances and weights that are carried. Rumours are rife. Its really simple: do the best you can and don't give up. If you do this, you will pass.

Olly was my boss and we would man some of the RV points on test week. We would set off together from the Storey Arms to climb Pen y Fan, where we could control the exercise. I would be on the summit with the tent erected, water boiling, and the radio working, before Olly staggered in carrying just the newspapers.

A new medic was posted in to us and I told him to pick up five newspapers. When he gave these to me, I couldn't believe it, he had three *Daily Mirrors* and two *Suns*. He thought I was going to give them to the students. He had so much to learn; I didn't want to give them rations, let alone reading material. The next day he gave me five different papers as requested, and I was pleased to see that he hadn't duplicated any. I started reading them at a lonely checkpoint where time really dragged, but kept thinking I already have heard about this, the news seemed familiar. It still didn't register till I found the crossword easy to do. It's then that I realised they were old papers. When I checked the dates, he had got last week's copies.

I love a laugh and admire anyone with a sense of humour. For revenge I told the medic that it was easy to get the dates mixed up as he was shortly to find out when he applied for leave. "Sorry, Hypo, but according to these dates on your leave records, you're a week too late."

The first couple of weeks were spent getting the recruits fit and teaching them map-reading. They got a brief introduction to the Brecon Beacons and quickly learnt what was required of them.

Next was test week where they had to complete different exercises within a set time. This is where we started thinning them out, and by the end of the week were down to a more manageable number. Up to now anyone could voluntarily withdraw which a lot did, but now they were RTU'd (returned to unit), or more affectionately known as a platform three job.

To see the lads at the finish of the endurance march was something special. After twenty hours of marching flat out, over mountainous terrain, carrying a heavy pack: it stays with you forever. The participants are so shattered that they only remember fragments of the final stages. The best quote I heard was from a Bucky who was the first Yank to complete selection. He said, "Lofty, I feel I have been chewed up by a nanny goat and shit over a cliff."

The officers got special attention. They had to pass officers' week which was very mentally as well as physically challenging. One exercise involved swimming the Wye. This was always cold, but especially so on the winter course. I was the agent contact who would direct the candidate to head for a red lamp that was the other side of the river. A young Rupert reported in and I directed him to the lamp. He headed in the general direction and returned two minutes later, saying, "Do I have to swim the river?" I said, "Unless you can walk on it, yes." Then I witnessed something I hadn't seen before. He stripped off all of his clothes and tied them up in his trousers. It was a bitter cold night, and as he bent to tie up his baggage, I swear I heard the wind making a deep humming sound as it whistled around his backside, much the same as the noise you make when blowing across the top of a beer bottle. I was wearing a parka and felt cold, so I knew how he must have been feeling. I thought, "I'm going to learn something here." I had never seen a buoyancy aid made of loose, unwaterproofed clothing.

He took a deep breath and entered the water and was immediately swept away by the current. I could hear his teeth chattering and a lot of gasping as he disappeared in the darkness. Because of his pile of clothing he couldn't swim properly and got swept under the safety rope. The safety boat that was standing by couldn't get to him as they fouled a propeller on the rope. Poor old Rupert was swept a long way before he could get back on dry land. Unfortunately his clothing never did. He was found eventually in a telephone box trying to hug the light bulb, covering his embarrassment with the Yellow Pages.

Sometimes there was a gap between officers' week and test week, so I would keep them busy and help prepare them for test week. They would be assembled in my office for a briefing and I would say, "I wonder what we can do till lunch." Drag, who was now demobbed, was our range storeman and still a superb long-distance athlete. He would casually walk past the door wearing a donkey jacket and tracksuit bottoms. I would say, "Mr Rowbottom, are you doing anything?" It was all prearranged and Drag would say he was just waiting for some new targets. I asked him if he would take the officers out for a run. He would take off his donkey jacket and say, "Alright, just a short one over the hill," and take the bemused-looking Ruperts out for what they thought was a doddle. When they came back they were in a state of collapse, walking on legs that behaved like those of a newborn Bambi. It set the standard. If the range storeman was that fit, what were the squadron guys like?

We played a game in the gym that was similar to basketball but everyone was wearing eighteen-ounce boxing gloves. The idea was to get the ball in the opposition's net. I selected the teams and gave the briefing. There was an arrogant guards officer who wanted bringing down a peg or two. I said, "The rules are simple: there are none. The only thing is you cannot run with the ball, and if you have it you will get punched, do you all understand?" Everyone was in a tight semicircle with fists ready, and the Rupert sarcastically said, "Even my tiny brain can comprehend this," and I gave him the ball. As soon as he took it all hell broke loose: the lads didn't need a second invitation. We all started punching. Comprehended or not, the damage was done. He was comprehensively given a good hiding: there is no place for arrogance in the gym.

On continuation we did a river crossing regardless of the weather. Often on the winter course there would be snow on the ground. The lads would strip off and place all their gear in a plastic bag and, using this as a floatation aid, swim the river.

As soon as they got out of the water they would dry themselves off and dress, then I would give every man a tot of rum. This was on the side of the river where cows grazed in lush, grassy meadows. To get the circulation going and restore some warmth to frozen bodies we would play murderball.

Two sides, which I picked, would face each other a hundred yards apart, and when I blew the whistle would charge to where I placed a medicine ball in the centre. The aim was to pick up the ball and get it by any means over the opposition's goal line. They used to hand me their watches and valuables for safe keeping, but they weren't that smart, because when I blew the whistle they would invariably leave the ball and attack me. No prisoners were taken: it was all-out aggression, and sometimes the game lasted thirty minutes or more. After the game everyone was shattered but very warm. On one occasion I was buried under a heap of struggling bodies, getting pushed deeper and deeper into the soft ground infused with cow muck. A filling was split by a stray knee, and when I managed to get to my feet I was covered head-to-toe in mud and muck.

I had to go to the dentist as my tooth was hurting. The receptionist, whom I knew well, was taken aback by my appearance. She got the dentist, who turned out to be a woman starting her first day on camp. I just stood and stared at her. She was young, pretty, had nice hair and makeup, wearing seamed stockings. She looked at me and said she knew what I was thinking. I don't think she did, otherwise she would have thrown me out there and then. The dentist she had replaced was a wizened old man who had served in the Crimea: this was a big improvement. She said something like, "Yes, I am a woman and also a dentist." When I finally found my voice I mumbled something about women drivers and apologised for the state I was in, saying I would return after cleaning up. She would have none of it, saying I was alright as I was. So with my breath stinking of rum, my body covered in filth, and my boots thick with cow's muck, I sat in the chair trying to look relaxed. A large tooth had split where it had been filled and the dentist said she would "just pop it out". My teeth don't pop out easily and two hours later she was still swinging on the stubborn molar. She started with a little spray that she puffed into my mouth to deaden the gum for the coming injection, humming a soothing melody. I was struck by how neat her make-up was, and how nice her hair looked. She started off very confidently, but as things went wrong she went downhill fast. The humming stopped and the grunting began. The tooth shattered and she had to dig for the roots. Her forceps came off the tooth and chipped another one above it. The side of my mouth was split and my tongue was marked. When I looked at her, she looked like I did when I first arrived. Most of her make-up was gone and what little remained had run and smudged. Her hair was an explosion of frizz, and the seams of her baggy stockings were wound around her legs, drooping like Nora Batty's. I was so glad to get out of the chair. When she got her breath back, she said she would phone me to make another appointment to ensure everything was alright.

When I got back to my office I told Paddy, who was my new clerk, that if the dentist phoned for me, to make an excuse and tell her I wasn't available. This had quite a consequence.

Three weeks later, I was walking past the QM's, when the dentist came around the corner. She looked at me, and went as white as a sheet, grabbing the handrail for support. She said, "I thought you were dead." I was taken aback and concerned for her condition as she was on the point of collapsing. I said something smart like, "I know you tried to kill me, but I recovered," and helped her straighten up. She said that she had phoned the office inquiring where I was and asked the clerk, "Where's Lofty?" Paddy, being the gifted clerk he was, obeying my wishes, came up with the superlative answer: "He's dead." This incident coincided with the death of twenty lads in the Falklands, one of which was also named Lofty. She thought she had seen a ghost.

After the survival phase the students went to Belize for their jungle training. Belize was formerly called British Honduras, and had every disease known to man. There were bugs, microbes and bacteria just waiting for us to arrive, so they could use our bodies to bite, infect and lay their eggs in.

Every man had a hepatitis B jab which was painful. The needle was of a large diameter and Hypo used to give it to us. He would try and cheer us up to take our minds off the forthcoming pain. When ready to give the jab he would say, "Say aagh." If you asked him why, he would say that his dog had just died. There was a sink in the MI room that had long-handled taps. The best position was to bend over the sink and grasp these. On several occasions the recipient would accidentally turn the taps on when jabbed, and hot water would splash up into the face, causing the needle to come out. This meant another prick: one was enough. We thought the same about Hypo.

We took a mycologist with us to study the bugs and try to develop an insect repellent. Leishmaniasis was common and the treatment for this was worse than the actual disease. Initially radiation treatment was given, but they found out that the common strain was self-containing and didn't need such drastic measures. This was after many men suffered unnecessarily and lost their hair. It was ideal to take Bugsy with us as he played a guitar. I also had him earmarked to give the insect lecture during the survival training.

He spent all day collecting specimens and putting them into jars. He thought he was in Heaven, he had never seen so many bugs. The larger insects he injected with formaldehyde to preserve them. One day I caught a big tarantula. Bugsy had an orgasm when he saw it, and injected it and put it in his pocket. When he gave his lecture to the lads he casually took it out of his pocket and dropped it on a lad in the front row. The lad never moved a muscle, he just sat there. Suddenly the spider came to life and started crawling. With legs extended it was bigger than my hand. The lad still never moved, only his eyes followed this hairy creature as it walked down his body and onto the ground. Bugsy was the one who nearly fainted: he had carried this round in his pocket all day.

We also ran a survival course for pilots. We always tried to fit one of these in at the end of selection as it guaranteed that we would get picked up on time. The pilots flew the helicopters and Harriers that were based on airfield camp.

To make the pilots aware of what it's like navigating in the jungle we used to cut a track from the LZ which meandered up and down spurs, crossed the river several times and took an hour to reach our camp. In fact the camp was less than a hundred yards from the LZ, but this was to teach them that the hour's hard march was less than one minute's flying time. It was a good way of introducing them to the jungle. They would land by heli and would be whisked away by the instructors. When asked where they were on the map, it was unbelievable where they thought they were and how much ground they actually covered. There were navigators who could guide an aircraft to a target in any weather thousands of miles away and drop a bomb with pinpoint accuracy. But here in the jungle, with nothing but a map and compass, they were pushed.

They were a great bunch of lads but were like fish out of water. They were used to their comforts and didn't like roughing it. Whereas we thought we were well off if we had last week's newspaper and a tea bag now and again.

There was deep-seated resentment between us and the RAF, as they lived off the fat of the land and had everything. When they picked us up after long, arduous operations you could smell their aftershave miles away. When they dropped us off at night they would return to a warm bed and regular meals. We would live like animals for the duration of the op. Now we had them on our terms and could exact revenge for all the times they were late picking us up, or delaying the airdrop, or dropping it in the wrong place.

They would arrive in base camp absolutely knackered after their one-hour familiarisation march from the LZ. We had to help them build shelters and settle them in, otherwise the Air Force would be short of pilots.

Although by their standards they got a hard time, by ours we were easy on them. We had to keep in with them, as they were the ones who dropped us off and picked us up.

One course had just landed, and while I was giving them a briefing, a trainee came running onto the LZ. He was very excited, mumbling about Neil cutting his kneecap off. I had sent Nasty Neil with some trainees to cut the track and had last seen him swinging this huge cane-cutter's knife that he had just bought. He looked more like a pirate boarding a ship with a cutlass than a soldier cutting a track. I was about to go and investigate when Neil emerged from the sticks walking stiff-legged with a blood-soaked shell dressing wrapped around his left knee. It was a dramatic entry worthy of any Shakespearean play. Neil was casevaced on the next chopper to have his kneecap sewn back on. It was a great introduction for the pilots.

Neil should never had been allowed to carry a knife. Every time he did he drew blood: luckily for us, his own. On the same trip while we were waiting to go home, I entered a team into a volleyball competition. We were in the finals in front of a big crowd when Neil appeared, clutching his stomach. He caught my attention as I was about to serve. I went to see what he wanted and he showed me his wound. When he let go of his stomach a spurt of blood emerged through a gaping wound. He had been sharpening his knife on the Armourers' grindstone, and the knife had gone around the wheel and come back and stabbed him. I had to substitute Hypo so he could go and suture Neil's wound.

I made a grave mistake when I told one of the pilots I didn't like low flying. We sat around a fire one night chatting away till the early hours, and the main topic was flying. The Harrier pilots had all been deployed down in the Falklands during the conflict, and told some great stories. We invited all the aircrews that supported us to our party that we always held at the end of the course back in airfield camp.

When they came to pick us up a familiar face in the chopper invited me to sit beside him in the front. It was the pilot whom I had told that I didn't like low flying. He took off and dived down a watercourse which led to the main river and followed this at zero feet. We flew under the canopy of overhanging trees, banking hard as the river twisted and turned. We flew into a deep gorge that got narrower and steeper and looked like it was a dead end. The pilot pulled up at the last second, forcing us to leave our stomachs behind at ground level, while the aircraft flew at a thousand feet. It took many miles before our stomachs caught up with us and I wanted to be sick, but my stomach didn't know where my mouth was. He swooped back to the river that had swung around ninety degrees, and carried on skimming the water. I thought, please don't sneeze or lose concentration. I wished I hadn't denounced the RAF and praised the Marine pilots now, and if I survived this flight I would be nice to pilots in future. It was some journey; I thought we were going to travel by air, not water.

When he approached the camp I requested him to land by our basha that had a good expanse of fine grass in front. He landed perfectly, planting his undercarriage well and truly on the cricket pitch. This would not go down too well with the camp commandant who was a very keen cricketer.

That night we had a very memorable party in the sergeants' mess. When we found out one of the pilots could play the piano, we sent a raiding party to the officers' mess who came back with a piano. At the end of the evening the pilots made their apologies and said they had to go, as they were flying in the morning. We said fair enough but have one more drink, which they agreed to. Fred got them each a bottle of Appleton rum. "Drink," he ordered. This was the finest rum that money could buy. It was so smooth and mellow to drink, but under its influence you could have a leg amputated and not know it till you tried to walk or kick a football.

Downtown in the bars they sold one barrel and two barrel rum. This was raw spirit that was blended with antifreeze and brake fluid. It was to be avoided at all costs; one made you blind, the other mad. But because it was cheap the temptation was there. A warning was given on our initial briefing, warning the lads of the perils of this drink. But we had to be careful, as the moment you say that a certain place is out of bounds or don't drink one barrel, the challenge is there, and the lads wanted to find out for themselves.

During jungle training we received a resupply every week. This was like Christmas and eagerly looked forward to by everyone. The students were given an easy day and time to cook and eat their fresh ration. We used to get last week's papers which were eagerly sought after. Doing the crossword was a major pastime. One of the advantages of having old papers is that you have the answers. The major would be studying *The Times* crossword, making heavy weather of it, and we would ask him to read out a clue so we could help. His natural reaction was to look down his nose thinking, 'How can this gang of miscreants help me?' but to humour us he would read a clue out. "Shakespearean character who married......." And someone would say, "That's easy: Desdemona." "Deciduous tree also named Corylus avellana." "That's easy: Hazel." We would take it in turns; he never twigged.

One night one of the lads asked, "Useful garden creature." Someone piped up: "Worm." "No, nine letters." He said, "Fiveworms."

Jeremiah was a nickname I gave to a medic who was Training Wing's medical instructor. He was very experienced and we took him to the jungle where he was in his element treating the lads. He would lance boils and dig out thorns, using our communal cook pot to sterilise his instruments. One minute it was full of curry, the next it was full of his bloody instruments.

I was sunbathing one day and he said, "Don't move." I froze, thinking there was a fer de lance about to bite me. He gave me a lengthy lecture on sunbathing and the dangers involved, and promptly fell asleep with no shirt on, with his hands on his chest. We let him sleep and when he awoke he was a deep shade of crimson, but where his hands had been, his skin was still white. He looked like he was wearing a bra. He wasn't very tall and we gave him a shotgun to carry; this was nearly as long as he was tall. He got a stick in his eye and was the world's worse patient. I called him Jeremiah after the mountain man, Jeremiah Johnson, but I was about to rename him Jemima because he acted like a big tart. He was a hypochondriac and swallowed half of his medical kit, before lying on his bed for the rest of the week, popping what pills were left. He wore a black patch over his injured eye, and to make him feel at home I had all the course do the same. They would march past his basha at every opportunity inquiring how Miss Nightingale was doing.

The highlight of the trip was our rugby match. When we came out of the jungle and had a few days off, prior to coming home, I would challenge the garrison to a game of rugby. I will elaborate on a classic game we had in the next chapter.

I would nominate an instructor each day whose duties would include making the morning brew and the evening meal, and cleaning the dixies afterwards. It was Nasty Neil's turn and he delivered an excellent curry which we all scoffed down in minutes. He put his shirt on to wash up, and suddenly started breakdancing. He ripped his shirt off and started jumping up and down on it, screaming abuse. He had been stung by something that was lurking in his shirt. After five minutes of continuous stamping and shaking he replaced his shirt. He took two paces towards the fire before screaming even louder than before and resuming his dancing with renewed vigour. He ripped his shirt off again and threw it in the fire. He had been bitten twice by a scorpion, but still had to wash up.

The students named him Nasty Neil as he gave them a hard time. He was an ex-Marine, and as a young lad was stationed in the Far East. An officer ordered him into the brush to recover a golf ball. Neil, out to impress, leapt into the undergrowth and came hopping out with a snake dangling from his big toe. He was only wearing flip-flops and vowed he would never ever wear them again. Another time he was on guard at Eastney Barracks, guarding the main entrance with bayonet fixed. A Wren walked past and stuck her apple core on the bayonet, resulting in Neil getting extra duties. He was a trifle unlucky was Neil.

On one trip Olly was diagnosed with worms. He wanted to sleep all day and had no energy. I told him that he couldn't afford to keep pets and got the medic involved. Bennie was not the brightest when it came to maths, and couldn't work out the correct dosage of medicine. The amount of powder given was determined by body weight, so many grams for every pound weighed. Benny had a large packet of worming powder that could have possibly dosed the whole of the Brigade of Guards. He used the old demo adage 'P for plenty' and gave Olly the lot. Olly came to me staggering, saying, "Eh, big 'un, I've got worms." Quick as a flash I said, "Come on, then, Olly, I'll take you fishing." He didn't see the funny side of this and collapsed. The powder killed everything inside him and he stank. There are good and bad bacteria which help protect us, but Bennie's dose had killed everything. He never passed the worms: they died inside his gut and for a week he was in a bad way and was sent home. I visited him when I got home and his wife had put him in the spare bedroom. He smelt like death and took a long time to recover.

There was a fly known as the botfly, which had the nasty habit of laying eggs in your scalp. This looked like a rash, and if untreated or went unnoticed, a maggot would develop. When the spot was squeezed or the hair combed, this maggot would emerge, very off-putting for the barber.

In between courses we had time off and most of the lads went moonlighting, I started a window cleaning round. Jimmy gave me a ladder that he acquired from the council, and I used a bucket that usually held dirty nappies. It started with me cleaning Molly and Jack's windows and their neighbours asked if I would clean theirs. Carolyn, their daughter, went down the street and got me more customers. I started doing windows around the married quarters, and before I knew it I had forty customers. It's true what they say about 'you should see what I can see when I'm cleaning windows'. Some of the sights were worthy of an X certificate. Soldiers coming home after four months abroad tend to go to the bedroom first and take their bergans off second. Returning warriors have been known to throw handfuls of hundreds and thousands into the long grass to keep the kids busy, while they got the wife's undivided attention. One lad came home and took advantage of his wife while she was busy at the kitchen sink. He was very upset afterwards, not for his animalistic instincts, but because she never looked around to check who it was.

Many of the lads played football for local teams, I played rugby for Credenhill, which was an RAF camp just outside Hereford. Every Wednesday afternoon we had a game and started winning most of our matches. They were only a minor unit, but we got in the quarter-finals of the RAF Cup after beating RAF Innsworth, who were former holders of the title. I would take a couple of the lads with me, depending on the fixture, and word quickly spread. The powers that be complained and we were stopped playing for them. This was a shame, as it was a lot of fun. We used to travel to away matches in a coach that also carried the girls' hockey team. They had a corresponding fixture with whoever we were playing. They were a scary sight, outweighing the rugby boys by stones, and knew better songs.

Billy put in his travel claim on Monday morning, claiming for a trip to Aberdeen. You were paid so much a mile so everyone migrated north on their leave to claim the maximum. The pay officer queried his claim and asked how he could have been there and back on the weekend, and play football on the Sunday. John was the pay bloke who was also a footballer. Billy apologised, saying, "Sorry, I meant Abergavenny." He was caught a week later eating a breakfast that he hadn't paid for, and an overkeen orderly officer reported him. For this he was fined forty pounds: he could have breakfast at Tiffany's cheaper than that.

We had a civilian admin officer who was an ex-QM, who butted into things that didn't concern him. To keep the peace we all steered clear of him, but occasionally I had to go into the office for the ration roster. The OC warned me not to laugh when I saw Hoppy, but this only aroused my interest further. I went in the office where the chief clerk and two typists had desks, with Hoppy's desk set apart in a corner. Behind the desk was a blond sixty-year-old swinger. He had what little hair he had combed forward and greased, so it stuck up like a farmyard rooster's. He was wearing a flowered shirt with a cravat tied loosely around his neck. He looked like a bowl of fruit salad and I couldn't help laughing. The typists were trying to keep busy but couldn't help suppress the odd giggle. His dyed blond hair looked like a well-worn sponge that had seen better days. He had fallen for a younger woman and became trendy overnight. He had met her at the ramblers' club and it was love at first hike.

Twice a year we would go to Southern Germany to instruct at a Special Forces School. Accommodation was scarce so the QM put us in a married quarters. We were told to behave and treat it like we would our own home. We promised faithfully to do this but that was before we found out that we could buy a two-litre bottle of Italian wine for the equivalent of fifty pence. We were on ration money so we fed ourselves. Each day we took it in turns to shop and cook the evening meal. We had a kitty and the duty cook could spend so much. It was cheaper drinking the wine than it was tea, and we soon got the taste of it. One night, the designated cook made egg and chips washed down by bottles of plonk. Someone complained that the meal was crap and a fight started in the kitchen between the cook and the protester. As they wrestled, the chip pan full of oil was spilt on the floor, which was quickly spread by these two pugilists. To see them slipping and sliding was hilarious. Covered in oil they couldn't stand up or throw any good punches, but what they succeeded in doing was spreading the oil everywhere. It was up the curtains, on the walls, over the floor, and on all the furniture. We all helped clean the kitchen, which after a fortnight still had traces of oil present. We kept on finding it when we opened a cupboard or drawer, or moved the fridge. It got trod into the lounge, making the carpet sticky. At certain angles traces of polyunsaturated fat could be seen smeared over the TV screen.

We could buy prime steak from the American PX cheaply, and another fight nearly erupted when I caught one of the lads cutting this up to make jerky for the survival course. Prime steak ruined, and given to the students, was too much for the lads. The culprit was nearly hanged, drawn and quartered, but I didn't want any more mess to clear up, so prevented it. Under the influence of the Italian wine they were capable of anything.

Part of the course was climbing the Zugspitze, the highest mountain in Germany. To access the mountain you have to pass through turnstiles where a fee is charged. To save paying this fee we used to climb over the fence early in the morning, and this was the hardest part of the climb. There was an exposed place high on the mountain that involved a traverse across a sheer drop of two thousand feet. This only required belaying to a preset cable, not climbing iron railings with spikes on top.

Another achievement was to get all the students on a parachute jump. I took them on ground training, and an aircraft from the Army Sport Parachute Club, Rhinedaling, flew down to drop them. It was on an airfield used by German paras. They were jumping while we were waiting for our aircraft. I was saying how safe it was, when two Germans got entangled and whistled into the deck. An ambulance sped to their assistance just as our aircraft landed. The students didn't know it at the time but there was a fatality.

I also ran a course in Berlin when the city was still divided. It was bitterly cold and the temperature well below zero. First thing in the morning we would parade outside, and after a brisk warm-up practice, unarmed combat. I was teaching instructors to be able to run their own courses. We always fight from the 'on guard position', which is the best way of defending yourself and also to launch an attack. To keep the students sharp I used to call out, "On guard," and the students had to immediately go into this fighting stance. If they were too slow, I would punish them with press-ups and crunchies.

One morning when the frost crackled underfoot, and every lungful of air hurt the lungs, I nominated Harry, a thickset Yorkshire lad, to take the class. I told him that if they didn't respond in time, give them a slap. He called out a young lieutenant with protruding ears and looked at him for several moments then smacked him full on the ear with an open palm. I think the noise of this started an avalanche downtown and the Lt's scream woke up the camp. "When I say on guard I mean on guard," said Harry. "You didn't say anything, you stupid ...." I think I got a hernia through laughing. The ears are as delicate as Dresden china in the cold and I still wince when I picture it even now.

I had a guy called Vince with me who looked like Neanderthal man. His knuckles touched his knees, and his nose was spread all over his face. He made Lon Chaney look handsome. His hair was ginger so I called him the Ginger Ninja.

We had a week to prepare a survival area and I got Vince to build a basha. It took him all week to do this while I did the rest. He was proud of his shelter and was horrified to find someone had used it as a toilet. Whoever did was never going to admit it for fear of their life. An American patrol was crossing the training area and one of the lads pointed to their leader, telling Vince that he had seen him in the shelter. Vince had the turd on his Iban parang and ran after the patrol. He flourished the blade under the captain's nose shouting, "What about this?" The Yanks couldn't believe it. There was some prehistoric madman jumping up and down threatening their boss with a Richard the Third on a cutlass.

Three of us went downtown. I paid for the bus tickets but only managed to get two; something was lost in the translation. This was ok till we changed buses and I was a ticket short. You could use the tickets for an hour going anywhere you wished; we were going to the Berlin Tattoo. I told Vince to get on the bus and mingle before me and Taff got on, and present the tickets hoping Vince had gone unnoticed – fat chance! He got on the bus and every passenger including the driver stared at Vince, following him to his seat. A Martian wouldn't have attracted so much attention, but poor old Vince stuck out like a turd on a snooker table. I think the conductor was too scared to ask him for his ticket.

A whiskey distillery sponsored the show and as invited guests we took full advantage of their hospitality. During the interval we retired to the VIP lounge where we were well looked after. Vince drew the sword belonging to the drum major of the Light Infantry. He threatened to decapitate a few guests before returning it to the sheath. The sword was curved and it was obvious which way it would fit into the sheath. Unfortunately Vince's logic was unsettled by a pint or so of whiskey which he had consumed courtesy of Bell's. He rammed the sword in the wrong way and got it firmly stuck, forcing the drum major to do the second part of the act without wearing a sword.

After the show we were going downtown, having convinced Vince that it would be great to take part in a live strip show. There was a place we were told about where you could get in a bath with half a dozen women. Vince growled his approval, lapping up the idea of naked bodies and bubbles.

Everyone in the VIP lounge was drunk and it was hard getting directions from them. Eventually the organiser volunteered his driver to take us. The driver would not have passed a breathalyser test, so took us downtown avoiding the main roads. He stopped in a backstreet and pointed to a large building, which was poorly lit.

We said our thanks to the German driver and entered the building. There were no signs or directions, so I knocked on the first door I came to. There was a flight of stairs going up to different landings with many doors on each side of connecting passages.

The door was opened by a big black guy who said, "Whad ya want?" I asked if this was the place where you got in a bath with the ladies. He seemed flummoxed and asked me to repeat myself. As I did so, doors started opening on all the landings. Someone shouted down the stairs, "What's going on?" The big black guy shouted, "There's some f…in' Limeys who want to get in the bath with my missus." The driver had dropped us off at some American married quarters, and we had a lot of explaining to do. We retired with all possible speed.

While we were waiting at a bus stop, Vince disappeared. We waited for him and was surprised when a crowded bus went by when Vince's unmistakable face materialised amidst a throng of commuters, strap hanging. We never saw him for two days, and when we asked him where he had been, he couldn't remember.

He gave a memorable lecture on fishing. He had a real country accent and spoke very slowly. He asked the class what was the first thing needed before going fishing. Various answers were called out by a spellbound audience, like, "A rod." He would ponder for a minute then say, "No." "Bait." Again a big pause. "No." "A river." Longer pause. "No." And so it went on. After about fifteen minutes of this he came out with the ultimate fisherman's tip, "You sharpen your hooks." The class erupted. I have never sharpened a fish hook in my life, by the time he gave them the reasons his time was up, lesson over.

We met many characters on selection and they all had the same desire to get away from their parent Regiment to join us. If they were borderline they got a second chance, coming back on the next course. Some would never pass as they made the same mistakes and never learnt. The officers were the most extreme: they were either very good or very bad. We used to say how can a man with only one head make so many mistakes. These men were supposed to be leaders but many were followed out of curiosity.

I've heard some good excuses for people being late. Having an injured leg is a lame excuse, and the number of times a certain individual's granny died got me believing in reincarnation. One guy said he had humming in his ears; I told him to teach it the words. Another guy said he couldn't sleep so I recommended he hand in his bedding. Sometimes the students got bad news from home and I had to break the bad news to them. I tried to be compassionate and thoughtful. The old story where the sgt major had to break the news of a soldier's granny dying comes to mind. His senior told him to be tactful, so he paraded the men. "Everyone with a grandmother two paces forward!" he shouted. "Where you going, Smith?"

In the jungle it was important that the students got their mail in the right order. One SQMS used to hold mail back if the soldier got a couple of letters to ensure he would get mail on the next resup. If he got this wrong, the soldier would read about the funeral before he knew about the death.

A padre was responsible for telling the next of kin if a guy was killed. When he appeared around the married quarters every curtain in the street would twitch as the occupants wanted to see where he was going. One day he went to the wrong house, consoling the woman and telling her to be brave. Sitting her down in the front room, he started to tell her that her husband was dead. She said, "You better go and tell him that, he's in the kitchen doing the washing-up." Fred, the padre, liked a drink and looking back, should have been locked up. To be told something depressing by a beery-breathed man of the cloth was outrageous. We did some things very well and some things very badly.

On one winter selection the weather was horrendous and we lost a man. At the inquest held in Brecon I was exhibit A. On a jungle course the same year a student died of sunstroke and at the inquest I was exhibit B. On the next summer selection I said to Olly, "I'm glad it's a summer course." It was the same time as the Fastnet boat race when they experienced the worst weather in history for the time of year. We lost a man on top of Pen y Fan. At the inquest I was exhibit C. I told Olly, "I hope we don't run through the alphabet." When you push men to extremes there is a price to pay. Everything possible is done to make it safe, but when man comes up against nature there is only one winner.

One of the lads was riding home on his motorbike when he spotted a milk lorry broken down in the road. He gave assist and got the lorry started. He was following it down a country lane when the lid of a milk churn came off and smacked him full in the mouth. Dusty lost control of his bike and crashed. The driver stopped and it was his turn to help. He said one good churn deserves another.

Dusty's bike was a write-off and he said, "I'm going to try a new prayer tonight and pray for a new bike." In the morning the milkman turns up with a brand new motorbike in compensation. Dusty couldn't believe it, it just goes to show:

NEW PRAYER BRINGS

CHAPTER SEVENTEEN

OPS RESEARCH

Operational Research was probably the best job in the Regiment, especially if you were coming to the end of your career. Ops Research was responsible for ensuring the Regiment got the best equipment. We would evaluate and test new weapons, boats, parachutes, clothing and rations – anything that the Regiment required. This meant working closely with Civvy Street where many contacts were made, which could be a help when finishing with the army. If any problems arose in the squadrons or the SP team, we would try and solve it. We were constantly looking for new ideas and better kit, and, as new tasks and roles were taken on, we had to supply the goods.

Ops research was always the envy of the sqns. I remember many moons ago seeing Clancy in the jungle lying under a poncho that was twice the size of mine. His hammock was lightweight that folded down to nothing, and his bergan had an alloy frame that weighed nothing. The pack had tons of zipped pockets. His boots were leather-soled with canvas uppers, and they laced up at the back, preventing twigs from snagging the laces. What technology, I thought at the time: soon we will be walking on the moon.

Our kit was tried and tested but there was always room for improvement. My envy of Clancy's kit was short-lived, as it gradually deteriorated as the op went on. The hammock rings broke and the material ripped, the poncho leaked at the seams, and the unbreakable lightweight frame on the bergan snapped. I remember the hammock tearing vividly. It must have been two in the morning when I was awoken by ripping cloth. Clancy went straight through the bottom and landed on all the sharp sticks he had left when clearing the ground. A sole came off his boot, and whether it was this that made him walk funny or the stick that nearly impaled him, I'm not sure. Back to the drawing board. The boots were a disaster. I think Clancy got fallen arches, hammer toes, corns and bunions, with a couple of blisters thrown in for good measure. The boots finished looking like something worn in the Bolshoi Ballet.

So this is what I had to live up to. The lads were keen on new gear and I had of plenty of great ideas.

My first project was solving the problem of cam cream. This washes off too easily in the jungle or when you sweat heavily, needing to be reapplied frequently. Max Factor produced some; it didn't last any longer, but it tasted better. We tried various powders, creams, lotions and paint, but all to no avail.

We experimented with a pill, that when swallowed, changed the pigment of the skin. After taking the pill a group of lads that looked like bottles of milk finished up like the Dixie singers from the Deep South. This was good news but, like every pill, there were side effects. It affected people in different ways. Some suffered severe headaches; others vomited. Everyone got swollen lips and the boffins said that long-term use would enlarge the breasts. We were already wary of wearing makeup and now there was a danger of the lads cross-dressing. We called this project 'Instant Abo'.

We used to talk about the one-tree hammock but this was a wind-up. We told the gullible that it was to be used where trees are scarce or too far apart. The colonel believed it and used to ask for regular updates. Looking back, he might have been winding us up.

A two-ounce dehydrated meat block was the basics of our ration. When mixed with water it would swell up. We always carried our rubbish back out with us, so someone suggested a bigger meat block that would save on packaging. We discussed the fourteen-day meat block in detail but it was a no-goer. Imagine if it got wet in the bergan and expanded. You would be followed by all the dogs in the world.

It reminded me of the story of Cinderella going to the ball when she started her monthlies. The fairy godmother changed a pumpkin into a tampon and said, "Don't dare stay out after midnight."

We had loads of kit being tested throughout the world which we called 'summer items'. When asked where they were, I would say, "Some are here, sum are there...."

What do you want? Common sense!

I took Paddy with me as my clerk, just in case the dentist phoned again. He couldn't type but was good company. We had an interest room with all the latest gadgets, equipment and clothing on display. As you went in the door we had three mannequins dressed in jungle, desert and Arctic kit. Every morning, Jack the cleaner would come round and dust the exhibits. One morning, Paddy stood between the jungle and desert models with a jungle hat on. Old Jack came as usual, whistling 'the shrimp boats are a-coming', armed with feather duster and cloth. When he got to Paddy he hesitated slightly, but before he realised something wasn't quite right, Paddy moved and growled. Poor old Jack fell through his own backside. We had to sit him down and pump tea into him all day. I think he smoked his tobacco ration in hours.

I set Paddy up a treat when I bought some onion sets. He asked me what they were for and I told him: you plant them in the garden, water them regularly, and large onions develop. He was a bit dubious, especially when I told him they would be mature in a week or so. He came round to pick me up one morning and I had planted a row of some shop-bought onions in the garden. I left a couple of sets in the kitchen to draw his attention to the subject without being too obvious. Sure enough, Paddy came round, saw the little sets and asked how they were doing. When I took him out to the garden and he saw this row of big Ailsa Craigs he was impressed. "Stop on the way back, I want to get some of them sets," he said. He wasn't as daft as he looked. He wanted me to plant them and keep him in onions, seeing they were so easy to grow.

We had some interesting trips, one of which was to Sellafield, the nuclear power station. This was a prime target not only for terrorists, but for protesters as well. They needed security advice and help with a new design to transport nuclear waste safely. Their first effort of a bombproof container was blown apart with ease. It had many small compartments that defeated conventional explosives, but if these became filled with gas and ignited, would blow the container apart.

Three of us drove up to Sellafield in a Ford Estate. Just short of our destination we climbed a steep hill. Halfway up we picked up two hitch-hikers who were glad of a lift. We only went a few more yards when the vehicle stopped and wouldn't start. We rolled backwards to jump-start the engine, but it just spluttered and was reluctant to start. We finished up back down the hill and the hitch-hikers left us to it and started their climb once more. After twenty minutes the car started again, so we attempted the climb for the second time. We got three-quarters of the way up and stopped to pick up the hitch-hikers. It was a bit awkward, as they had to get in the back with their packs through the passenger door. They settled in, Paddy took off the handbrake, and the engine spluttered and died. The same thing happened when we rolled backwards trying to restart, but without success, finishing back at the bottom of the hill. The hitch-hikers, trying to remain civil, wished us luck and set off once more. It was some form of fuel starvation, and Paddy came up with the idea of reversing up the hill. He had seen this in the film *Ice Cold in Alex*. This is what we eventually did and the hitch-hikers were pleased that we didn't stop to offer them a lift as we went past them backwards near the summit.

Albert looked after us, giving a detailed visit around the plant. We stood on the nuclear reactor once he convinced us it was safe. He got me to put my hands in a pair of gloves that were fixed inside a metal container with a glass front. This is where they handled plutonium, and using the gloves you could operate a remote arm. I was getting the hang of moving the radioactive materials when Paddy said, "Is that a hole in the glove?" I nearly died and couldn't get my hands out quick enough. I've got a thing about gloves. I wouldn't let anyone on selection wear them, probably because I didn't have a pair. There's nothing worse than trying to do something fiddly with gloves on. I encouraged everyone to keep their hands warm by exercising them. Trying to fire a weapon or operate a Morse key was not practical when wearing gloves.

Albert took us out for an evening meal and I finished up ordering the cheeseboard. A young waitress brought a variety of cheeses to the table which include a whole Wensleydale. She went away to get some biscuits and I got stuck in. The Wensleydale was outstanding and I made the big mistake of telling the others. They got stuck in, and when the waitress came back the whole cheese had gone. She said we were not supposed to eat the lot, and I said, "Got any more?"

Mick, who was the other one with us, made notes of everything. He jotted the name of the cheese down so he could get his missus to buy some. He wore a coat that had large pockets which were filled with a variety of items. He always carried an apple which he ate differently from any other human I've known. He started at the stalk, eating down through the apple. He couldn't tell us why he did this: his father was probably a Gloucester Black Spot. One day I asked him about a certain street in Birmingham. He opened up his jacket and rummaged around an inside a pocket, coming out with an A-Z of Birmingham: he was the boffin on the team.

Olly joined us from selection and headed the team. We now had a new camp, and his office was directly above the boiler house that heated the swimming pool. This was on most of the time, producing a high-pitched whine. There's bound to be settling cracks in new buildings, but the one in the wall by his office was an inch and a half wide. I could look through the wall and see Olly at his desk. It was so hot in his office, it was like working in a volcano.

The three of us had an early morning start for an appointment at Bow Street nick with the Chief Commissioner of Police. I was driving, Paddy was sleeping, and Olly was moaning. Nothing seemed to go right for him. He bought a suit with two pairs of trousers, and burnt a hole in the jacket. We were in civilian clothes all of the time and Olly spent a lot of time at the War Office. He wore a suit with collar and tie, and me and Paddy were in jeans, a cheap anorak with orange lining, and chukka boots. He had to carry a briefcase that he kept on losing. Wherever we went I ensured he didn't leave his briefcase behind.

Bow Street nick is on one of the busiest roads in London. We arrived as rush hour was at its height, so I pulled in front of a pair of large double gates. Olly got out, going to the main entrance to make inquiries. I asked him not to hang about gossiping, which he was a master at, and to get these gates open so we could park up, allowing me to find a toilet that I urgently required. Paddy was good company, lying there making zzz's. Ten minutes or more passed when a car pulled up behind me. The driver tooted his horn and, using sign language, I told him I was waiting for the doors to open. I don't think he understood my sign language and carried on tooting. I changed my sign language to one that everyone understands, the old two-finger salute. He jumped out of his car and came to my window which I wound down. "If you don't move, laddie, I'll get you moved," he threatened. I told him to f… off. He left his car where it was and went to the main entrance. Two minutes later the large double doors opened and a policeman waved me through. I explained to him who we were seeing and asked if he had seen Olly. He went away to find out and a coach arrived. It was from the Scrubs, and a string of manacled prisoners de-bussed and were ushered inside. I asked Paddy if he noticed anything unusual about them. They could have been wearing stilettos and Paddy wouldn't have noticed. Every one of the prisoners was wearing jeans, with orange-lined anoraks, and chukka boots. After what seemed like hours we were reunited with Olly on the top floor where he was drinking tea with the Chief Constable. He got up to introduce us. "Sir, this is Lofty and Paddy, and this is Chief Constable….." I interrupted him before he could finish. I said, "We've already met." It was the driver of the car who blew his horn downstairs…. Oops.

Once in a lifetime you meet a character like George. He was an inventor and specialised in plastics. It's a very thin line between genius and lunatic, and I will let you make up your own mind.

He phoned one day saying he had a bulletproof material that was lighter and cheaper than Kevlar. I invited to bring it to the camp where I would test it. He brought three samples and I fired different calibre rounds from various ranges. All three samples stopped the rounds, which was very promising. The next phase was for George to make up some new samples and I would get someone from the Home Office to witness the results and endorse it if successful. George returned with his new batch, and with the guy from the Home Office we went to the range. I fired exactly the same weapons as before but everyone of the samples failed. George was devastated.

He returned to his workshop and asked his assistant, who had made the panels, if he had followed George's formula exactly. The assistant swore he did, but on further questioning admitted that the first batch he made that were successful, he used what was available. He said, "There was none of that so I put this in. You had loads of this so I doubled up, and you only had so much of this." So George knew it was possible to make a lightweight bulletproof material, but didn't have a formula. He is still searching to this day.

George was born in India where his father was serving in the army. His parents never registered him, so when he came to the UK he didn't exist. He had a hard time to get a passport.

He had two older brothers that didn't like George, as he was his mother's favourite. I suppose someone had to love him. They played tricks on him and teased him relentlessly. They had a monkey tied to a stake that they threw stones at. The monkey would fly at them with yellow fangs bared, frothing at the mouth. They would stand on the edge of a carefully measured circle, keeping them just out of range of gnashing teeth. George used to cower miles away, terrified. They convinced George that it was good fun, and after demonstrating how it was done, gave George some stones. He stood on the edge of the circle and threw a stone, getting the ape's attention. The second stone caused the primate to fly, but before George could throw the third stone the ape had fastened his teeth around George's calf. The brothers had moved the circle in. He was in bed for months getting over this; he had a massive infection and was lucky to recover. The monkey wasn't so lucky: his father shot it.

It's a wonder he survived his childhood, because when they came back to the UK the brothers made a raft. George was made captain and bribed by sweets to get aboard. The brothers promised faithfully that they would join him after they launched the raft. George was pushed out as the tide was turning and disappeared on a spring tide in a solo attempt to cross the Irish Sea. His brothers went home, and when his mother asked where he was, they said he was messing about by the river. She received a call from the coastguard saying they had picked her son up halfway across to Ireland. He was picked up by the Isle of Man ferry.

Another trick they played on George was to load him into a steel tub that was used to take rocks away from a quarry. It ran on a narrow-gauge rail, and when full would run down a slope and hit some buffers, automatically emptying the tub. They gave the reluctant driver a pair of goggles salvaged from a gas mask case, and convinced George he would enjoy it. Again they promised to ride with him once they got the tub rolling, but when George was underway he looked behind to see two figures getting smaller rapidly, waving. He hit the buffers and couldn't remember anything for two weeks. He fell a good thirty feet, landing on a soft bed of rocks.

He came with another example: he wanted me to fire an M1 carbine at from point-blank range. The first question I asked was, "Is there any metal in it?" George assured me there wasn't, so I went ahead with the test. The carbine is very high velocity so I made sure there was only sand behind the plate. Reluctantly, I fired with the muzzle half an inch away, thinking the sample was heavy for Glass-Reinforced Plastic (GRP). My worry was justified. The bullet hit the sample, flattened, came back and hit me right between the eyes. This didn't hurt much but it didn't end there. The bullet dropped into my mouth and, being red-hot, burnt my lips and tongue, which did hurt, a lot. This may sound way out, but with George anything was possible. He admitted later that he had put some high-tensile steel rods in the sample.

Another trial I conducted for him was on a safe door. It was made from GRP, reinforced with metal bars. We were very keen on anything that could stop bullets or the effects of blast.

I placed the door in an old building on our demolition range. It was a nice day with the sun shining and birds singing. The range was on high ground and had a great view over the valley with the Black Mountains in the distance. The colonel and adjutant were making one of their monthly visits, and took an interest in our activities. I rigged up a small charge and went to the firing position where the colonel and adjutant were emptying their bladders. I warned them of the pending explosion and they carried on their activity, but placed both hands over their ears. To see two senior officers standing with todgers out with fingers in ears was a sight to behold. I delayed it as long as possible, savouring the moment.

After the bang I let the dust settle before investigating the sample. I was surprised to see it burning, as George had stated that it was fireproof. The building quickly filled with black toxic smoke, so I advised everyone to clear the building. George had spent seven hundred pounds on the sample and was trying to salvage what he could. I had to drag him away coughing and spluttering with his face as black as a coal miner's.

His next stroke of genius was to produce a GRP skullcap that fitted under a policeman's soft hat. He got an appointment with the Chief Constable of West Mercia. He took his son along with him who carried an engineer's ball-peen hammer. George introduced himself, telling the chief he wanted to give a short demonstration of his invention but didn't elaborate. He was wearing a cap with the insert underneath and gave his son the nod. His son, Graham, stood up, producing the hammer which was concealed down the waistband of his jeans, and gave his dad a sharp blow on the top of his head. George slid under the desk with only the whites of his eyes showing. The Chief Constable wasn't aware of the skullcap and thought he had witnessed a murder. He was about to disarm Graham when George reappeared clutching the desk and levering himself up on the chair, pretending he wasn't affected. His slurred speech gave it away and he suffered headaches and a stiff neck for weeks. They had practised this many times before the actual demo, trying to get it right. So George was probably suffering from concussion from the accumulated blows anyway, but on the day his son gave it a bit extra, probably due to the adrenalin flowing.

I was home most nights on this job so caught up with a lot of jobs around the house. I was into Do It Yourself. The wife would say, "Put that shelf up," and I would say, "Do it yourself." Our front room had three sets of wall lights which made the room too dark, so I disconnected these and pushed the wires in the wall. I installed a light in the middle of the ceiling; the only trouble was, it stayed on all the time. I finally worked out the correct wiring and was very pleased with myself. When papering the walls where the wall lights used to be, I got a strange tingling feeling through my arms. The wiring was shortening out, making the wall live.

The coffee table I made had one leg shorter than the others. I didn't ever think of cutting the other legs in case it finished up Japanese-style. Using my airborne initiative I drove a large, headed tack into the short leg. I then placed the table where we wanted it and banged it down till it was level. The wife was impressed that the table was solid and didn't rock, but not so much when she tried moving the table. The head of the tack went through the new carpet and ripped it when moved. Stick to what you know: if at first you don't succeed, leave it!

The carpets we bought were never the best quality, but were the best we could afford. A brand new carpet was destroyed on day one after laying. I bought my lad a pair of football boots which he proudly wore, strutting around like Bobby Moore. He took a penalty from the centre of the room and a stud went straight through the carpet and created a ladder-like rip that kept on snagging and got larger. We couldn't afford to replace it, so in front of the fire it looked like an African waterhole.

Army mess tins have been in service since the First World War. The only change made was they introduced wire handles in the fifties, but reverted to aluminium which gets very hot when cooking. They are very uneconomical on fuel as they have no lid, so I went to Tidworth to talk to a retired brigadier who was responsible for such items. He was ex-Indian Army and was responsible for putting a pocket in the front of every pair of trousers that the army wore. It was designed to carry a small field dressing, but being in front it was very uncomfortable when you tried bending. So no one ever used this pocket and we never carried small field dressings. We carried the large field dressing which you can use to treat all wounds big and small. Gunshot wounds are never small, so the smaller dressing was inadequate.

We talked about mess tins and his pride and joy was a set coated with Teflon. We weren't interested in this as, more often than not, we had nothing to burn or stick. We needed to be able to boil water efficiently, that was our priority.

A week later the military police phoned and wanted to know what we were talking about. The brigadier had blown his brains out over the weekend, but this was nothing to do with me or mess tins.

Everything we tried to develop came under the eagle eye of different departments within the army. We would want something light, robust and efficient. By the time the army finished with our basic design it was over-engineered, finishing up heavy and impractical, defeating what we were trying to improve on in the first place. An elephant was the result of these boffins trying to design a horse.

Paddy and I went to Belize to lift some caches that were buried when confrontation with Guatemala was on the cards. Now all the sabre-rattling had died down we wanted to lift these caches and test them for deterioration. They had been in the ground for two years, and contained ammunition, radio batteries and food. They had to remain sealed only to be opened under laboratory conditions back here in the UK.

Paddy's run of bad luck started on the aircraft. He was reading a book and had a cup of tea on his tray that was pulled down from the back of the seat in front of him. I watched the cup creeping nearer to the edge as the aircraft vibrated. It took an age to reach the edge and tip the contents into Paddy's lap. He shot bolt upright, managing to save half of the tea. As the hot liquid soaked through his jeans raising skin temperature, so did his agitation. He was just about in control of the pain when he slammed the tray upwards but it hit the seat and rebounded, hitting the cup and spilling the rest of the tea back in his crotch. You may wonder why I watched this happen. It's boring on a nine-hour flight and anything that helps pass the time is good news.

After a drink Paddy always fell out of bed and finished up kneeling like Christopher Robin saying his prayers at the foot of the bed. This is how I found him on the morning we were flying in to lift the first cache. The night before I told him that we were going to abseil in, which didn't impress Paddy. He was terrified of heights; even the bed was too high for him. We finished up fast-roping from twelve feet: this is basically sliding down a thick rope. Paddy managed the first eight feet but let go for the remainder. I was down first and heard something crashing through the bushes. The heli was hovering over a small peak, and when Paddy let go it was off to one side. When I found Paddy he was thoroughly stirred and shaken. The shovel that he had strapped to his back had hit him on the head when he finally came to rest, after falling through the foliage and rolling down the slope. We still had a short march to the cache, and I had to tread carefully to ensure the cache was not compromised. It's common practice for the enemy to strip the cache and booby-trap it. Paddy wasn't used to this high-octane living. He was a clerk and missed the office. I promised him some good times when we finished our work: I knew a friend who had a yacht.

Finding a cache from someone else's sketch map is difficult. A grid reference gets you into the area, but then you must have a distinctive feature from which accurate bearings and distances are taken. We found this one without much difficulty and carried it to an LZ where the chopper could land the next day and lift us out. The heaviest thing to carry was Paddy. He had hurt his ankle and even threats of burying him in the cache couldn't get him walking. We didn't take him on any more recoveries.

As promised, we took Paddy on a yacht for a spot of rest and recuperation. He needed it after lying in his pit for two weeks. He had at least a fifty-yard walk to the cookhouse, and didn't know where his next beer was coming from. Barry and his wife had sailed a catamaran from the UK, and anchored alongside the army jetty in Belize. Barry was ex-Regiment and took the troops out to the Cays for recreation training.

Paddy came aboard, and in his haste to get a beer, tripped up the threshold and disappeared head first down below: he hadn't got his sea legs yet.

We tied up to pier on one of the Cays and went swimming. We all dived off the boat into open water, but Paddy decided to dive between boat and pier. He hit his head on an underwater stanchion. He kept us in stitches so I reciprocated and put four stitches in a big gash on his forehead. He spent the rest of the day with an ice pack on his head nursing a can of Tennent's.

Selection had just finished their jungle training so I organised a rugby match against the garrison. I only had twenty-five men to pick from but I did acquire two ringers; one was a combined services prop, the other a Navy winger. The garrison had a choice from over a thousand and played regularly.

The selection guys were super-fit but not rugby-fit. They had been on the go continuously for four months. So with two stars and thirteen willing hearts we took the field. All the lads knew that anything short of an outstanding performance could end in an RTU. To come second in a marathon is very commendable, but to come second in a fight, which this was, is despicable. They were all willing to die for the cause, but I said this wasn't good enough, I wanted more.

The opposition were all dressed the same, in smart, hooped shirts, matching shorts and socks. This is the sign of a good team: they even had proper rugby boots. We were wearing white T-shirts with different logos on, a mixture of shorts, cut-off OGs, and swimming trunks. Most had trainers; a few were in jungle boots. The referee and linesmen looked the part, resplendent in formal kit.

When the whistle blew, the first kick put the ball deep into our half. The second kick was delivered by our full back, who put the boot deep into their scrum-half's midriff. He was nowhere near the ball at the time and we got penalised. The ref awarded them a penalty and one of the lads called him a wanker. He immediately awarded them an extra ten yards and another voice said, "I wished his father was."

They were a good side and were twelve points up at half-time. We did have a good chance of a try, but the winger dropped the ball at the crucial moment. Someone in the crowd said he must have had a blackout. This was answered by his mate saying, "That's the trouble, he's taking her out again tonight, that's why he can't catch a ball."

By half-time we had run ourselves stupid. The heat and physical exertion took their toll, but we were not finished yet. We still had a secret weapon we called Hypo. He was the medic who had made up a concoction for us to drink. It certainly reached the parts that other drinks couldn't. As soon as it was swallowed you could feel your mind clearing and fatigue getting replaced by energy. The other stroke of genius was applying Algipan to the legs and finish up wiping the hands around the genitals. Algipan was deep heat and really burnt delicate tissue.

By the time the whistle started the second half we were raring to go. We ripped into them like a band of dervishes. We never stopped running for forty minutes, tackling anything above the grass, whether they had the ball or not. We brushed them aside, winning the game twenty points to twelve. We never found out what was in the drink but suspected witchcraft and Mogadons. There was a side effect, however: we couldn't sleep.

After the match the celebrations started, and the star turn was Fletch. He knew more songs than Rodgers and Hammerstein: he never stopped. After a gallon or two, we left the camp in taxis, heading for the Big C, a local nightclub. The drivers were promised a big tip to be the first there, so a race began between six big American cars. The roads are not the best: large potholes and subsidence is the norm. Donkey-drawn carts take up a lot of road and are always in the wrong place. The taxis, which had seen better days thirty years ago, were overcrowded, taking them longer to stop than a super oil tanker. Big engine, no brakes, faulty steering, nine imbeciles leaning out of the windows – it all added up to an exciting ride. Include a driver who was under the influence of either rum, drugs or both, and you get a good idea of the scene.

Fletch took over the cabaret and led the singing. He organised the waiters to keep up a constant flow of drinks and snacks when required. He was brought up in Argentina and could speak Spanish. The locals loved it when he sang "Eskimo Nell" in their native tongue. It was a night to remember, and all too soon we watched the sun come up. We went back to camp at a more leisurely pace, looking forward to a good kip. But try as we might, sleep wouldn't come. Before we knew it, another party had started in one of the bunks. This went on long into the night and I was getting fed up of Fletcher's singing: he was still at it. I left the party wandering around the camp to my bunk. I flopped down on the bed exhausted, but could still hear Fletch singing; the party was next door. If you can't beat them, join them, so back I went to carry on the movement. It was three days before I got any sleep and this was on the aircraft on the way home. When we landed I sleepwalked through customs and vaguely remember seeing my wife, before falling into a stupor. Let this be a lesson to everyone: beware of the demon drink and don't take drugs. Everyone who had drunk the potion suffered the same way; when we finally got to sleep it was like a short course in death.

I had to go back to the airfield to pick up the caches and clear them through customs. They got a bit shirty when I said they couldn't open the boxes. I gave them a phone number to ring and all was cleared. Looking back, I could have smuggled anything I wanted. I should have taken an empty cache box out with me and filled it with goodies.

The wives' club was raising money for a local charity, and the colonel's wife came round for donations. They were asking all departments for anything unusual, rare and not used very much. I offered them Paddy's brain, but we couldn't find it.

She bumped into Pete who was visiting me, and asked him why he hadn't turned up to help put up a tent, which he had promised to do. He sneaked away to the back room to make a brew while I made up some excuses for him. She asked me why my wife didn't attend the wives' club. To wind her up I told her that I was the warrior and my wife had to stay at home, washing and ironing, to look after me, and had no time left to gossip. She said, "Lofty, I think you are a male chauvinist pig. There is nothing a man can do that a woman can't." A voice came from the tearoom: "Well, put your own f…ing tents up."

Visiting the people responsible for rations was always a challenge. The brigadier was deaf and his advisor was a woman whose false teeth were two sizes too big for her gums. I wanted a more substantial ration, and all she could talk about was obesity. There was never any danger of our lads getting fat on what they lived on in the field. The food pouch had a tab which you pulled to open, and it wasn't big enough. We told the woman "to make it larger". The brigadier chipped in: "Who wants a tin of lager?"

The infantry wanted a ration they could eat when in a close observation role. It couldn't be cooked and had to be eaten straight out of the packet. I was asked what we did in similar circumstances, and I told them we took sandwiches. The brigadier asked me to elaborate so I described two pieces of bread with a lump of meat or cheese in the middle. He kept repeating, "Sandwiches, sandwiches, they must taste awful after a couple of days." I said, "To the contrary, they taste delicious." You are that hungry you would eat your boots if you could.

Hilda's teeth kept on moving after she finished talking, looking like a woman in a badly dubbed movie. Her answer to raising the calorific value of our ration pack was to put more sweets and chocolate in. We didn't want this: we wanted things like cheese, nuts and granola bars. I told her, "The men are sick of goodies." The brigadier said, "Who's been kicked in the goolies?" It was all food for thought.

We had a code word which I used when we wanted to get away from such meetings. If I said, "Four candles", it meant don't ask any more questions where we are going.

This backfired on me when I gave the code at a conference and the chairman told me to sit down. I forgot that I had told him our code when he came with us to a previous meeting.

Olly had a flat in the Cromwell Road as he spent most of his time at the War Office. I stayed with him at least once a week and we would walk to Chelsea together in the morning. Olly would be in a pinstriped suit carrying a briefcase. I would be in jeans carrying a bin liner full of rubbish. This just about sums my life up. It took me twenty-seven years and fifty-five days to be able to move that rubbish unsupervised.

I'm glad to say I'm still grinning and would do it all over again.

Hilda and the brigadier retired and were replaced by a younger couple who were caught in a compromising position in a larder. The charge sheet read:

NEW PAIR SINS

CHAPTER EIGHTEEN

LIFE AFTER DEATH

One of the last projects I did in Ops Research was to write a survival manual. This was initially for the Regiment, as the survival course notes were rubbish. I showed it to the colonel who advised me to go and get it published. I met a guy who was doing a book on the regiment and he introduced me to his son-in-law who was working at Fontana Books. This was the softcover book department of Collins. I left it with him with a threat of men in black overalls and gas masks coming for him if I didn't hear back in two weeks. He fed it into Collins and my book went to number two bestseller. It's now in nineteen languages and in all forms selling over two million copies.

Number one at the time was a young Welsh girl who wrote about music discs and tapes. Her book was the "Gwyneth Book of Records".

All the publicity surrounding the book gave me a good start when I started the School of Survival. When you leave the Army aged forty-five no one wants you. The only valid piece of paper I had was HGV 2. This allowed me to drive a ten-ton truck. Who wants a Malay-speaking, free-falling, knackered demolitionist? I didn't want to go on the circuit looking after people; I wanted someone to look after me. On the pre-release info the army give you there is a list of expectations. As a WO1 I could run a garage forecourt, but because I was Special Forces I could become a bingo hall manager.

I had to survive: I had a wife, seven kids, cat and mother-in-law to look after. So I opened the school. It was not only wilderness survival that I taught, but also urban and corporate. Urbane survival included self-defence, dealing with floods and disasters. Corporate survival was teaching teamwork, leadership and tenacity.

When I left the Army I promised myself that I would never eat out of a mess tin or sleep in a sleeping bag ever again. I found myself on survival without even these items, sleeping rough and eating out of a rusty tin can if I was lucky.

I met some amazing people who came on the courses. Belly dancers, lawyers, doctors, magicians – just about every profession came. I learnt as much off them as they did off me. One couple who stick in my mind were Billy and Don. I was running a weekend course waiting for the students when I heard an irate voice shouting abuse. When I went to investigate I saw a woman dressed up to the nines carrying a large suitcase. She had eyelashes 2 inches long, stiletto heels 5 inches long, using a tongue 6 inches long. She was shouting at her partner, Don, who had promised her a dirty weekend. Her suitcase was full of frillies, and she wasn't too impressed with Don's idea of a dirty weekend.

Each year I did expeditions to Alaska, Nepal, Oman and Borneo. It was great going back as a civvy and seeing how much these places had changed. Old habits die hard, and I took Mick to the jungle in Borneo. We stayed in Kuching on the first night so I took him to the market. I started bargaining with the stallholders over the price of a bottle of Tiger. Mick asked me what I was doing, and when I explained he said, "If you think I've come seven thousand miles to haggle over a penny…", and he put everyone on the firm, buying all present a drink. I thought, he's in for a shock when he finds out that I use tea bags twice.

I ran courses with Dennis who used to look after the Miss World beauty competition. He was asked so many times how he got such a job that we decided to run a course. There was no training in those days, and security was a new word. It was the first course in the country to teach VIP protection.

I ran courses for the Petroleum Training Federation, who sent prospect engineers all around the world in search of oil. Their safety record was appalling, so we trained them in medical, survival, small boat handling, use of helicopters, chainsaws, map-reading and the effects of extreme climates like deserts, jungles and the Arctic.

The book gave me credibility and opened many doors for me. It was a new subject and it caught the public's imagination. I did many TV and radio interviews, taking a few stars on survival. My first TV appearance was on *Elinor*, a Welsh programme. I turned up in jeans and T-shirt carrying a carrier bag of goodies. I was shown a dressing room with a clothes rail six feet long and told to hang my things up. I couldn't have filled it with all the clothes I had at home. This was the first time I was forced to wear makeup, and am glad to report that it didn't become a habit. Elinor was the female presenter who nearly died when I told her what she had just sampled from my bag of goodies. I made an omelette from moorhen's eggs laced with worms and gentles. She actually enjoyed it till I told her what it was. It's all in the mind, but in her case all in the mouth, which she tried to empty as she called for water. What won't fatten will fill.

I got involved when they filmed *Memphis Belle*. I took the actors who were playing airmen on survival. Harry Connick Jr was so impressed when I fed him a worm omelette that he composed a tune for me called, "Lofty's Cockroach Soufflé".

Peter Duncan from *Blue Peter* did a two-week survival course with me. This made two one-hour programmes. He found it a struggle but I looked after him. He got his revenge back in the *Blue Peter* studio. They had the world's biggest teddy bear all wired up and supported which they were going to film the next day. Peter encouraged me to do a flying break fall on the bear. I carried out his wish and amidst a cloud of dust and twanging wires. I got the biggest bollocking of my life from one old bat in the studio. I didn't realise that they had spent all day fixing the bear.

I had good fun with Dawn French, showing her how to survive in the woods. After a day of eating rabbit and fungi she challenged me to show her how to survive in Birmingham. Just outside New Street station is a small park where I dug a hangi pit. I went shopping with her to buy meat and vegetables to cook in the hangi. We attracted quite an audience, including the park keeper who wanted to know who gave us permission to light a fire and dig a hole. I left this to Dawn to explain.

I took her husband Lenny Henry up the Amazon to survive in a tropical rainforest. He had never been camping in his life and was very apprehensive. I gained his confidence so he could have complete faith in me. He said that anyone who could get his wife to eat worms was OK. In the jungle I would go to bed at night and still be able to hear my voice. Lenny used to impersonate me, but my jokes were better than his.

The Castaways was a big production, a group of people living on a remote island in Scotland for a year. I helped with the selection of the party and trained them in various survival techniques. Ben Fogle became a star from this programme. He got a bit arrogant on the island and the film crew wanted to bring him down a peg or two. He had a young dog which he idolised, and every morning would wake up, look at the scenery and say, "Wonderful." He would take the dog for a walk and that was it for the day. I suggested we have a big curry for the evening meal and, while he was asleep, hide his dog. In the morning when he couldn't find it, the crew could tell them that it was in last night's curry. For some reason they didn't take this option.

Gary Rhodes did a *Round Britain* cookery programme. He dropped in at my training area where I prepared a hangi for him. I asked him how he could cook three types of meat, with potatoes, cabbage, onions, parsnips, swede and carrots with no containers. He was at a loss so I unearthed the hangi which I already had in the ground, just waiting to dig it up when he arrived. A hangi is a pit about a metre deep and a metre wide. A fire is started in it with rocks on top. As the fire burns these rocks get very hot and drop to the bottom of the pit. Once the fire is burnt out and all embers removed, the food is placed on top. Leaving an airspace and placing sticks across the top covered by a cloth, the whole thing is buried with earth and left for two hours.

Up in Scotland we made a programme *The Heat Is On*. It was one of the first programmes to have a selection process and to feed the participants on bush tucker. They also handled snakes, scorpions and spiders. The lucky ones failed and were sent home, but the unlucky ones selected went to Peru to carry out a long jungle trek.

I was an advisor on a couple of programmes and enjoyed giving advice on many subjects, from tracking and bodyguards to evasion. It was nice to have Jon Pertwee and Carole Lombard in my kitchen, where we discussed the script of *The Bodyguards*.

The phone never stopped ringing when the Regiment was in the news. I choose not to comment on any matters that could affect security. Various members of the press attended my courses and were not very discreet. I told them to be careful when they fished in a couple of pools as these were not mine, belonging to a local villain. One reporter wrote when he returned to work which made the front page and read something like, "Not only did I dare attend one of Lofty's courses, but I also survived poaching from the local villains' pond." Another guy from the TV I told that if he caught any fish to hide them. But he stood along a busy road in front of camera, proudly displaying his catch, and was stopped by a water bailiff who was responsible for the stretch of river and pools that the fish came from. Charming!

For his fiftieth birthday, Ron Dennis, McLaren's Formula One boss, hired Studeley Castle where he had the misfortune to have me as his party organiser. I had six lads helping me and we treated Ron and his party to an introduction to national service. We treated Ron and all his guests like conscripts and gave them a hard time. Among his gusts were Andrew Courtard, Keke Rosberg and Mika Häkkinen. I really enjoyed myself but I don't know about them.

More recently I had Bradley Walsh come and have a chat. He took his son on an SAS-type mission, and I gave him some history of the Regiment and some survival tips.

Well, that's all the name-dropping done with. I have really enjoyed writing this book: it still brings me many laughs. I wrote this in my kitchen and every time a visitor came I gave them a reading. It was great to hear their laughter.

FOUR CANDLES